# ALCOHOL, OTHER DRUGS, AND ADDICTIONS

## A Professional Development Manual for Social Work and the Human Services

# ALCOHOL, OTHER DRUGS, AND ADDICTIONS

## A Professional Development Manual for Social Work and the Human Services

**Allan E. Barsky**
*Florida Atlantic University*

BROOKS/COLE
CENGAGE Learning™

Australia • Brazil • Japan • Korea • Mexico • Singapore • Spain • United Kingdom • United States

**BROOKS/COLE**
CENGAGE Learning

**Alcohol, Other Drugs, and Addictions:
A Professional Development Manual for
Social Work and the Human Services**
Allan E. Barsky

Executive Editor: Lisa Gebo

Assistant Editor: Shelley Gesicki

Editorial Assistant: Sheila Walsh

Technology Project Manager: Barry Connolly

Marketing Manager: Caroline Concilla

Marketing Assistant: Rebecca Weisman

Advertising Project Manager: Tami Strang

Project Manager, Editorial Production: Mary Noel

Art Director: Vernon Boes

Print/Media Buyer: Doreen Suruki

Permissions Editor: Chelsea Junget

Production Service: Simone Payment, Stratford
     Publishing Services

Copy Editor: Kristen Bettcher

Cover Designer: Larry Didona

Cover Images: (top to bottom) Masterfile;
     Ingram Publishing/Alamy; Thinkstock/
     Getty Images; Enrique Algarra/Pixtal;
     (poppies in background) Bjorn Svensson/
     age Fotostock America

Compositor: Stratford Publishing Services

For product information and technology assistance, contact us at
**Cengage Learning Customer & Sales Support, 1-800-354-9706**

For permission to use material from this text or product,
submit all requests online at **www.cengage.com/permissions**
Further permissions questions can be emailed to
**permissionrequest@cengage.com**

Library of Congress Control Number: 2004109567

ISBN-13: 978-0-534-64125-2

ISBN-10: 0-534-64125-3

**Brooks/Cole**
20 Davis Drive
Belmont, CA 94002
USA

Cengage Learning is a leading provider of customized learning solutions with
office locations around the globe, including Singapore, the United Kingdom,
Australia, Mexico, Brazil, and Japan. Locate your local office at
**www.cengage.com/global**

Cengage Learning products are represented in Canada by Nelson Education, Ltd.

To learn more about Brooks/Cole, visit **www.cengage.com/brookscole**

Purchase any of our products at your local college store or at our preferred
online store **www.CengageBrain.com**

Printed in the United States of America
2 3 4 5 6      21 20 19 18 17

To my daughter, Jocelyn Adelle,
divine inspiration for my work
and blissful diversion from working too much

# Brief Contents

# Contents

# Preface

This manual has been designed to facilitate the professional development process for anyone interested in social work or counseling with people affected by addictions. There are four primary ways to use this manual: (1) as a required co-text for a graduate or upper-level undergraduate addictions course, matched with a textbook or package of readings that is focused on theory, research, and practice knowledge (see Appendix C for Table of Concordance between this manual and matching textbooks); (2) as a stand-alone book for a training course that is part of a certificate program in which the students have already completed coursework on pharmacology and theories of addictions; (3) as a recommended reading for an addictions course or social work practice course, using particular modules in mandatory practice courses to ensure that students have some addictions content in their core courses; and (4) as a reference text in libraries located in universities with substance-abuse courses, addictions services, or social-work agencies that serve people with addictions problems.

I have written this manual based on the assumption that all who use it have been or are still affected by alcohol, other drugs, or addictions (AODAs). Some have faced AODAs themselves, while others have been affected by the AODA experiences of family members, friends, neighbors, or prior clients. This statement has a number of implications. First, it demonstrates the pervasiveness of AODAs, as virtually everyone is touched by AODA issues, whether directly or indirectly. Second, it normalizes the experience of being affected by AODAs, allowing students to reflect on their AODA experiences as they learn from the academic literature and experiential exercises. Though an AODA course must not cross the bounds of therapy, there are times when appropriate personal disclosures can contribute to the learning experience of the entire class. Third, this assumption acknowledges that everyone in the class has some knowledge of AODA problems. Personal knowledge can help students learn how to help clients with AODA issues, but such knowledge must be put into context through self-awareness and critical thinking. The information an individual has learned from personal experience may or may not apply to clients globally, or to certain clients in particular. This manual, therefore, encourages students to be aware of their prior experiences, attitudes, and understandings of AODA issues so that they can build on what they know and be open to new knowledge, challenging biases, and developing professionally sound practices.

When I began to work in the field of AODAs in the mid-1980s, I had little substance abuse or addictions training. I was dependent—so to speak—on my clinical supervisor, Patti Juliana, and my other coworkers at the Albert Einstein College of Medicine Division of Substance Abuse in Bronx, New York. These experienced colleagues helped guide me through what to do and how to do it. Unfortunately, some of my original clients suffered through my learning, which was to some extent by trial and error. I still remember the initial meeting with my first client, a Vietnam War veteran who was physically and psychologically addicted to heroin and wanted to participate in our methadone maintenance program. The agency policy book said that before the physician could prescribe and administer methadone, the client had to complete a 30-page psychosocial assessment questionnaire administered by the caseworker. Dutifully, I welcomed the client into my office and explained that we needed to complete the questionnaire before he could meet with the physician. The questionnaire included a series of multiple-choice and closed-ended questions that I coded on an electronic-scanning form so that a computer could compose the assessment for me. The process seemed simple and straightforward, with little room for me to make an error as long as I followed the forms. My client was compliant, knowing this was a prerequisite, though he seemed somewhat irritable. As I asked about his criminal record, he gave me so much information that I ran out of room on the form and he pleaded with me to just let him bring in copies of his rap sheets (about 25 of them) for the next meeting. I finally decided to exercise some discretion and not insist on all the information at this first meeting. What I did not comprehend at the time was that he was going through withdrawal as our interview lingered on into the second hour. Looking back, I realize how insensitive this whole interviewing process was. I wonder whether I was more helpful or hurtful. I wonder about the appropriateness of providing opiates to people addicted to opiates. I also wonder about the political forces that promoted the vast increase in methadone clients at the time. This was a period when the AIDS epidemic was first being noticed among the intravenous-drug-using population. Many of our clients were already infected. Sure, methadone might have prevented people from sharing needles for heroin use, but many were still shooting cocaine or using other drugs. Also, counselors had caseloads so large that some clients commented that the counselors were glorified "drug pushers," because they provided access to opiates but had little time for actual counseling or talk therapy. Fortunately, my beginning caseload was small and I eventually learned how to personalize and individualize my work for the clients I served.

Learning on the job provided me with many of the skills and strategies that form the basis of my professional competence to this day. At the time, I was participating in a Master of Social Work program that provided me with generalist and ecosystemic approaches to social work. The MSW program had an elective in substance abuse, which provided specialized knowledge about substance abuse and addictions. As with most MSW programs, the field experience provided the best opportunity to integrate knowledge, skills, values, and reflective self-awareness. Our textbooks and classroom exercises focused on learning specific pieces of information rather than how to apply, critique, and continue to develop our knowledge base in practice. This student manual is intended to be a tool to aid not only students, but also their field instructors and their classroom teachers. Field and classroom instructors can use this manual to help students link what they are learning in the classroom and through their readings with what they will face as practicing professionals, based on the principles of conscious use of self, evidence-based practice, critical thinking, and ongoing professional development. My hope is that this manual will not only help social workers and related professionals prepare for beginning practice with people affected by AODAs, but it will be useful as a tool to consult during the ongoing process of professional development.

This manual does not espouse a single theory or model of practice, but encourages students to look at AODAs from a range of perspectives and models of helping. As the saying goes, "If the only tool you have is a hammer, then every problem looks like a nail." By exploring a range of theories and models, students will be equipped with many tools, and will learn how to consider critically which approaches are most likely to be appropriate with which client situations, rather than apply a single approach simply because that is the only one they have learned. This manual will also allow professors to tailor their courses in a way that emphasizes theories and models of intervention that the professors believe are most important, most prevalent, or most effective.

This manual contains exercises geared toward serving seven functions for students:

1. Identifying their current attitudes, skills, and knowledge base, to enable them to individualize their learning plans and experiences during classwork and beyond
2. Enhancing understanding and reinforcing the AODA knowledge base gained from the classroom and readings
3. Learning how to apply this knowledge base
4. Developing critical thinking, including understanding the strengths and limitations of various approaches to practice, and how to ensure that practice is based upon sufficient research evidence
5. Integrating various levels of AODA practice, including work with individuals, families, groups, organizations, communities, and public policy
6. Providing a framework to guide analysis of ethical and value dilemmas common to the AODA field
7. Fostering methods for continuous acquisition of new knowledge, skills, and professional awareness

This manual contains more exercises than could ordinarily be completed in a typical one-semester, three-credit course. This will enable the course instructor and students to select exercises that fit with students' progress in the curriculum, as well as their special needs and interests. The additional exercises could be used in a second course, or could form part of each student's plan for ongoing professional development.

This manual strives to reach a balance between learning specialized skills and knowledge for specific levels of practice with learning the principles of generalist social work that promote integration across all levels of practice. Chapters 1 and 2 build on generalist social-work knowledge by providing exercises that will reinforce basic skills, information, and attitudes that form the foundation for micro, mezzo, and macro practice[1] in an AODA context. Chapter 3 focuses on change processes with individuals in order to introduce the basic theories and models of practice that are used in the AODA field. Chapter 4 on engagement, Chapter 5 on assessment, and Chapter 10 on termination and follow-up, include exercises for these phases of help with

---

1. Micro refers to practice with individuals and families, mezzo refers to practice with small groups and organizations, and macro refers to practice with communities or development of social policy.

examples at all levels of practice, encouraging students to view client situations from various system levels and building their understanding of the importance of interventions at different levels. Chapter 6 on families, Chapter 7 on groups, Chapter 8 on communities, and Chapter 9 on health promotion and policy provide specialized exercises for the work phases of each of these levels of practice. Chapter 11, on research and evaluation, cuts across all levels and phases of practice. Appendix A provides answers to the multiple-choice questions. Appendix B provides a table that cross-references key themes throughout the manual. This allows you to follow the sequence of exercises for each major Case Profile and refer back to particular topics of interest. Appendix C provides a Table of Concordance between this manual and five AODA textbooks that are commonly used in social work addictions curricula (van Wormer & Davis, 2003; McNeece & DiNitto, 2005; Johnson, 2004; Lewis, Dana, & Blevins, 2002; Fisher & Harrison, 2005). Many of the multiple-choice questions and exercises are based upon material from these five textbooks. The Table of Concordance will also enable the instructor and students to match required readings with exercises throughout the course. Students are encouraged to use additional scholarly readings so that they do not rely solely upon information from any single textbook.

The chapters and exercises in this manual can be completed out of sequence. Chapter 1, which contains the primary Case Profiles that will be used throughout the manual, and Chapter 3, which contains the overview of theories and models, should be completed early in the course. Further suggestions for using this manual are provided in the Instructor's Manual, available to instructors from Brooks/Cole.

Some exercises from this course could be saved for other courses in the curriculum, which will encourage students to transfer knowledge from one course to another. For example, some ethics exercises could be used in an ethics course or some diversity exercises could be used in a course on culture, sexual orientation, or other aspects of diversity practice.

The perforated pages of this manual can be torn out so that they can be handed in to the instructor for feedback and evaluation. Upon return, students can keep them in a three-ring binder. In addition, students should keep a journal or loose-leaf pages for their notes, answers to journal questions, and other assignments. Each chapter has at least one longer exercise that can be used as a major assignment for grading during the course. The role-plays used throughout the manual follow one of four different client profiles. Each working group of three to six students should select a primary Case Profile to use throughout the course. By following a particular scenario, each group will get to know the issues raised by that Case in detail, while still being exposed to the other issues as other students discuss or present their experiential exercises within the larger class.

Students are encouraged to individualize the course for themselves. Review the course requirements at the beginning of the course, as well as the other exercises within this manual that are not required. Remember that course requirements are a minimum—you can initiate your own learning by doing additional exercises or by talking to your instructor about whether you can do an additional assignment in lieu of one required by the original course syllabus.

## Acknowledgments

As an educator and a helping professional, I have come to appreciate the many lessons I have learned from others—clients, students, teachers, family, coworkers, and mentors. Three of my former clinical supervisors stand out among the many people who have contributed to my knowledge of practice with people affected by alcohol, other drugs, and addictions: Patty Juliana of the Albert Einstein College of Medicine Division of Substance Abuse in Bronx, New York; Martha Bragin of the Children's Aid Society PINS Project in Brooklyn, New York; and Charlynn Rhea of the YMCA Youth Substance Abuse Program in Toronto. All three shared their wisdom and practice experience, guiding me with patience as I began my work in this field. As I moved into academia, Ellen Sue Mesbur, then Director of the School of Social Work at Ryerson University in Toronto, entrusted me with teaching my first Substance Abuse courses in the early 1990s. My students at Ryerson, University of Calgary, and Florida Atlantic University have often taught me as much as I have taught them, sharing their professional and personal experiences. I am indebted to these students for allowing me to test a range of role-plays and exercises, determining which ones contributed to professional development, particularly how best to translate theory and academic knowledge into practice. I am also grateful to Dr. Michele Hawkins and the students of the Florida Atlantic University School of Social Work for allowing me to pilot-test the materials in this book while teaching substance-abuse courses.

The staff of Brooks/Cole has been very supportive of my work throughout the writing and production processes. From Lisa Gebo's unshakable support (even through an actual earthquake), to the insightful assistance of the reviewers, to the professional services of Simone Payment, Kristen Bettcher, and the rest of the editorial and production staff, I could not ask for a better team to help me take this textbook from a rough idea to the finished product you are now reading.

Finally, I must thank those around me—my partner Greg, my daughter Adelle, my mother Edith, and the rest of my extended family who provided me with incredible love and support in a very trying period when I was writing this book. I spent two months at the Special Care Nursery at Credit Valley Hospital, helping nurture a 3-pound newborn into a healthy young girl. Fortunately, we had wonderful nursing and medical staff, so I was able to work away on my laptop between feedings, tests, and kangaroo care, well aware of both the fragility and vigor of life.

# About the Author

Dr. Allan Edward Barsky has a background in law, social work, mediation, and addictions counseling. He has taught at a university level since 1989 in four different schools of social work (University of Toronto, Ryerson University, University of Calgary, and Florida Atlantic University where he is presently Full Professor). Dr. Barsky's books include *Conflict Resolution for the Helping Professions* (Brooks/Cole, 2000), *Counsellors as Witnesses* (Canada Law Book, 1997), *Interdisciplinary Practice with Diverse Populations* (Greenwood, 2000), *Clinicians in Court* (Guilford, 2002), and the upcoming book, *Successful Social Work Education* (Brooks/Cole). His addictions practice experience includes work with the YMCA Youth Substance Abuse Program in Toronto and Methadone Maintenance with the Albert Einstein College of Medicine in the Bronx, New York. His addictions research has been published in the *Journal of Drug Education*, *Canadian Social Work Review*, and *Revista Treball Social* (Spain). He has also published a chapter on addictions in John Poulin's *Strengths-Based Generalist Practice: A Collaborative Approach* (Brooks/Cole, 2005).

CHAPTER

# 1

$\sim\!\!\wedge\!\!\sim$

# Introduction

This manual is about integration. The exercises in this book are designed to help you bring together your present value and knowledge bases with the skills, attitudes, knowledge, and values that you will need to foster your development as an effective and ethical addictions practitioner.[1] If you find the materials in this book clear and simple, then I have failed. If you find the materials to be confusing, challenging, complex, and troubling, then you will know that you are learning something new and significant. Trust the process. Take risks. Enjoy the ride.

If you are looking for answers in this manual, you might be very disappointed. This manual provides questions and sends you on missions in search of answers.[2] To find answers, you will need to rely on additional resources: a primary textbook, supplemental reading, your community, your instructor, your class, and yourself. This manual contains some information about addictions, but rather than repeat the materials that are in your primary textbook, this manual is meant to supplement your textbook. You will find yourself referring back and forth—taking concepts that you are learning from your textbook and seeing how they apply to cases, role-plays, debates, and discussions that will help you relate the materials to real-life situations and practice questions. Although your textbook is a useful resource, no single textbook is a sufficient resource for a developing-addictions professional. You will need to explore supplemental readings—not only readings suggested by your instructor or this manual, but supplemental readings that you identify to satisfy your own learning interests and needs. To localize your

---

1. I will use the terms *practitioner* and *social worker* throughout to indicate human service professionals who work in the field of addictions. Given my own social work background and interest in developing a manual for developing social workers, this manual contains some terminology and perspectives specific to social work. Although not all people who use this manual will have a social work background, the majority of the materials and exercises apply across disciplines (e.g., psychology, family counseling, and psychiatric nursing).
2. Answers to multiple choice questions are included in the Appendices.

knowledge base, since every community is unique, you will need to go out into your community to gain knowledge of its people, addictions problems, resources, and strengths. Finally, because addictions work requires human interaction, learning about how to help people with addictions issues will require you to interact with your classmates. By learning from one another and reflecting upon your own attitudes, skills, and beliefs, you will learn how to use your skills and capacities in more intentional, ethical, and effective manners.

This chapter is designed to help you explore your basic attitudes and understandings of addictions, as well as to introduce a definitional framework for key terms used by addictions professionals. Chapter 2 deals with the categorization of substances, as well as the physical, psychological, and social effects of alcohol and drug use. Chapter 3 focuses on theory and intervention with individuals affected by alcohol, other drugs, and addictions (AODAs). Chapter 4 provides exercises to help you learn how to engage individuals, families, groups, and communities affected by AODAs. Chapter 5 delves into assessment. Chapter 6 deals with families. Chapter 7 looks at the use of group work to promote change. Chapter 8 explores how to help communities change. Chapter 9 provides exercises on health promotion and public policy. Chapter 10 deals with termination and follow-up, including maintenance and relapse prevention. Chapter 11 concludes with research and evaluation issues regarding AODA clinical practice, policy, and programs.

# Attitudes Toward Alcohol, Other Drugs, and Addictions (AODAs)

## Personal Attitudes

Before you read other's perspectives on AODAs, it is helpful to gain a sense of your own attitudes toward drug use and people affected by AODAs. For each of the following statements, indicate with a check mark (√) whether you agree or disagree. Do not spend time thinking about the statements. Write down your first impression.

1. People who use illicit drugs have a moral defect. _____ Agree __√__ Disagree
2. Alcoholism is a disease. __√__ Agree _____ Disagree
3. "Hard" drugs such as heroin and cocaine are worse than "soft" or "organic" drugs such as marijuana and magic mushrooms. __√__ Agree _____ Disagree
4. People who have an addiction need help from social workers or other professionals. __√__ Agree _____ Disagree
5. The primary cause of substance abuse in the United States is the oppressive nature of the structures in this society (e.g., racism, homophobia, capitalism, patriarchy, religious institutions, criminal justice system, or welfare system). _____ Agree __√__ Disagree
6. Addicts have an essential character flaw that cannot be changed. _____ Agree __√__ Disagree
7. Drug use is a voluntary choice for people who are addicted. _____ Agree __√__ Disagree
8. Fines or incarceration for possession of illicit drugs is needed in order to deter drug use. __√__ Agree _____ Disagree

9. Drug addiction can be controlled, but not cured. _____ Agree __✓__ Disagree

10. Employers should have the right to test employees for illicit drug use. __✓__ Agree _____ Disagree

11. When working with a substance abuser, the primary role of an addictions counselor is to help the client become abstinent. _____ Agree __✓__ Disagree

12. Social workers and other helping professionals who are themselves in recovery tend to be more effective for clients with addictions problems than helping professionals who have never had an addiction. __✓__ Agree _____ Disagree

13. Society should put more money into *prevention* of addictions, rather than *intervention*. __✓__ Agree _____ Disagree

14. An eating disorder (such as anorexia or bulimia) is a form of addiction. __✓__ Agree _____ Disagree

15. People who are involved in sex-related crimes such as exhibitionism should be punished, even if they have been diagnosed as having a sexual addiction. __✓__ Agree _____ Disagree

16. The child welfare system has a responsibility to remove children from the care of parents with serious alcohol problems until the alcohol problems are under control. _____ Agree __✓__ Disagree

17. Smokers should pay higher premiums for health insurance than nonsmokers. __✓__ Agree _____ Disagree

# Reflective Exercise

Attitudes are internal perspectives that affect the way a person sees the world and interacts with it. Addictions professionals need to become conscious of their attitudes so they do not impair their ability to work effectively and ethically with clients. Attitudes underlie each of the 17 prior statements. **Identify the source of your attitudes for each of the prior statements and how it might impact (positively or negatively) your work in the field of addictions.**

> For example, if I agree to statement 6, I might identify the source of this attitude as my personal experience (e.g., having a parent who was unable to change regardless of how hard she tried) or something I have read (in newspapers or research). This attitude might make it difficult for me to work with clients who are addicted because I do not really believe that they can change.

The purpose of this exercise is not to change your attitudes, just to identify them and raise your awareness of them as you work through this course. With new information and experiences, you may change your attitudes. Refer back to this exercise when you want to reflect on your attitudes and how you are integrating new knowledge, values, and skills. When you are determining how to intervene with clients, remember to focus on your conscious beliefs and values, rather than allow unconscious attitudes rule your decisions.

## Attitudes Conveyed in the Media

Now that you have a sense of your own attitudes toward AODAs, let us consider attitudes conveyed in the media. Select a movie, television show, novel, advertisement, or other form of popular media that portrays a fictional character or community affected by AODAs. Identify how the character or community is conveyed. What attitudes, assumptions, and stereotypes (if any) underlie how the character or community is conveyed? How realistic is the portrayal?

> Consider, for example, the character of Homer in *The Simpsons* television series. Homer gulps large quantities of beer at home and at a neighborhood bar. He is portrayed as irresponsible, bumbling, and not too bright, but somehow still loveable or pitiable. Beer seems to have no long-term effects on him, other than perhaps a "beer gut." The assumptions underlying this portrayal include the notion that binge-drinking beer is a social phenomenon of the everyday, working-class person, acting as an escape and having few if any negative consequences. How realistic is this, given what you know about AODAs so far?

> The way that AODAs are portrayed in the media is important because this affects your clients and how they are seen by family members, peers, employers, and other important people in their lives. If the media stigmatizes people with AODA problems, for instance, this can easily translate into stigmatization of your client. If the media portrays accurate messages about people affected by AODAs, then family members and significant others will be more likely to provide positive support.

# Definitional Framework

The language used by the media and others to describe people affected by AODAs has an impact on the way we think about them. As a developing professional, it is important to know the meaning of different terms and to choose language that fits with the theories and models of helping that you will be using with clients. This manual uses the term *addiction* in the title rather than *drug use, substance abuse,* or *chemical dependence* in order to include problems with nonsubstance-related dependencies, such as gambling addiction and other behavioral dependencies. Each term has important differences in meaning, use, and implications for practice and policy. The following exercises are intended to provide you with a greater understanding of each of these terms. It is not sufficient to simply memorize definitions. You will need to be able to compare, contrast, critique, and apply these terms to real-life situations.

## Who Is an Addict?

How do YOU define the term *addicted*? Consider the following three cases in the sequence provided. Provide definitions using your own words. Do not look up or use definitions from your textbook or other sources.

1. Siggy is a 45-year-old woman from Boston, MA. She is unemployed and her major pastime is drinking. She drinks five to six beers per day, but does not drink to the point of getting drunk.

◇ Is Siggy addicted?
◇ Why? Why not?
◇ How do you define addicted?

2. Xavier has diabetes and takes insulin every day. If he does not, he would become very ill. He lives in Albuquerque, NM.
◇ Is Xavier addicted?
◇ Why? Why not?
◇ How do you define addicted?

3. Fran is a survivor of child sexual abuse. She has flashbacks and panic attacks on occasion but uses Valium to help her deal with the pain. She lives in a rural area of Idaho.
◇ Is Fran addicted?
◇ Why? Why not?
◇ How do you define addicted?

Why is it so difficult to come up with a single definition of addiction that captures the people you think should be identified as addicted, but does not capture people who you do not think should be identified as addicted? What are the reasons that some professionals and lay people use the term *addict*? What are the practical and ethical criticisms of using this type of terminology? How do culture and gender affect how people define who is an addict?

## Compare and Contrast

As you were trying to define *addiction*, you probably used other terms such as *dependence, compulsion, tolerance,* and *withdrawal.* Fortunately, these terms have more specific and commonly accepted definitions than addiction. Identify definitions for each of the following sets of terms from your textbook or another reliable source of information. Write down definitions for each of the terms in language that YOU CAN UNDERSTAND and that you could convey to a client who had a 10th grade education and little knowledge of substance abuse. Compare and contrast the terms in each set by identifying the similarities and differences among each of these terms.

Set 1: Addiction—Dependence—Codependence—Compulsion—Obsession—Weak-willed
Set 2: Tolerance—Withdrawal—Cross-tolerance—Reverse Tolerance
Set 3: Physical Dependence—Psychological Dependence—Social Dependence
Set 4: Substance—Drug—Medication—Pharmaceutical—Chemical
Set 5: Substance Use—Substance Abuse—Substance Misuse—Substance Dependence
Set 6: In Recovery—Recovered—Cured—Controlled—Abstinent
Set 7: Stress—Cope—Adapt—Oppress—Discriminate[3]—Internalize—Interact—Role

Different terminology fits with different models or perspectives of practice. For each of the following models or perspectives, identify which terms from Sets 1 to 7 (above) a practitioner would generally use. Provide rationale for each of your decisions.

---

3. Including sexism, racism, heterosexism, and other forms of bigotry.

Moral Model




Medical Model




Psychoanalytic Model




Cognitive-Behavioral Model

Family Systems Model



Ecological Model



Feminist Perspective



Radical or Structural Perspective

## Application

The following exercise builds on the definitions you have just written by asking you to apply them to a practice situation. For each of the following client examples, select the terms that you think apply most accurately and explain how your selected terms relate to the case scenario.

1.  Justin thinks about sex all the time—at work, at home, and virtually every moment of the day. He sometimes skips work so that he can go to a club to watch exotic dancers. If he goes without having sex or watching sex for more than 24 hours, he starts to feel very anxious and upset.

    Addiction—Dependence—Codependence—Compulsion—Obsession

2.  Janine is 84 and has been using sleeping pills for the past eight years. During her first seven years of using them her doctor had to increase the dosage or switch the type of sleeping pill every year because they seemed to lose their effect. In the past year, her health has deteriorated, and the doctor has decreased her dosage to prevent an overdose.

    Tolerance—Withdrawal—Cross-tolerance—Reverse Tolerance

3. Cory has tried to stop smoking for the past 5 months. Whenever he goes to a bar, however, he starts to feel cravings for cigarettes. If he doesn't give in to his cravings, he starts to feel queasy and sick to his stomach.

   Physical Dependence—Psychological Dependence—Social Dependence

4. Police have reported an alarming number of accidental deaths by overdose of Oxycodone. Doctors prescribe Oxycodone as a time-release painkiller for people with severe and chronic pain problems. Some people have been selling Oxycodone on the street as a recreational drug. If an Oxycodone pill is crushed before swallowed, the person feels the full impact of the drug at once, rather than in a time-release fashion.

   Substance—Drug—Medication—Pharmaceutical—Chemical

5. Apply the following terms to the facts in 4.

   Substance Use—Substance Abuse—Substance Misuse—
   Substance Dependence

6. Hanna used to snort cocaine every day. She has stopped for the past week, but continues to feel strong urges to use it again. She plans to stop using for at least a year, but may try to use cocaine recreationally after that if she gets through the first year without using.

   In Recovery—Recovered—Cured—Adapted—Controlled—Abstinent

7. Ophelia is an 82-year-old woman who has been using sleeping pills for the past 10 years. During this period, she has lost significant weight and has become quite frail. She also has exhibited signs of liver disease. Her doctor recently reduced the dosage of her sleeping pills in order to reduce the chances of an overdose. Ophelia is unable to fall asleep unless she has her pills. She does not really have cravings for them, but if she does not use them, she suffers from trembling, sweats, and increased sensitivity to light and smells. Sometimes, Ophelia takes only half a pill or combines the sleeping pill with a diet pill so that she will not be as drowsy when she wakes up.

   Tolerance—Substance Dependence—Substance Misuse

8.   Rena comes from a family in which women are treated as subordinate to men. Men make the major financial and family decisions. Women make babies and take care of their husbands. Rena has done what was expected of her, but at the expense of fulfilling her own dreams. Rena is depressed that she never had an opportunity to go to college. She drinks to drown her sorrows.

   Stress—Cope—Adapt—Oppress—Discriminate—Internalize—
   Interact—Role

## Critique

Now that you have an understanding of various AODA terms and how to apply them, consider how different agencies select and use different terms. Identify an agency or facility in your community that provides assessments or diagnoses for people with possible addictions or substance abuse problems. Find out what terminology it uses and whose definitions it uses (e.g., DSM, World Health Organization, or Person-In-Environment). Find out why it uses those definitions. What are the advantages and limitations of those definitions (consider funding availability, who is included and excluded, and the validity and reliability of those definitions)? How would their program be affected if they used one of the other sources of terminology and definitions?

## Discussion Questions: Labeling the Person Versus the Behavior

Some practitioners criticize the type of AODA terminology discussed above because it reduces people to a label and reinforces stigma around AODAs. Consider the following scenario: A client refers to herself as an addict and an alcoholic. She says that, as a member of AA, she believes that she has a disease and that the first step is to admit that she is an alcoholic. Assume that you do not believe in labeling the person as the problem, but rather focusing on the behaviors that need to be changed—for example, helping her to stop using alcohol. You believe that labeling the person is demeaning and damages a person's sense of self-efficacy.

1.  How would you proceed to work with this client (i.e., what strategies would you use)?

2.  What clinical and ethical issues would you need to take into account?

3. How could you avoid the use of labels if the client's public or private health insurance requires a specific diagnosis in order to fund treatment?

4. If you do not label a client's problem with a pathological label, does that mean that you do not give the client any responsibility for the problem or the choices that the client continues to make?

# Educational Needs Assessment and Professional Development Plan

At this point, you have explored your attitudes about AODAs, and you have considered the importance of the language that is used to discuss AODA concerns. The next exercise turns your attention to the future, specifically, what you want to learn about helping people affected by AODAs. Using the following chart, identify your educational needs and interests as they relate to your professional development as a practitioner who plans to work with people, organizations, and communities affected by AODAs. For each item, rate your current level of proficiency using the following scale:

1. Very limited proficiency—"I need substantial improvement"
2. Partial proficiency—"I need moderate improvement"
3. Full proficiency—"I do not need any improvement"

The *Level of proficiency* column is divided into three columns so that you can rate yourself at the beginning (B), middle (M), and end (E) of the course. In the *Time frame* column, indicate whether you plan to work on proficiency in that area during this course (C),[4] during your field placement (F), during other courses (identify them), following graduation and during the first few years of practice (P), or if it is not important for your professional development (N/I). This chart is meant to be comprehensive, but not overwhelming. Feel free to highlight a few areas that you want to focus on. You can come back to the other areas of competence later in your career. After all, professional development is a lifelong process.

| Areas of competence[5]—the ability to . . . | Level of proficiency B   M   E | | | Time frame |
|---|---|---|---|---|
| 1. Understand, differentiate, critique, and apply key AODA *terminology* (e.g., substance abuse, misuse, psychological dependence, physical dependence, tolerance, or codependence) to client situations. | | | | |
| 2. Understand and articulate the *desired and undesired effects* of particular substances (e.g., alcohol, heroin, cocaine, amphetamines, cannabis, inhalants, _____, _____, and _____. | | | | |
| 3. Articulate a *theoretical understanding* of the causes and effects of substance abuse and addictions. | | | | |
| 4. Raise awareness of my *attitudes, beliefs,* and *affective responses* regarding AODAs so that I can ensure that personal or professional biases do not interfere with effective and ethical work with my clients. | | | | |
| 5. Describe and assess the various *motivations* for substance use and abuse. | | | | |
| 6. Identify and apply *engagement* strategies for clients at various stages of change and motivation, including genuineness, unconditional positive regard, empathetic understanding, and "here and now" orientation. | | | | |
| | | | | *(continued)* |

4. Check your course syllabus to see what objectives your instructor has established for the course. Also, consult your instructor if you want to individualize your learning objectives to see how these might be accommodated by the course and instructor.

5. The competencies identified in this chart are derived from Benjamin S. Bloom's "Taxonomy of Educational Objectives" (1956), which is based on the belief that professional development requires education in the cognitive, affective, and psychomotor domains. The competencies also require integration of understanding, critical thinking, self-reflection, and interpersonal skill-building.

| Areas of competence—the ability to . . . | Level of proficiency B M E | | | Time frame |
|---|---|---|---|---|
| 7. Demonstrate an ability to *screen clients for risks* such as suicide, homicide, domestic violence, and accidental death related to AODAs. | | | | |
| 8. *Select assessment tools* that are appropriate to client needs, given their presenting problems and diversity. | | | | |
| 9. Assess client systems *using specific assessment tools* (e.g., SASSI, DSM, PIE, _____). | | | | |
| 10. *Help clients assess* their own needs for intervention using differential assessment skills. | | | | |
| 11. Differentiate between *intervention needs of select populations* affected by AODAs. Identify particular groups that you intend to focus on: _____. | | | | |
| 12. Identify and apply *intervention strategies* for clients at various stages of change and with various personal and social resources. | | | | |
| 13. Develop *prevention strategies* to reduce specific risks related to AODAs. | | | | |
| 14. Conduct a *needs assessment for an organization or community* affected by AODAs. | | | | |
| 15. Identify *local resources* for people with AODA problems and critically evaluate which resources are appropriate for certain client groups and presenting problems. | | | | |
| 16. *Facilitate change for individuals* by helping clients tap into internal motivations to change; assisting them through a problem-solving process based on informed, self-determined, and realistic goals; building on client strengths; developing more functional coping mechanisms; and applying appropriate models of intervention. | | | | |
| 17. *Facilitate change in family systems* by helping family members recognize dysfunctional roles and negotiate more functional roles; assessing for intimate partner abuse, elder abuse, child abuse, and neglect; helping family members identify and change behaviors and interactional patterns that support or maintain AODA behaviors. | | | | *(continued)* |

| Areas of competence—the ability to . . . | Level of proficiency | | | Time frame |
|---|---|---|---|---|
| | B | M | E | |
| 18. *Facilitate change in groups and communities* by raising awareness of AODA issues, building internal capacities to work on self-determined goals, and providing education on how to prevent or resolve AODA issues. | | | | |
| 19. *Facilitate change in organizations* by raising awareness of risks and resilience in relation to AODAs; helping the organization to build on resiliencies and reduce or eliminate these risks; and promoting knowledge, skills, and attitudes that foster positive health and social functioning. | | | | |
| 20. *Make appropriate referrals* and ensure that clients gain access to the services and supports they need. | | | | |
| 21. Understand, critique, and apply *specific models of AODA intervention* (select those of particular interest):<br>◇ Cognitive<br>◇ Behavioral<br>◇ Motivational Interviewing<br>◇ Transtheoretical Model (Stages of Change)<br>◇ Harm Reduction<br>◇ Pharmacological (e.g., Antabuse, Naltrexone)<br>◇ Functional<br>◇ Family Systems (Strategic, Structural, Bowen, Minuchin)<br>◇ Narrative Therapy<br>◇ Resilience/Capacity Building (individual/community)<br>◇ Environmental Modification<br>◇ 12-Steps<br>◇ Hypnotherapy<br>◇ Other: _____ | | | | |
| 22. *Terminate* effectively, including reviewing progress on AODA issues, assessing ongoing needs, dealing with feelings about ending, and making appropriate referrals. | | | | |

*(continued)*

| Areas of competence—the ability to . . . | Level of proficiency B M E | | | Time frame |
|---|---|---|---|---|
| 23. Plan and implement *follow-up* with clients to ensure maintenance of goals and deal with potential relapse. | | | | |
| 24. *Evaluate* clinical practice and program effectiveness in terms of goals identified by clients and other interested constituencies. | | | | |
| 25. Identify the ways that addictions *policy and practice* affect each other. | | | | |
| 26. Develop srategies to *influence public policy* and resource usage for AODA concerns. | | | | |
| 27. *Work together* constructively with AODA practitioners from other disciplines and professions. | | | | |
| 28. *Identify laws and policies* that affect practice in the field of AODAs. | | | | |
| 29. *Identify and resolve ethical dilemmas* in the field of AODAs (specifically: _____). | | | | |
| 30. List other educational objectives: | | | | |

This list of objectives can be overwhelming, so here is an approach to making your major learning goals more manageable. On a separate piece of paper, select three of your top learning priorities from the list above. For each objective that you identified as a priority, write a plan of action for how you intend to improve your proficiency. Include learning activities such as readings and specific types of exercises (e.g., role-plays and videotaped demonstrations, tests, papers, critical thinking, field placement, additional courses, conferences, library or Web-based research, empirical research). This exercise will help you individualize your learning plan for the course, identifying areas for self-directed learning that can supplement the required portions of the course.

## Good Source of Information (GSI)

In order to develop into a practitioner who uses sound knowledge to guide assessment and intervention with various client systems, you will need to know how to identify "Good Sources of Information" (GSIs) (Gibbs, 2003). Possible sources of information include research articles, textbooks, experts, videotapes, and the Internet. What makes a source of information "good" depends on the reason that you need the information. If you need information about a particular individual or community, then you may need to go directly to that source, asking questions and/or making direct observations. If you want to know about the comparative effects and risks of two different substances, then you might be advised to rely upon empirical research conducted with a large sample, using scientific sampling procedures and other rigorous research methodologies. Ideally, practitioners would use primary sources of information, such as research and theory articles written by the people who conducted the research or developed the theory. By going to these primary sources, you can evaluate the research methods in order to check the reliability, validity,[6] strengths, and limitations of the research findings.

Textbooks and other writings that summarize research, theory, and other information are called secondary resources. If you are going to rely upon these sources then you need to explore whether the writer(s) is an expert whose writing is reputable. Has the source undergone a process of peer review before it was published? Does a reputable professional or scientific body back up the source? Does the source have a particular bias? Finally, if you want to apply the information to a specific situation, what precautions or adjustments are required (e.g., to take ethnic diversity into account)? When writing a paper, remember to cite your sources accurately, enabling people to check the trustworthiness of your conclusions.

## GSI Exercise—Addictive Liability

Let us try a couple of exercises to ensure you have a solid understanding of how to use GSIs for different purposes. First, assume that your course instructor says, "Cocaine is highly, physically addictive," but your textbook says that, "Cocaine is psychologically addictive, but it is not physically addictive." How will you determine which information to rely upon? Identify two or three GSIs, write down their findings, and describe why you believe that their information should be relied upon.

---

6. *Validity* and *reliability* are terms drawn from quantitative research. For qualitative research, consider *dependability*, *trustworthiness*, and *transferability*.

## GSI Exercise—Selecting an Assessment Tool

For this second GSI exercise, assume your textbook includes an assessment tool called *Addiction Severity Index* (ASI). You are working with a client who is 68 years old and identifies herself as a male-to-female transgender person of Slavic background. How will you determine whether the ASI is an appropriate and effective tool for assessing this client's addiction severity?

## GSI Exercise—Community Enhancement

This time, assume you are hired to help the city of Scottsdale, Arizona, develop a drug prevention program. You have been told that this city has a high percentage of elderly people and a high percentage of Latin Americans. What GSIs will you use in order to help make informed decisions? Explain why you can rely upon these GSIs.

## GSI Exercise—Information on the Internet

For this GSI exercise, find the Web site for a major AODA research organization, such as the National Institute for Drug Abuse. Identify three pieces of information on that Web site that you know you can rely upon, and provide your reasons for why it is reliable. Identify three pieces of information that you think require further verification before you can rely upon them, and explain your reasons for why you have questions about their reliability.

Too often, people rely upon the most easily obtained source of information rather than the best. Try using a general Internet search engine (e.g., http://www.google.com) and insert the words *addict* and *sex*. Critique one of the top ten Web sites in terms of currency, validity, and reliability of information.

*Web site:*

*Critique:*

What other online databases could you search in order to find scholarly literature on this topic? (If you are unsure, ask your college librarian for assistance.)

## Information Versus Knowledge

*Information* refers to data, facts, or material that has been gathered. *Knowledge* refers to information that has been learned and integrated in such a manner that it has relevance and can be applied to a life situation. As a professional, you cannot simply gather various sources of information. You must determine whether and how that information has any practical use. To illustrate, fill in the following blanks using a GSI:

Did you know that, according to statistics compiled by _____, there were ___ people who were current users of illicit drugs and ____ people who were dependent on illicit drugs in the year ____? This represents a ___ percent increase/decrease in the number of current users and a ___ percent increase/decrease in the number of dependent people since 10 years earlier. In my own state of _____, there were ___ current users and ____ dependent people in the year ____.

The greatest number of deaths and health costs linked to substance abuse are not caused by illicit drugs but by _____ and _____. These substances are regulated by the government through the use of _____ and _____.

Once you have filled in the blanks, answer the following questions: What knowledge can you draw out of this information? As a professional, how will this information be useful (consider work with individuals, families, groups, organizations, and communities)?

# Basic Facts for Primary Case Profiles

Many of the assignments for this course are based on the model of *problem-based learning*. The following four client profiles will be used for the purposes of role-plays, case discussions, and other hands-on learning exercises throughout this manual. Different work-study groups in the class can focus on different client profiles throughout the course. By following these client systems through various presenting problems, you will learn:

♦ how to view client situations from various levels of practice
♦ how to integrate theory (from your readings, class discussions, and lectures) with values, reflection, and conscious use of skills and self
♦ how to intervene at various phases of the helping process
♦ how to use time as a medium for change

In order to use these case facts, you may want to detach the pages and keep them in a separate binder so that you can refer back to them easily. Each client has been assigned various diversity factors such as age, ethnocultural background, socioeconomic status, gender identity, and sexual orientation. Each working group should feel free to add or change diversity factors to allow you to learn about addictions issues among specific population groups that you intend to work with. Be sure to write down the new diversity profiles so that group members can refer back to these throughout the course.

## Profile A: The Torres Family

### Presenting Issue and Agency Context

Maria has an appointment with a social worker at ODAAT, the One Day at a Time treatment program for people with substance abuse problems. She wants to discuss getting help for her sister Julia, who has a problem with alcohol. Maria is concerned about Julia's ability to take care of her two children because Julia goes off on weekend binges and Maria has to help take care of Julia's children.

### Background Information

The Torres family consists of Teresa (72), her husband Raphael (71), and their four adult children, Maria (49), Julia (42), Roberto (41), and Robertito (39). All were born in Puerto Rico, but have lived in mainland America for the past 27 years. Teresa and Raphael still live in the apartment that the family moved into 27 years ago, but the children have long since moved out. Raphael is a self-described alcoholic. He cannot make it through the day without drinking. A bottle of whiskey is his best friend. Teresa has stood by him through the years, believing that he could not survive without her. She sees him as a good provider for the family, although she has had to cover for him at work on a regular basis. She has also grown used to cutting back on the food and household budget after Raphael has blown his paycheck or pension money on one of his drinking and gambling weekends. Teresa comes across as a very harried but well-intentioned woman. These days, her main pastimes are playing bingo at the local church or going to a neighborhood restaurant to play the video lottery terminals (VLTs).

None of the children are married, each having had difficulty maintaining any type of stable relationship. Maria works long, hard hours at an employee placement firm. For the last four years, she has been rewarded with the highest commissions in her company (based on the number of clients she has placed in jobs). Maria is goal oriented and takes failure very personally. In addition to being successful in her career, Maria is known to her friends as someone they can depend on for a shoulder to cry on or a sound piece of advice. While Maria is not involved in any intimate relationships, she passes this off as unimportant and really no problem. Maria says she doesn't have time for a relationship at this point in her life, and it would probably just mess up her other goals. Besides, she has lots of friends.

Maria remembers her childhood as being very chaotic. Her father would frequently come home in the evening and drink to the point of passing out in the living room. But that wasn't the worst of it. She remembers how alcohol always meant yelling and fighting in the house. She doesn't recall any physical violence directed at her or her siblings, but she does remember how she was afraid when things got out of control. For a long time, Maria blamed herself for her father's need to get drunk. Now, she just thinks of him as a "pathetic animal" (she holds back from using more profane language to describe him). She feels sorry her mother, but at the same time resents that her mother was not stronger. Maria was the oldest of the children, so it was her responsibility to cook or clean when her mother was unable to take care of household chores. Maria cannot remember certain parts of her childhood, and she'd just as soon keep it that way. Maria used to go stay with her godparents, Christina and Richard, when things really got out of control at home. Although Christina and Richard are not biological relatives, Maria considers them family.

Julia was always the wild one in the family. She was continuously getting in trouble at school for "acting out" and had her first confrontation with the law when she was 13. At that time she was caught shoplifting makeup from a drugstore. Julia has had lots of jobs, but never one for very long. Roberto was like an identical twin to Julia. If Julia was into trouble, Roberto was not far away. As an adult, Roberto stayed in one line of work quite consistently: trafficking small quantities of pot and other drugs on the streets. He has been charged and convicted on two occasions. While in custody, he was able to make connections with drug suppliers who helped him operate when he returned to the community. He feels the justice system didn't really help rehabilitate him, except to make him smarter about not getting caught. Besides, with a criminal record, what else is he to do for a living? Roberto, as the oldest son, has a strong sense of machismo and sees himself as the one who needs to take care of everyone. Unfortunately, he doesn't really have the skills or self-discipline to follow through.

Julia and Roberto have had problems with alcohol for a number of years. Maria has tried repeatedly to get them into Alcoholics Anonymous and residential alcohol treatment programs. Maria believes that she never abused alcohol because she didn't want to end up like her father. In fact, Maria hardly ever touches a drink. She "snorts a little coke now and then." It gives her feelings of power and confidence. Maria says, "A little coke isn't hurting anyone, not like alcohol. My brother and sister are the ones who need help." She says she is willing to do anything to prevent them from turning out like her parents. She feels sick to her stomach when she sees them repeating her parents' mistakes, but she knows she has to be strong for them.

Julia's son's names are DJ (3) and Dominic (1). Both may have developmental problems related to either Fetal Alcohol Effects or inadequate parenting.

## Profile B: George Favel

### Presenting Issue and Agency Context

George has been referred to a substance abuse treatment program called YODA, Youth Off Drugs and Alcohol. A youth worker named Kerry had been trying to help George get off the streets. Kerry referred George to YODA because he was involved in a lot of risky behavior, including unprotected sexual intercourse, drinking to the point of blackout, and living in unsafe environments (vulnerable to violence on the street). George initially sees his problem as a need for stable housing.

### Background Information

George Favel is a 17-year-old man who has been traveling around America for the past 6 months and is currently living in an abandoned house. He is emotionally reserved and relatively "street smart," although he just finished grade nine. Even though George ran away from his most recent foster parents without giving them any notice, he didn't leave because he felt he was treated badly by them. They didn't beat him or anything, but he had been with them for a couple of years and he still didn't feel like they were family. All his foster siblings were older, did well in school, and seemed to have their lives set out for them. George didn't know what direction his life was going to take. Staying in school certainly didn't offer him much. He'd put up long enough with disdain and derision from his teachers and racial taunting from other students.

George's biological parents are from a Cree reservation in the northern plains, but George has lived in various foster homes and group homes since he was 5 years old. George was taken into foster care after a report that a male neighbor was sexually abusing him. The department of child welfare determined that his parents were unable to ensure his safety or provide for his basic needs due to their alcoholism. He has had no contact with his parents since then. George says he doesn't care about his parents, believing they just abandoned him and never tried to regain contact.

When George first hit the streets, the only substances he had abused were glue, nicotine, and alcohol. He usually drank alone, and it was mostly to try to forget all the garbage that was going on in his life. He preferred drinking to huffing, but sometimes glue was the only painkiller he could get his hands on.

George found a few odd jobs—pulling a rickshaw for tourists and selling souvenirs for the local baseball team—to pay for food, booze, etc. He has not been able to earn enough to get a room or an apartment. A youth worker he met on the street tried to hook him up with welfare, but he felt he kept getting "jerked around" by the "welfare bureaucraps," as he called them. George did not understand all their rules and had trouble reading all the forms. He spends most of his time trying to figure out where his next meal is coming from and does not have time to wait for "some uppity worker" in a social assistance office. He has been thrown out of a few supportive housing units due to his drinking (he destroyed property, did not clean up, etc.).

Last week, George went on a real bender, to the point of blacking out. When he woke up in a hospital, he did not remember what he was drinking or how he got there. George's youth worker convinced him to go speak with a counselor at a substance abuse treatment center about his drug and alcohol use. The worker said the counselor would not try to make him give up drugs or do anything else he did not want to do. George is ambivalent about what to do. In some ways he'd like to turn his life around; in other ways the prospect of giving up drugs, alcohol, and street life is scary.

## Profile C: Marge and Randy Lang

### Presenting Issue and Agency Context

Marge Lang (36) is a recently divorced woman who has become concerned about certain changes in the behavior of her son, Randy (a 14-year-old student at Snowflake Middle School). Things reached a crisis point last week when Marge and Randy were arguing over his poor school performance, and Randy started to throw his books through the kitchen window. She suspected he must have been high on "something," so she decided to make an appointment with the school social worker at Snowflake.

### Background Information

Marge and her former husband, Steve Lang (40), were born and raised in Beijing, China. They came to America as political refugees shortly after they were married. They only had one son, Randy, who was born in America. Steve and Marge grew apart when Randy was very young, but they tried to stay together for his benefit, never arguing in front of him and trying to keep his life as normal as possible. They finally told Randy that they were breaking up because Steve had a job opportunity in another state that he could not refuse. Marge did not want to leave her job or community. Marge works as an information officer for a large electronics company.

During the first meeting with the school social worker, Marge feels comfortable talking about Randy and his problems, but she is hesitant about discussing anything concerning herself or her ex-husband. Marge sees Randy as a very good son, but thinks he started hanging out with a new group of buddies that have been getting him into more and more trouble. While she has never seen Randy using any drugs, she strongly suspects that drugs are the root of his problems. Marge does not know what types of drugs that Randy is into. When the social worker asks about his moods, she says he sometimes comes home really "hyper," and within half an hour, he falls asleep. There are also occasions when he gets agitated and leaves the house to go to "who knows where." When she asks him about drug use, he denies it and tells her that she should just "lay off," and if she wants to see a shrink, she should "go without me." Marge never found any signs of drugs in his room. Randy never comes home smelling of smoke or alcohol. At first she thought he was "just drinking or something" at parties on the weekend, but now his mood swings seem to last the whole week.

On further discussion, Marge notes that from an early age Randy had a mild learning disability and had trouble making friends. He lacked confidence and was a bit of a loner. Although both his parents were born in China, Randy identifies himself as American rather than Chinese or Chinese American. Randy was really close to his father. This changed when the marriage started to break up and Randy's father moved out of town. Randy rarely sees his father now. He blames his mother for his parents' divorce. It seems that all of Randy's problems have been snowballing over the past year.

Randy refuses to talk to the social worker. He says he's got things under control, and he's old enough to make his own decisions. When the social worker asks Marge why she wanted Randy to see a social worker, Marge responds: "I'm worried about my son. Wouldn't you be? I want to know if Randy is using drugs. Tell me what he's using and how I can make him stop."

Although Randy is average weight and height for his age, Marge is very gaunt and thin. She wears a dress that covers most of her legs and arms. She chews sugarless gum. Her teeth seem unusually stained for a woman of her age. Throughout the interview she has a nervous twitch in her eyes.

## Profile D—Dionne Thevenin

### *Presenting Issue and Agency Context*

Dionne went into a general hospital for what she thought was "just a case of pneumonia," but while there learned she was HIV-positive. Dionne refused to accept this diagnosis because she did not think that she fit into the risk groups for people with AIDS. In her mind, since she never traveled in places with high rates of HIV such as Haiti or Africa, she never shared needles, and she never had sex with a gay man, how could she have AIDS? When Dionne was released from the hospital, she refused to seek additional help for AIDS. The hospital social worker contacted an outreach program called Life Goes On (LGO). The LGO worker assigned to reach out to Dionne is named Connie.

### *Background Information*

Dionne is a 63-year-old accountant who works for the Evercharge Oil and Gas Company. She considers her job somewhat boring, but it has given her financial security. This security has proven to be very important, as Dionne has suffered from pneumonia and a number of other illnesses over the past 18 months. Although she tested positive for HIV and has been diagnosed as having AIDS, Dionne does not believe she has AIDS. She does not have "that blotchy skin," and she said she "feels well, except when I am sick." Dionne lost about 20 pounds during periods when she was sick. She always thought she was too fat and is actually pleased to have been able to lose this weight.

Although Dionne does not believe she put herself at risk for HIV, she has had unprotected sexual intercourse with six or seven men over the past three years. Dionne shoots heroin on occasion but has her own set of works. She lives alone in a suburban townhouse. No one at work or in her family knows about her drug use, her sexual behavior, or her health status. Dionne is African American and is the choir leader at a local Black Church. She feels quite ashamed about her drug use and "sexual promiscuity," given the conflict with what she has learned from her moral and cultural upbringing. Dionne feels alone in her troubles. The only person who knows the details of her health and lifestyle is her physician. Her firm has an employee assistance program, but she is worried about how the company would react if she spoke to someone there.

Dionne has been a long-time user of heroin. Her college buddies first introduced heroin to her at weekend parties. Her frequency of heroin usage gradually increased to almost daily. She does not see the heroin use as a real problem because it is steady and does not affect her work. She does not really even feel much of a high off it anymore, but it does make her more relaxed around men. She believes she could stop using it if she wanted to.

Dionne's doctor prescribed painkillers and tranquilizers to help her relax and get some sleep. She sometimes takes more than the prescribed amounts, particularly when she gets depressed. Sometimes, all Dionne wants to do is sleep.

## Assignment 1.1: What I Need to Know

For this assignment, you and your work-study group should select one of the four Profiles. Review the Profile and identify essential information and concepts that you believe you need to know in order to understand and work effectively with the client system described in the case (do not go into techniques or phases of intervention). For your analysis, include the following information:

1.  Identify six to ten AODA-related issues that are potentially important for you to explore in order to provide effective help to the clients in the Profile. Of the issues identified, select three or four that are of particular interest to you. Explain why you are interested in learning more about these issues for your professional development. [1 to 2 pages]

2.  Identify six to ten AODA terms or concepts that you will need to understand in order to assess and intervene effectively with the client systems. (Consider the terms listed in the subsection Definitional Framework, as well as terms from your course syllabus and textbook.) Explain why you think it will be important for you to learn each of these terms. For each term, identify one or two GSIs that you will use in order to find an appropriate definition and explanation of the term. [2 pages]

3.  Identify the substances used or abused by clients in the Profile. For each substance, identify two or three GSIs that you can use to help you learn about the biological, psychological, social, and spiritual effects of using these substances. [1 to 2 pages]

4.  Identify any nonsubstance behavioral addictions raised by the case. For each of these addictions, identify two or three GSIs that can help you understand the dynamics of these addictions. [1 page]

5.  Identify two or three diversity aspects of the profile that you will need to take into account (e.g., age, ethnicity, culture, sexual orientation, gender, disability, or co-occurring mental illness). For each diversity aspect, identify at least two GSIs that you can consult to learn how this diversity aspect might affect your assessment or intervention with the relevant client systems. [1 page]

6.  Prepare an annotated bibliography of the GSIs that you identified for the prior questions. In this bibliography, identify the major topics or question(s) addressed, type of methods used to generate knowledge (e.g., theory building, quantitative research, qualitative research, literature review), and briefly critique the strengths and limitations of the information generated by the GSI (write 3 to 6 sentences per GSI). [4 to 7 pages]

7.  Include a list of the databases that you searched (e.g., Social Work Abstracts or PsychARTICLE), as well as the key words that you used in your literature search (e.g., addiction, eating, bulimia).

**Evaluation** will be based on the following criteria: effectiveness of literature search, selection of relevant readings and GSIs, engagement of the reader, format, literary competence, accuracy of information from the literature, clarity of description of key concepts, application of theory to practice situation (where appropriate), creativity and contribution of original thought, logic of inquiry, critical analysis, linkages to social work perspectives (or your own professional perspective if it is other than social work), and synthesis of material. The paper should be 10 to 14 pages in APA format.

### SAMPLE CASE—"All About Eva"

The following excerpt is provided to illustrate how you can approach Assignment 1.1 for this course. The research cited below is fictionalized, and the analysis is abbreviated. Your research will be authentic and in substantially greater depth.

**Sample Profile:** Eva is a 42-year-old air traffic controller who likes to fly in her spare time. The problem is that she likes to fly without a plane. Eva's substance of choice is cocaine, which she freebases. Her mottoes since high school are: "Party hearty" and "Life is too short to be sober." How she became an air traffic controller with this attitude and lifestyle choice remains a mystery. Somehow, she has been able to do her job and keep her drug use separate from her career.

Eva started to use illicit drugs when she was 14. Although her parents raised her with strong Mormon values in a small-town Utah home environment, Eva rebelled hard when she became a teenager. When her parents first discovered her drug use they threatened to ground her for life. Eva took off and moved in with a hippie cousin in the big town, Salt Lake City.

**Sample Assignment 1.1:** *The facts in the Case Profile describe a woman whose substance abuse began during early adolescence. In order to gain a better understanding of the relationship between these issues, I plan to study the impact of developmental issues on substance use, abuse, and addictions (Elder, 1999; White, 2002).*

*Since I am unfamiliar with the effects of cocaine and how to freebase, I will refer to two of the more recent texts on pharmacology (Stone, 1941; Crank, 1962). I do not plan to experiment with cocaine myself, although some authors suggest that only people who have used drugs can understand their use (Tsu, 2003). I will try to be aware of the limitations of learning about drugs through reading, and will reflect upon clients from my fieldwork who have used drugs. I will also look at the debate on the addictive liability of cocaine (Lesser, 2001; More, 2004).*

*I am planning to live in a community with a large Mormon population, so I am interested in learning more about their beliefs and culture as they pertain to substance use and addictions. My literature searches on PsychINFO, Sociofile, Social Work Abstracts, and Medline have only identified two articles in this area (Fasken, 1994; Hilden, 2001). I will speak with social workers in my community who have worked with the Mormon community, as well as Mormon clerics, in order to try to identify more information.*

*The case facts state that Eva is an air traffic controller. This is an extremely stressful job that is associated with high rates of suicide (Prudent, 2000). This is not an angle that I am interested in pursuing. I believe that addictions are related to biological and psychodynamic factors rather than systemic or environmental factors. I will use the following resources to explore biological and psychosocial factors. . . . In order to explore an alternative perspective, I will read the following articles from structuralist and feminist literature on addictions . . .*

**Sample Annotated Citation:** *Hilden, J. (2003). Fourteen-year-old women who leave the Mormon faith and use cocaine. Journal of Fantastic Drug Issues, 34, 12–33.*

*This article presents a qualitative study of the experiences of six 14-year-old women who left the Mormon community and became addicted to cocaine. It provides a rich description of their experiences, and provides insightful recommendations for prevention and intervention. Given the small sample size and the specific location of the study (Provost, UT), any transfer of its conclusions to Eva's case must be made with caution . . .*

# Introductory Role-Play—World's Worst Addictions Counselor

Role-plays are intended to help you put theory into practice. Rather than wait until you are practicing with real clients, role-plays provide you with the opportunity to take risks and try out new ways of intervening with simulated clients. Sometimes, we learn more from making mistakes than from performing perfectly. This role-play is intended to be a fun way to introduce the concept of role-plays and show how safe it is to perform "poorly," as long as your group provides supportive, constructive feedback.

For this role-play, one person plays client, one person plays worker, and the others play observers and provide positive feedback. Each person should read only his or her role. Role-play this scenario for 2 to 3 minutes, debrief using the questions below, switch roles, and role-play it again.

> Client: You are playing a client named 045736 (36 for short). Actually, that's your student number, and you feel more like a number than a person. You are a workaholic. You love to work. Can't get enough of it. That's why you've started your master's program, even though you already have a job as a stockbroker and are the primary caretaker for three lovely, preschool-aged children. What else is there to do with your spare time? Anyhow, a friend says you'll burn out if you don't get help. You've agreed to see a counselor—for at least 15 minutes. You don't want to quit any of your jobs. You just want some advice on how to get more done in less time. Burn out? Never.

> Worker: A client who is a self-described workaholic has come to see you for counseling advice. This is a first meeting. You work in a family service association. You are playing a social worker who is absolutely awful. Make a list of seven things that you could do in this type of counseling session that are completely inconsistent with your professional values and code of ethics or what you have learned about psychology or social work theory and intervention. When you are role-playing, try to incorporate as many of these seven items as you can. Have fun (nothing too abusive to the person who is playing the client, please).

> Observers: During the role-play, take notes of key interventions and client responses, and keep track of time. After the role-play, one of the observers should facilitate debriefing, using the following questions as a guide.
> > ◇ To the client: How did you feel in the role of client? What felt comfortable? What felt uncomfortable? Use "I" statements. Do not ask for criticism of the worker's performance.
> > ◇ To the worker: What were the most dysfunctional or unethical things that you did in the interview? In spite of trying to do a terrible job, what were some of the positives that came out of the way you conducted the interview?
> > ◇ To all the observers: What did you learn about effective and ineffective interviewing of people with AODA problems from this role-play?

# Journaling Exercise

In order to monitor and direct your learning process, it is useful to keep a journal of your thoughts, feelings, questions, and concerns about AODAs and your process of professional development. Write a journal entry between each class, or at least once a week—if structure is helpful, make an appointment on your calendar once a week to write a journal entry. Consider including responses to the following questions (and feel free to tailor the questions to your own concerns).

1. What are two or three key pieces of learning that I have gained over the course of the past week? What *facts, theory, skills, or interventions* will I want to remember 5 years from now when I am a practitioner working with people with AODA problems?

2. What are two or three *questions* about people with AODA problems and AODA interventions that I would like to explore during the next few weeks? How are these related to my goals for professional development?

3. How have my *attitudes or feelings* toward people with AODAs changed during the past week? What biases or attitudes do I need to work on in order to become an even more effective worker?

4. What have I learned about AODAs from *other members* of my work-study group and class?

## InfoTrac College Edition®

### Key Words

◇ Alcohol
◇ Drug
◇ Addiction
◇ Substance Abuse
◇ Physical Dependence
◇ Psychological Dependence

CHAPTER

# 2

⌒⌒⌒⌒

# Pharmacology

For some social work and human service professionals, the most arduous task for developing competence in AODA work is learning the pharmacology of various substances. Is it absolutely necessary for a generalist practitioner to memorize all of the biological and psychological effects of every substance that people use or abuse? Probably not. Knowing where to find sound pharmacological information is more important, because you can often look up the effects of substances on a case-by-case basis. However, some *rote memory* work will be necessary in order to serve clients effectively and be able to work with other professionals who specialize in this area.

This chapter is designed to help you not only remember the effects of various substances, but also to *understand* their effects and how to *apply* your understanding of the pharmacology of drugs to client situations. It begins by looking at ways that substances are classified and how you can learn about different effects of substances by how they are classified.

## Categorization of Substances

Substances are categorized in a number of ways: by their legal classification, by their pharmacological effects, or by their functional usages.

## Legal Categorizations

The laws treat different types of substances differently. Some substances, such as coffee and chocolate, are regulated as food items. Anyone can purchase, possess, or sell these items, with relatively little government regulation (e.g., labeling and packaging). Supposedly, these substances have little regulation because they pose little risk.[1] Medicinal drugs have a much higher standard of regulation, including restrictions on who can prescribe and sell these items. Social or recreational substances such as cigarettes and alcohol have different types of regulations, restricting the ages of people to whom the substances can be sold; controlling the packaging, advertising, contents, and taxes; or requiring licenses for selling these substances. Finally there are drugs that are deemed illicit—that is, it is a criminal offense for people to possess, buy, sell, grow, or produce these substances. In the United States, the Comprehensive Drug Abuse Prevention and Control Act is one of the primary sources of substance control laws. Locate a copy of this act, online or in print.

1. The legislation has five schedules, which are basically five lists of drugs. Describe how the legislation distinguishes among different types of drugs in its five schedules. How are the drugs grouped? What types of legal restrictions are placed on drugs in each group regarding possession, production, purchase, and sale? What is the rationale behind grouping drugs in this manner?
2. Which schedule does each of the following drugs fall into: Valium, Pot, Heroin, Morphine, and LSD?
3. What are the justifications for treating these five substances differently? To what extent do the legislative distinctions relate to the actual risks of each of these substances?[2] What other factors might be affecting the policy decisions behind how these drugs are regulated?
4. In addition to federal laws, what other laws regulate substance use, possession, sale, and production? Identify at least two state laws and two international laws or conventions. Why is it important for practitioners to be aware of these particular laws?

## Categories by Effects

*Categories by effects* refers to dividing substances into different groups according to their primary physiological effects when ingested. Categories such as stimulants and depressants are based on the effects on the central nervous system. Categories such as hallucinogens are based on the effects on perception. Categories such as opiates, cannabis, and inhalants are grouped based on common molecular structure and common effects for these classifications of substances. As you will see, if you can identify which category a drug fits into according to pharmacological effects, you will have a good, general understanding of the effects of the particular drug. Knowing the differences among substances within a category can also be important, but at least you will know the general effects of the particular substances.

1. Identify one or two GSIs that explain the pharmacological effects of psychoactive substances. Ideally, your GSI should answer the following questions for each substance or category of substances: what are the short-term effects that users generally intend to achieve; what are the short-term side effects or risks of use; what are the long-term risks of use; and what is the addictive liability of each substance?[3]

---

1. Consider food items such as peanuts, which can cause severe allergic reactions and even death. Is labeling sufficient to ensure safety or should growing and selling these substances be limited or prohibited?
2. That is, risks supported by empirical research, including the *types* for negative physical, psychological, and social consequences, and *level* of risks for users of these substances.
3. See Chapter 1 for an explanation of Good Sources of Information (GSIs).

2. Identify 7 to 15 substances that you want or need to understand (from the Profile you selected in Chapter 1, from your instructor, or from other needs identified in Chapter 1). Here is a sample list that you can draw from, but try to individualize it to your needs: Depo-testosterone, Haldol, wine, hash, crack, gasoline, morphine, phenobarbital, LSD, PCP, Xanax, Geritol, cigars, Ecstasy.

3. Using the GSIs and substances you have identified, complete the following charts. As you complete the charts, be sure you understand each of the terms you use (e.g., it is of little use to know that Wernicke-Korsakoff Syndrome is a long-term risk of alcohol use if you do not know what Wernicke's is). Photocopy a blank chart if you need additional pages.

| Substance | Categories[4] (include all that apply) | Intended effects[5] (from user's perspective) | Short-term risks[6] (acute, during intoxication) | Long-term risks[7] (chronic, months or years of use) | Addictive liability (physical psychological, high, low) |
|---|---|---|---|---|---|
| Example: alcohol | Depressant, controlled substance (regulations on sale, advertising, age of purchasers, licensing of vendors) | To relax, to overcome social anxieties, to quench thirst, to block psychological pain | Accidents while operating cars or machinery due to impaired coordination and judgment, blackout, coma, or death from overdose | Wernicke-Korsakoff Syndrome; cirrhosis; ulcers, weakened heart muscles, severe withdrawal effects (see below), memory loss, Fetal Alcohol Effects | High physical and high psychological addictive liability |
| | | | | | *(continued)* |

4. Examples of categories: psychoactive, nonpsychoactive, stimulant, depressant (sedative-hypnotic, tranquilizer, alcohol, anesthetic, benzodiazepine, barbiturate), opiate, hallucinogen, antidepressant, antibiotic, anabolic steroid, other/mixed, illicit, regulated, generally unregulated.

5. Examples: relieve anxiety, induce sleep, combat fatigue, kill bacterial infection, reduce appetite, induce appetite, provide energy, keep awake, socialize, relieve thirst, relieve depression, create euphoric feelings, dull emotional pain, relieve physical pain, replace testosterone, treat endometriosis, treat blood anemia, reduce panic reactions, treat disinhibition, relax muscles, enhance feelings of self-esteem.

6. Examples: heart attack, stroke, accidental death, memory loss, HIV or other communicable disease (through needle sharing), hangover, blackout, overdose, coma, asphyxiation, hallucinations, loss of balance, respiratory arrest. Note that certain effects that some people categorize as risks may be viewed by others as desired effects. For instance, is it necessarily a problem to forget things? Some people profess that cannabis helps people focus intensely on one thing and ignore others.

7. Examples: cancer, permanent damage to brain/liver/kidneys/lungs/reproductive system, vitamin depletion, weight loss, weight gain, damage to memory/attention/learning, insomnia, tremors, suppressed immune system, FAS/FAE.

| Substance | Categories (include all that apply) | Intended effects (from user's perspective) | Short-term risks (acute, during intoxication) | Long-term risks (chronic, months or years of use) | Addictive liability (physical psychological, high, low) |
|---|---|---|---|---|---|
|  |  |  |  |  |  |
|  |  |  |  |  |  |
|  |  |  |  |  |  |

*(continued)*

| Substance | Categories (include all that apply) | Intended effects (from user's perspective) | Short-term risks (acute, during intoxication) | Long-term risks (chronic, months or years of use) | Addictive liability (physical psychological, high, low) |
|---|---|---|---|---|---|
| | | | | | |
| | | | | | |
| | | | | | (continued) |

| Substance | Categories (include all that apply) | Intended effects (from user's perspective) | Short-term risks (acute, during intoxication) | Long-term risks (chronic, months or years of use) | Addictive liability (physical psychological, high, low) |
|---|---|---|---|---|---|
|  |  |  |  |  |  |
|  |  |  |  |  |  |
|  |  |  |  |  |  |

*(continued)*

| Substance | Categories (include all that apply) | Intended effects (from user's perspective) | Short-term risks (acute, during intoxication) | Long-term risks (chronic, months or years of use) | Addictive liability (physical psychological, high, low) |
|---|---|---|---|---|---|
| | | | | | |
| | | | | | |
| | | | | | |

| Substance | Signs that person is feeling the initial effects of recent use[8] | Signs that person is coming down from use | Signs of withdrawal effects (if any) | Usual route(s) of administration[9] (how substance is ingested into the body) |
|---|---|---|---|---|
| Example: *alcohol* | *Giddiness, mental and physical relaxation, depressed heartbeat and breathing, impaired motor coordination, slowed blood pressure, slurred speech, sleepiness* | *Tired, dehydrated, hangover (from larger quantities)* | *Anxiety, nausea, irritability, tremors, fever, rapid heartbeat, hallucinations, coma, or death (medical supervision for detoxification is advised)* | *Swallowed through drinking* |
| | | | | |
| | | | | *(continued)* |

---

8. Examples: increased/decreased heartbeat, breathing, or blood pressure; dilated/constricted pupils; slurring of speech; impaired motor functioning and reaction time; flushed/bluish skin tone; hyperactive/lethargic behavior; delusions; hallucinations; dissociation of ideas.

9. Examples: applied to surface of skin, subcutaneous injection, intravenous injection, intramuscular injection, applied to mucous membranes, inhaled through nose, inhaled through mouth or nose, smoked, swallowed, inserted into anus.

| Substance | Signs that person is feeling the initial effects of recent use | Signs that person is coming down from use | Signs of withdrawal effects (if any) | Usual route(s) of administration (how substance is ingested into the body) |
|---|---|---|---|---|
|  |  |  |  |  |
|  |  |  |  |  |
|  |  |  |  | *(continued)* |

| Substance | Signs that person is feeling the initial effects of recent use | Signs that person is coming down from use | Signs of withdrawal effects (if any) | Usual route(s) of administration (how substance is ingested into the body) |
|---|---|---|---|---|
| | | | | |
| | | | | |
| | | | | |

*(continued)*

| Substance | Signs that person is feeling the initial effects of recent use | Signs that person is coming down from use | Signs of withdrawal effects (if any) | Usual route(s) of administration (how substance is ingested into the body) |
|---|---|---|---|---|
| | | | | |
| | | | | |
| | | | | *(continued)* |

| Substance | Signs that person is feeling the initial effects of recent use | Signs that person is coming down from use | Signs of withdrawal effects (if any) | Usual route(s) of administration (how substance is ingested into the body) |
|---|---|---|---|---|
|  |  |  |  |  |
|  |  |  |  |  |
|  |  |  |  |  |

## Research on Specific Risks

We often hear general messages about drug risks, such as "Smoking causes cancer," "Drinking by pregnant women can lead to birth defects," "Ecstasy can trigger strokes," or "Heroin is highly addictive." But not everyone who smokes gets cancer; many women who drink during pregnancy have healthy children; the vast majority of people who use Ecstasy do not have strokes; and not everyone who uses heroin becomes physically dependent. Select one of these substances and find a GSI that describes the specific risks of these substances. Summarize your findings about the actual risks of these substances (e.g., for smokers, what is the specific level of increased risk of lung cancer; how does the level of risk change depending on the frequency of use, period of use, gender, or other significant factors?). When it comes to public education about the risks associated with your chosen substance, what message should we be providing? Why have we often used simple slogans, such as "Just say no" or "Speed kills," rather than more specific information?

## Effects Versus Experiences

A person's experience of alcohol and other drugs (AOD[10]) goes beyond physiological AOD effects. AOD effects are relatively automatic responses or involuntary physical reactions to substances, such as dilation of pupils and loss of coordination. AOD experiences include AOD effects, but they are affected by many idiosyncratic factors, such as the social environment, expectations, and cognitive processing by the individual. Which of the following describe AOD experiences that go beyond involuntary physical reactions?

- Increase in heartbeat
- Feelings of euphoria
- Giddiness
- Perspiration
- Shakes
- Shallow breathing
- Memory lapse
- Connection to higher spirits
- Blending of senses such as hearing and vision

---

10. The AOD abbreviation refers to alcohol and other drugs. AOD will be used when referring specifically to alcohol and drugs, whereas AODA will be used when talking about behavioral addictions whether or not they involve the use of substances (e.g., gambling or shopping addictions).

# Functional Categorizations

Categories of substances according to function include substances used for hunger and thirst (e.g., food and beverages), substances used for medicinal purposes (e.g., antibiotics for bacterial infections, anesthetics to block physical pain, and psychotropic drugs for mental conditions), substances used for ritual purposes (e.g., sacramental wine), substances used for recreational drugs (e.g., hash and LSD), and substances used to cope with psychosocial problems (e.g., substances that block painful memories or help a person with social inhibitions to be more gregarious). These categories are problematic for a number of reasons. Different substances can fit into more than one category. The reason for using the substance often depends on the individual who chooses to use it rather than the substance itself (e.g., although Ritalin is a medicine usually prescribed for Attention Deficit Disorder, it can be used as a recreational drug). Finally, the nature of use is often culturally defined (e.g., wine is used only as a sacrament for some religious groups, whereas other religious groups sanction its use for social purposes). Accordingly, it is generally more useful to look at the functions that substances serve particular individuals, families, or groups in society than to generalize the functions of certain substances for all people.

## Role-Play: Social Worker as Drug Pusher

This role-play involves a *psychoeducational group* in which 11 clients each present a different psychosocial problem. The clients will ask which specific substances are best able to help them cope with this problem. The social worker will help each client describe the problem and will then educate the client with information about the "best" substances for the client's stated needs (use information from the *Intended effects* column of the drug chart you completed above). The social worker will explain how the particular substances work to alleviate the presenting problem and the differences between the substances, so that the client can make an informed decision. The worker will not explain the risks of the substances unless a client asks for this information. The worker does not want to lose any clients, so the worker will try to explain how to use the substances safely, reducing any risks of use. Have fun with this learning exercise, in which the practitioner takes on a role similar to a "drug pusher."

1. Mariah has recently witnessed a horrible accident that has given her nightmares and caused extreme sleep disturbances. She is looking for a substance that can wipe the accident from her *memory*.
2. Ned is very *nervous* when it comes to dating. He wants a substance that can calm his nerves so that he doesn't sweat, stutter, and shake when he goes out on a date.
3. Eduardo is in a panic about his studies. He is falling behind in all his readings and just can't study late into the night. He asks for a substance that can give him more *energy* and keep him awake for long hours.
4. Fatima is an artist who just can't *focus*. Her thoughts have been very scattered and she is looking for a substance that can help her become fully involved in the subjects of her paintings.
5. Constance hates public speaking and is supposed to do a presentation at work next week. She desires a substance that will make her feel more *confident*.
6. Bluto is just plain *bored*. He hasn't felt excited about anything for a long time and requests something to make him feel overjoyed.

7. Felice is unhappy with her life and wants to end it all. She is looking for drugs that can help her *commit suicide* painlessly, quickly, and efficiently.

8. Jiminy wants a *quick boost* and he wants it now; yesterday is already too late. He wants something that will make him sing "I'm on the Top of the World" and really mean it.

9. Demi has cancer and is going through chemotherapy. The chemo makes her nauseous. She'd like something that helps her mellow out and *reduce the nausea*.

10. Spike says he's a reformed alcoholic. He hasn't used alcohol for 30 days and says he'll never go back to it again. Now that he's in control, he'd like to find a type of pill that can do pretty much the *same thing as alcohol*. Something in a cool blue color would be nice. Any suggestions?

11. Kruger would like something to help him *lose weight and feel more energetic*.

**Debriefing:** Although this exercise is contrived, consider its relevance to a real-life situation. What is the role of a social worker, if any, in terms of helping a client select substances that are more helpful and less harmful? What are the differences or similarities between an effective social worker and an effective drug trafficker? Does the ethical principle of client self-determination mean that a social worker should help a client use substances if the client wants to use them to cope with psychosocial problems? What other ethical principles does a social worker need to consider in determining how to respond?

### Profile: Identifying Functions

For each of the individuals using substances in your chosen Profile (from Chapter 1), identify the possible functions that the substances serve. (In Chapter 5, when you will be conducting an assessment interview, you will have an opportunity to check whether your hypotheses about the functions of the substances fit with the clients' perceptions of why they are using.)

# Biophysiology of Substance Use

Doctors and other medical practitioners take several courses in order to understand biophysiology, including the way that substances are processed and affect the body. As a helping practitioner, your task of learning at least the basics can be made easier if you can simultaneously learn why this information is relevant to your work.

1.	Define each of the following terms in language that could easily be understood by a 12-year-old student:[11] central nervous system, sympathetic nervous system, parasympathetic nervous system, homeostasis, agonistic, antagonistic, endorphins, dopamine, serotonin, epinephrine, metabolism, digestive system, reproductive system, cardiovascular system, allergy, toxicity.

2.	Provide one or two reasons why it is important for a social worker working with AODAs to know about each term.

Example: *Neurotransmitters—1. These are different types of chemicals in the body that send messages from the brain down the spine and to different parts of the body. Some of these chemicals speed up body functions (heartbeat, breathing, and so on) and make the person feel excited. Other chemicals slow down body functions and make the person feel tired or relaxed. 2. Social workers need to know about neurotransmitters because different drugs have different effects on neurotransmitters—for example, some drugs increase the effects of neurotransmitters and other drugs prevent neurotransmitters from having their ordinary effects. Sometimes, a drug that blocks neurotransmitters can be used to help a person stop using more harmful drugs.*

## "Natural Drugs"

Is drug use inherently "evil" or "bad"? Consider chemicals such as endorphins and adrenaline, which naturally occur in the body. What illicit substances provide similar effects to endorphins and adrenaline? Should society distinguish between drugs that occur naturally in the body and drugs that people take? (Provide your reasoning.)

Are particular substances necessarily all good (e.g., a magic pill or new cure for cancer) or all bad (dangerous, risky, or addictive)? How would you articulate a more realistic perspective on drugs such as AZT (used to treat people with AIDS) and nicotine (one of the most addictive drugs available)?

# Progression of Substance Use

Some social workers believe that people who use AODs go through a common series of specific stages called a "Progression of Substance Use." Locate a GSI on a particular model that explains the *Progression of Substance Use*, for example, the Jellinek Curve on the Stages of Alcoholism or Washton's Course of Cocaine Addiction.

1.	To what extent is the model you identified supported by research?

2.	Once a person begins to use or abuse substances, does the person necessarily move down to the next stages of the progression?

3.	How can the Progression of Substance Use be used to help a client stop using AODs?

---

11. Try to describe the substance as accurately as possible without using complicated language.

# Exercise: Applying a Model on the Progression of Substance Use

For *each* of the following vignettes, answer these questions:

    a. Which of the following concepts apply and how: tolerance, addiction, substance abuse, substance misuse, or dependence?

    b. What are the negative effects or possible risks of client's substance use (if any)?

    c. Where is the client on the Progression of Substance Use? What additional information would you need to know to make a proper assessment?

    d. What are the positive functions or effects of client's substance use (if any)?[12]

    e. How typical or realistic is this vignette? Why?

1. Ivan is 35 years old. He works as a data processor, has been married for two years, and has a newborn child. Ivan has led a relatively calm lifestyle, but once in a while he likes to party. His circle of friends at these parties is into snorting a little coke. Ivan will usually do a couple of lines over the course of an evening. He's only tried pot or hash once or twice (and even inhaled). He nurses one or two bottles of beer over the course of an evening. He usually feels pretty good at the party. If he stays sober at one of these parties, he feels like everyone else is in another headspace and he can't relate to them. Ivan doesn't think he has a drug problem because he never does coke alone.

2. Vlada is a 20-year-old student at American Intoxic University. He was brought up in a culture that prohibited the ingestion of any intoxicating substance. Vlada himself was not even exposed to caffeine or nicotine until he and his family moved to the United States two years ago. On the way home from classes one evening, Vlada was offered some crack from a local "street pharmacist." Having heard so much about crack in the news, Vlada was very curious about this drug. He purchased what he was told was an 8-ball. That night he smoked it. The experience "blew his mind." The next day when he told a friend about this experience, he said that the crack gave him this big rush. He felt like he was Superman for about 6 hours. The experience was so good that he wondered why there was such a big fuss about crack.

3. Igor is 40 years old. He's been using coke now for more than five years. At first, it was just a few times a month, at parties. Now, he likes to do a couple of lines in the evening so he can work late into the night. There's been a lot of pressure to produce at White Rock Enterprises, where they're threatening to lay off half the employees. The more Igor tries to get ahead, however, the more he seems to fall behind. He's been quite irritable and tired lately, and the coke is the only thing that keeps him going. The last time he went for a few days without coke, he just about went off the deep end, really feeling down and out. He says he could stop using cocaine if he wanted to, but there's no reason to stop. Besides, he's no druggie. He has never shot up or anything.

4. Boris, 46 years old, has been shooting coke for the past 3 years. For a while, he was really hurting at the end of an evening, but some buddies taught him how to "speedball" (using cocaine and heroin). His habit has grown to be quite expensive—he's way behind on rent and bills and support payments to his ex. He says he

---

12. Look at the effects from the client's perspective, that is, what the client currently sees as either a positive or negative consequence of using drugs.

doesn't care. She left him, so why should he save money just for her to spend. He hates the tracks on his arms, so he always wears long sleeves. That's not much of a price to pay compared to how he'd feel if he stopped using—shakes, sweats, nausea, the runs.

5.   Valerie is 42 and has been seeing an ear, nose, and throat physician for a nasal problem—a deviated septum he thinks. While left alone in the doctor's office for a few minutes he noticed a container marked "Cocaine." Curious, he picked it up and read something about it being an anesthetic. He laughed because whenever he'd used cocaine it certainly didn't put him to sleep right away. Just then, the doctor walked back in. Valerie was embarrassed and put the container in his pocket so the doctor wouldn't think he was trying to steal something. Later, when Valerie went home, he tried inhaling the cocaine he picked up. No reaction. Valerie was disappointed and called up a friend for some real rock.

Write down your answers for each of the vignettes before reading on. Now, reread the vignettes, but in the following sequence: 2, 1, 3, 5, 4. Refer to the client as Ivan throughout the five vignettes, so that the client is the same person who goes through a series of stages. Reconsider the Progression of Substance Use. In what ways does this sequence of vignettes fit with the Progression? In what ways is this sequence unrealistic or untypical? How would this analysis be different if the substance used by Ivan were alcohol rather than cocaine?

## Discussion Questions

1.   How can a social worker determine whether a client's substance use is experimental use versus social use?
2.   How can a social worker help a client determine when social use is becoming problem use?
3.   Can someone be in the chronic stage and still have family and friends? Do you have to have all the symptoms to move into the next stage?

# Gateway Drugs

Cigarettes and marijuana are sometimes referred to as *Gateway Drugs*. What does the concept of a Gateway Drug mean? Find a GSI on Gateway Drugs to determine whether there is research to support the notion that certain drugs act as gateways. Given the research that you have found on Gateway Drugs, what are the implications for how to design an effective prevention program? Given the research on Gateway Drugs, which of the following statements are true?

1.   Smoking cigarettes is one of the primary causes of illicit drug use, such as marijuana.
2.   People who do not use cannabis will not go on to use harder drugs.
3.   Most people who use cocaine or heroin have used alcohol or other Gateway Drugs prior to using cocaine or heroin.
4.   The same factors that encourage a person to use marijuana may be factors that cause some marijuana users to use other drugs (e.g., social stress, availability).
5.   Some drug users switch to stronger drugs because they have built up tolerance to the drugs that they were initially using.

Compare and contrast the concept of Progression of Substance Abuse with the concept of Gateway Drugs.

# Jeopardrugs

In earlier exercises you have located GSIs on the pharmacological effects of different substances. Although it is useful to commit at least some of these effects to memory, memorization can be an arduous and boring task. The following exercise provides a fun way to learn more about the effects of different substances, as well as test your memory about the pharmacological effects of specific substances. You can do this exercise at home or in class. Designate one person to act as quizmaster and divide the rest of the group into teams. Each team will take turns selecting a topic and point value from the table below. The quizmaster will read an answer and the team selecting the topic will have an opportunity to provide a question that fits the answer. The quizmaster will rule on whether the response is correct, using the answers at the back of this manual. Points are awarded for correct responses. If one team provides a wrong answer, the next team gets a chance to respond.

| Uppers | Downers | Opiates | Hallucinogens | Pot Pourri |
|--------|---------|---------|---------------|------------|
| 100 | 100 | 100 | 100 | 100 |
| 200 | 200 | 200 | 200 | 200 |
| 300 | 300 | 300 | 300 | 300 |
| 400 | 400 | 400 | 400 | 400 |
| 500 | 500 | 500 | 500 | 500 |

*Note:* The answers and questions for the quizmaster are in the Appendix.

# From Information to Knowledge

Whereas Jeopardrugs tested your ability to recall basic pieces of information, the following multiple-choice exercise will test your ability to apply pharmacology knowledge to situations relevant to practice.

1. A client has been prescribed Ritalin. In order to research its effects, you will look under the category of:
   a. Opiates.
   b. Decongestants.
   c. Carcinogens.
   d. Stimulants.
   e. Hallucinogens.

*Feb 16th*

2. Librium is classified as a benzodiazepine or tranquilizer, but it is sometimes used therapeutically as a:
   a. Drug to replace heroin so that the person does not go through withdrawal.
   b. Treatment to control glaucoma.
   c. Treatment for alcohol withdrawal.
   d. Rat poison.
   e. Diet pill.

3. A client describes having hallucinations and flashback memories. Her parents think she has schizophrenia. In order to rule out the possibility of substance use as the cause of these symptoms, you should ask the client whether she has used:
   a. Cocaine or similar drugs in its class.
   b. LSD or similar drugs in its class.
   c. Amphetamines.
   d. Nicotine.
   e. Opiate antagonists.

4. You are working with a client who is on a methadone maintenance program to treat a heroin addiction. You should educate the client about the risks of using other drugs while on methadone because:
   a. All drug use is illegal.
   b. Using other drugs means that the dosage of methadone has to be increased.
   c. Combining methadone with other drugs will enhance the power of the methadone.
   d. Methadone increases a person's desire to use other opiates.
   e. Taking methadone with other drugs could have unpredictable results, including death.

5. In order to relieve depression, a psychiatrist should prescribe:
   a. A stimulant, such as methamphetamine.
   b. A barbiturate, such as phenobarbital.
   c. An antidepressant, such as Prozac.
   d. A hallucinogenic, such as PCP.
   e. An antibiotic, such as tetracycline.

6. A client asks about some of the negative effects of inhalant use. You advise that inhalants can cause:
   a. Constipation.
   b. Confusion.
   c. Poor concentration.
   d. Tooth decay.
   e. Both b and c.

7. A client says she is "speedballing." You know that this is a street term that generally means using:
   a. An antidepressant and a hallucinogen.
   b. An inhalant and a designer drug.
   c. A cannabinol and a depressant.
   d. A stimulant and an opiate.
   e. None of the above.

**50**

Chapter 2

8. A client advises you that he has taken a drug that causes a blending of colors, sounds, and smells. Of the following substances, this effect is most likely caused by taking:
   a. Insulin.
   b. Morphine.
   c. LSD.
   d. Ritalin.
   e. Lomotil.
9. To improve speed performance (without concern for accuracy), a typist might be tempted to use:
   a. Barbiturates.
   b. Benzodiazepines.
   c. Valium.
   d. Methadone.
   e. Amphetamines.
10. Someone who has recently inhaled gasoline is most likely to present with:
    a. Hyperactive movements and dilated pupils.
    b. Frequent nodding off combined with disturbed eating patterns.
    c. Slurred speech, giddiness, or dizziness.
    d. Clammy skin and emotional agitation.
    e. Paranoid delusions and flashbacks.
11. A woman who is intoxicated from heroin use is most likely to present with:
    a. Euphoria.
    b. Drowsiness and slowed respiration.
    c. Nausea.
    d. Nodding off.
    e. Any of the above, depending on when she took the drug.
12. A man who smoked pot about 2 minutes before seeing you is most likely to present with:
    a. Euphoria.
    b. Greater inhibitions and shallow breathing.
    c. Tremors and chills.
    d. Extreme depression.
    e. All of the above, depending on the day of the week.
13. Carla has used heroin 15 times in her life. She likes the effect, although certain friends who do not want to associate with someone who uses hard drugs have cut her off. She can easily go without heroin for weeks at a time and does not experience cravings. Based on this information, which statement reflects the most accurate assessment?
    a. Carla is misusing heroin.
    b. Carla is physically dependent on heroin.
    c. Carla is a chronic user of heroin.
    d. Carla is abusing heroin.
    e. Carla is psychologically addicted to heroin.

14. When you are conducting a psychosocial history with a client, he tells you that he has been going to a group for codependents. From your knowledge of codependence, you surmise that this is a group for:
    a. Two or more family members who are physically or psychologically dependent on a substance.
    b. Individuals who have a strong craving to use two related substances.
    c. Individuals who depend on the approval from others in an attempt to find safety, self-worth, or identity.
    d. Individuals who have a compulsion to use a substance, in spite of detrimental effects.
    e. Individuals with toxic psychosis or other medical complications that occur during the abstinence phase of alcoholic recovery.
15. Assume that you subscribe to a theory that people with alcohol problems have the greatest motivation to change when they "hit bottom." You can assess whether a person has hit bottom by identifying whether the client:
    a. Uses alcohol to relieve physical or psychological pain in amounts greater than allowed under normal social rules (an Alpha Alcoholic).
    b. Drinks periodically, including binge drinking to the point of blacking out (an Epsilon Alcoholic).
    c. Suffers from alcohol-related physical problems such as cirrhosis of the liver, but without physical or psychological dependence (a Beta Alcoholic).
    d. Is a chronic, progressive drinker, who is developing increasing tolerance and psychological dependence (or alcohol dependent according to the DSM).
    e. Believes from his own point of view that he has hit bottom.
16. You are using a harm reduction approach with a client, Jorge, who does not want to become psychologically dependent. Which of the following substances could he use without risking psychological dependence?
    a. Amphetamines, cocaine, and caffeine.
    b. Alcohol, heroin, and barbiturates.
    c. Pot and acid.
    d. Paint thinner.
    e. None of the above.
17. Psychological dependence to hallucinogens is more likely to occur when:
    a. The client is in denial about the effects of the drugs.
    b. The client has a high level of ADH.
    c. The substance used has a powerful positive effect for the client.
    d. Stimulants are used to counteract negative effects of hallucinogens.
    e. The client participates in psychotherapy from a well-trained social worker.
18. You have been asked by a drug-law reform committee to act as a consultant on the effects of drugs. They want to differentiate between substances that are more likely and those that are less likely to produce physical dependence. Which of the following substances is most likely to produce physical dependence?
    a. Caffeine.
    b. Cannabis.
    c. Barbiturates.
    d. Magic mushroom.
    e. Glue.

19. A public policy group wants to know where to allocate resources for a substance abuse prevention program. You suggest that they target the substance that is associated with the greatest total health costs to society:
    a. Crack/cocaine.
    b. Heroin.
    c. Narcotics.
    d. Amphetamines.
    e. Nicotine.

20. Predicting the specific effects that substance abuse will have on a particular client is difficult because the effects of a particular drug depend on:
    a. Pharmacological processes, such as the type of drug and its strength.
    b. Physiological processes and individual differences, such as the person's rate of metabolism and level of tolerance.
    c. Psychological processes, such as the person's mood and expectations.
    d. Social processes, such as whether the person is using drugs alone or with a certain group or in a particular type of public setting.
    e. All of the above.

21. You are working with a client who is at risk of committing suicide. Which of the following situations would put the client at the greatest risk of being able to commit suicide by overdosing?
    a. The client has access to large quantities of barbiturates and plans to use them.
    b. The client has recently purchased 5 mg of cannabis.
    c. The client has a plan to drink 2 bottles of beer and take 4 aspirin.
    d. The client has never used drugs before, but plans to drop acid at a party tonight.
    e. The client regularly drinks 5 to 8 bottles of beer in an evening and plans to drink 8 bottles that particular night.

22. The parents of a teenager are concerned that their child is using LSD, which they have heard is a lethal drug. You explain to them that the most common form of fatality associated with LSD is the result of:
    a. An overdose by an inexperienced user.
    b. Liver damage as a result of prolonged usage.
    c. Sudden withdrawal reaction.
    d. Accidental death arising from altered perception from use.
    e. Transmission of HIV or hepatitis from sharing needles.

23. You are working with a client who uses drugs to boost his confidence to compensate for feelings of inferiority, shyness, and insecurity. Which of the following drugs is most likely to give him the effects he seeks?
    a. Benzodiazepines.
    b. Barbiturates.
    c. Methamphetamines.
    d. Either a or b.
    e. Either b or c.

24. You are working with a group that is considering whether cannabis should be legalized for medical purposes, specifically to help patients cope with nausea and prevent vomiting. If cancer patients required a method of administering cannabis in a manner that produced effects very quickly, the preferred method of ingestion would be:
    a. Application to nasal passages.
    b. Intramuscular injection.
    c. Smoking.
    d. Swallowing.
    e. The time it takes to feel high is the same for each method of ingestion, since it is the same substance being ingested.

25. You are assessing a client for possible long-term effects of chronic alcohol use. Which of the following is *not* an indicator (or risk) of prolonged alcohol use?
    a. Permanent loss of memory.
    b. Cirrhosis of the liver.
    c. Chronic malnutrition.
    d. Cancer.
    e. Constriction of the arteries.

26. You are working on an advocacy brief to encourage the government to provide more resources for treatment programs for people who abuse cocaine. To highlight the need for these services, you identify the common social consequences of prolonged cocaine abuse, including:
    a. Involvement in criminal activity.
    b. Deterioration of family relationships.
    c. Loss of support from one peer group and development of support from groups that are involved in criminal activity.
    d. All of the above.
    e. Only a and b.

27. You are working with a client who smokes hash. One of your strategies is to help the client figure out why he uses hash and then determine if there is a healthier behavior that can produce the same effects. Which of the following effects are normally achieved through hash use?
    a. Helps the individual to relax when feeling anxious.
    b. Helps the individual to suppress appetite and lose weight.
    c. Helps the individual to develop more accurate memory.
    d. All of the above.
    e. Only a and b.

28. You are working with a truck driver who is concerned about falling asleep at the wheel. You review his eating habits and medication use. Of the following, which one contains a central nervous system depressant that might cause drowsiness?
    a. Lomotil (used in the treatment of diarrhea by slowing the digestive system).
    b. Chocolate (used by people who love the sweet, melt-in-your-mouth taste).
    c. Nutmeg (used in baking).
    d. Nicotine (used in cigarettes).
    e. Antibiotics (used for bacterial infections).

29. Medical doctors sometimes use cocaine for:
    a. Patients who are depressed.
    b. A local anesthetic.
    c. A cure for obesity.
    d. Treatment for jaundice.
    e. All of the above.

30. You are working as a discharge planner with a hospital. The medical staff is concerned that patients do not follow their prescriptions properly upon release. Many patients do not even know what substance misuse means. You design an educational brochure that provides examples of substance misuse. These examples appropriately include:
    a. Taking medications three times a day when they were prescribed for two times a day.
    b. Eating before taking pills when they are supposed to be taken on an empty stomach.
    c. Stopping medication earlier than prescribed because the person feels better.
    d. Taking a suppository orally when it is supposed to be taken anally.
    e. All of the above.

31. Rather than ask a client, "Are you addicted to alcohol?" or "Are you an alcoholic?" a social worker could focus on physical and emotional responses that indicate whether the client is physically dependent on alcohol by asking:
    a. "How much alcohol do you drink in a week?"
    b. "How often do you drink alcohol?"
    c. "Do you view yourself as an alcoholic?"
    d. "Think about the last time that you didn't drink alcohol for 12 to 24 hours. How did you feel and what were you experiencing?"
    e. "Have you ever passed out or had a hangover from drinking large quantities of alcohol?"

32. Fran started sniffing cocaine 5 years ago. To get the same effects today, she shoots cocaine. This change in drug use is most likely due to:
    a. Psychological dependence.
    b. Increased tolerance.
    c. Wanting to avoid flashbacks.
    d. Codependence.
    e. Not enough base in the cocaine.

33. When Belinda is out in the mountains, she has a strong urge to smoke pot. This may be an indication of:
    a. Physical dependence (withdrawal effects).
    b. Ecological dependence (person is not supported well by social environment).
    c. Psychological dependence (associational learning).
    d. Spiritual dependence (controlled by the client's higher power),
    e. Codependence.

34. Cecil has not used LSD for over a week. He is having flashbacks. This is most likely due to:
    a. Physical withdrawal from LSD.
    b. Psychological withdrawal from LSD.
    c. Increased tolerance to LSD.
    d. A one-time overdose of LSD use.
    e. Long-term effects of LSD use.

35. A client who is using diet pills to suppress her appetite has been advised that she should avoid taking other central nervous system stimulants, which could have additive effects. Which of the following substances act as stimulants?
    a. Cocaine.
    b. Caffeine.
    c. Nicotine.
    d. All of the above.
    e. Only a and b.

36. A client who has been prescribed sleeping pills is concerned about developing tolerance to them. In order to avoid increasing tolerance to a drug, he would be best advised to:
    a. Use large dosages.
    b. Use only opiates.
    c. Combine stimulants and depressants for the synergistic effects.
    d. Use the drug infrequently.
    e. All of the above.

37. Barbiturates are used medically as:
    a. Sedatives, to induce sleep.
    b. Short-term anesthetics, to stop pain during surgery in a specific area of the body.
    c. Anticonvulsants, for people who are trying to abstain from alcohol.
    d. Treatments for psychiatric problems, such as major depression or multiple personality disorder.
    e. All of the above.

38. In order to avoid physical withdrawal effects from magic mushrooms, a client could use:
    a. Benzodiazepines.
    b. PCP or a similar hallucinogen.
    c. Muscle relaxants such as Carisoprodol.
    d. Librium.
    e. There are no physical withdrawal effects from magic mushrooms.

39. Gerry is prescribed Prozac by his physician. Gerry sells it to a friend to use for similar symptoms. This may be described as an example of:
    a. Substance misuse.
    b. Codependence.
    c. Classical learning theory.
    d. Structural theory.
    e. Psychoanalytic theory.

40. You are developing a program for at-risk youth, designed to prevent them from using drugs. If you want to target first-time users, then your program needs to focus on:
    a. Chronic use.
    b. Problem use.
    c. Experimental use.
    d. Critical use.
    e. Antisocial use.

41. In a residential treatment program, your group members have remained abstinent for 3 weeks. You are working on a relapse prevention program. To help members

identify when they are at highest risk of relapse, you advise them that they are at this point when:

    a. They start to feel good about themselves.

    b. They are no longer codependent on a loved one.

    c. They return to old patterns of behavior, common to their drug abusing days.

    d. Their tolerance to the substance is starting to decrease.

    e. They make use of new social supports.

42. A client is confused because you have said that alcohol is a depressant, but the client says she feels great when she uses alcohol. This may be because, depending on the individual and the situation, alcohol use can produce:

    a. Depressant effects.

    b. Euphoria or other stimulant effects.

    c. Thought distortion.

    d. Sense alteration.

    e. All of the above.

43. Your client has been able to remain abstinent from cocaine for 1 year. The client still has urges to snort cocaine. Although the client knows how cocaine has been harmful, these urges are powerful because:

    a. He will still have cocaine in his system for 2 more years.

    b. After 1 year, he is just beginning to have withdrawal systems.

    c. The positive, euphoric effects from past use remain in his memory, and there is no specific time frame to get over a psychological addiction.

    d. The client has developed a reverse tolerance to cocaine.

    e. The client doesn't really have an ability to judge what is best for him.

44. Doctors prescribe certain opiates for patients who require:

    a. Weight loss.

    b. Relief from pain.

    c. Vaccinations for HIV.

    d. Antidepressants.

    e. Doctors cannot prescribe opiates, since they are illicit substances.

45. Paula says that she feels euphoric when she uses heroin. This feeling is caused by:

    a. The fact that heroin is a central nervous system stimulant.

    b. Her level of tolerance to heroin from past exposure.

    c. Misinformed expectations about the effects of heroin.

    d. Euphoric effects that occur before depressive effects are experienced.

    e. Effects of coming down from heroin.

46. Frequent crack users tend to:

    a. Have a period of enhanced social and psychological functioning during their first 6 months of use.

    b. Avoid negative effects of crack use as long as they increase the frequency of use to compensate for increased tolerance.

    c. Suffer from financial, health, and social problems more quickly than frequent alcohol users.

    d. Have conditioned cravings and compulsive urges only in late stages of the course of cocaine addiction.

    e. Suffer from cocaine psychosis and chronic severe depression during experimental use.

47. A social worker can use the Jellinek Curve (or another model of the stages of alcoholism) as part of an intervention with an alcohol-dependent client by:
    a. Injecting alcohol agonists into the client.
    b. Exploring the risks of progression of use so the client might choose to change behavior before really "hitting bottom."
    c. Facilitating ways of using alcohol for its numbing and escape effects as ways of coping with stress.
    d. Teaching family members ways to enable the client's use.
    e. None of the above.

48. Chewing coca leaves is considered a low-risk behavior, whereas smoking crack is considered to be a high-risk behavior. The reason for this is:
    a. South American Aborigines who chew coca leaves have an innate tolerance for cocaine, whereas most people in the United States have no innate tolerance for cocaine.
    b. The active ingredient in crack comes from a different class of drugs than that found in coca leaves.
    c. Not known to science.
    d. Coca leaves are more toxic than crack, which discourages people from chewing them.
    e. The form of administration and level of concentration of crack brings higher risks, including greater risks of dependence, heart attack, and stroke.

49. OxyContin can be more dangerous than other pain killers such as morphine and codeine because:
    a. OxyContin is a barbiturate rather than a benzodiazepine.
    b. OxyContin has no medical uses.
    c. Although OxyContin is offered as a time-release medication, a person can get the entire effects very quickly by breaking up the pill before swallowing it.
    d. All of the above.
    e. None of the above.

50. In order to determine what type of psychoactive substance exists in a pill, a social worker would be best advised to:[13]
    a. Put the pill on the tip of her tongue—salty pills contain depressants, woody pills contain THC, and sweet-flavored pills contain stimulants.
    b. Grind up the pill and put it in a solution of vinegar and water—benzodiazepines will bubble up, whereas barbiturates will turn the solution blue.
    c. Cross-reference the number printed on the pill with a list of pharmaceutical drugs, such as books published for law enforcement or for pharmacists.
    d. Consider the shape of the pill—square pills are depressants, round pills are stimulants, and pills with holes in the middle are hallucinogens.
    e. Check the color of the pill—blues are sedatives, pinks are cannabis, and reds are amphetamines.

---

13. Other possibilities include asking the client, reading what is written on the label of the pill bottle, showing the pill to a pharmacist or other expert, or taking the pill to a laboratory that can test for what is contained in a pill.

51. A client who drinks 8 to 12 cups of coffee per day wants to know if he is physically addicted to caffeine. In order to help him determine this, you could ask him:
    a. Whether he has any triggers for drinking, such as smoking cigarettes.
    b. Whether he has any psychological cravings for coffee.
    c. Whether he puts cream and sugar in his coffee.
    d. How he feels when he has not had coffee for a prolonged period of time.
    e. How he feels when he has just had a cup of coffee.

52. You have helped a client to stop using alcohol, only to find that she has switched to "reds" (a barbiturate called Seconal). You help the client understand that:
    a. She has successfully cured herself of her alcohol addiction.
    b. She has avoided going through withdrawal from alcohol because Seconal is a similar type of depressant, but Seconal abuse has many of the same risks as alcohol abuse.
    c. Alcohol is less risky to her health than Seconal, which is an illicit substance.
    d. If she wants to switch drugs of choice, then amphetamines are more similar to alcohol than Seconal.
    e. She should combine alcohol and reds for a period of 6 months and then try to cut down on both.

53. Some people argue that cannabis should be legalized because its short- and long-term effects are no more harmful than the effects of smoking nicotine cigarettes. As you are formulating your opinion on this issue, you know that the risks of cannabis use include:
    a. Impaired ability to drive a car or other vehicle.
    b. Lung damage.
    c. Suppressed immune system.
    d. Adverse effects on the reproductive system.
    e. All of the above.

54. An important reason for a social worker to be able to assess whether a client is physically addicted to substances such as alcohol, barbiturates, or heroin is:
    a. To determine whether the client needs to go to a specialized detoxification program when she first stops using drugs.
    b. To know whether to report the client to the police.
    c. To determine whether the client is immune from criminal conviction because she has a disease.
    d. To identify the risk of suicide.
    e. To diagnose whether the person is clinically depressed.

55. AOD use can contribute to aggressiveness and violence by:
    a. Diminishing ego controls over comportment, releasing submerged anger.
    b. Impairing judgment.
    c. Creating a craving to obtain and use the drug, which can result in criminal behaviors, such as assaulting a person to get money to buy drugs.
    d. Creating feelings of bravado or omnipotence to obliterate one's ordinary sense of caution.
    e. All of the above.

# Converting Jargon Into Client-Appropriate Language

When studying pharmacology, it is easy to get caught up in technical language and forget how to speak in language more appropriate for dealing directly with clients. For each of the following examples, construct a reframed question or statement in clear, simple language that you could use with a real client.

1. What intoxication effects are produced when you ingest smokeable methamphetamine?

    Sample reframe: *Please describe what happens to you when you use ice.*

2. Which route of administration do you use when you consume your drug of choice?

3. What functions do benzodiazepines serve in your life?

4.   Pharmacologically speaking, Valium is classified as a sedative-hypnotic.

5.   You demonstrate the classic signs of physical dependence on alcohol, because you experience nausea, delirium tremens, insomnia, and hallucinations upon prolonged periods of abstinence, and you show a high level of tolerance when you are using alcohol.

6.   Adolescents using cannabis tend to be in the experimental or social stages of the progression of substance abuse, though some may be self-medicating boredom and anxiety for desired effects such as social inclusion and relaxation.

7. Given that feelings of insecurity trigger your desire to nasally ingest cocaine, I hypothesize that you are psychologically addicted and need to find alternate strategies for coping with this type of effect.

## Role-Plays: Nigel/Nicole and Roberta/Robert

The following two role-plays will help you put plain language into practice. Each involves a social worker and a client. The person playing the social worker should *not* read the client's confidential facts.

### Nigel's/Nicole's Case

In this role-play, the social worker is interviewing a new client (Nigel or Nicole) who is using a drug called "Sludge," but doesn't know its real name. The social worker's role is to explore the client's frequency of use, onset of use, desired and undesired effects, psychological dependence, physical dependence, and route of administration.

**Confidential facts to be read only by Nigel/Nicole:** You are 42 years old. Your drug of choice is called "Sludge," which is a brown, slimy substance that you glob onto tobacco, roll like a cigarette, and smoke like a joint. You smoke Sludge 10 to 12 times a day. The first time you used it was when you were 13 and at a party with your older brother. You haven't gone a day without Sludge for the past 8 years. You enjoy Sludge because it makes you feel mellow and detached—a great escape from the pressures of work and family. You don't like everything about Sludge. It gives you Sludge breath, yellow teeth, and difficulty breathing, especially during exercise. You have smoked the same amount of Sludge over the past 8 years, with no noticeable change in effects (though it did take you 4 years to initially get used to Sludge, by the time you were in college you could easily blow eight Sludge in an evening).

**Debriefing (to be read by observers in advance of the role-play so they can take notes during the role-play):** What questions seemed particularly useful in eliciting information that the worker wanted? Write down two or three worker questions or statements that included too much jargon or did not sound genuine. Reframe each of these responses so that they are more appropriate, given the context of the interview. What category of substance does Sludge seem to fit into?[14]

---

14. Sludge is a fictional substance.

Sleet.com, Inc., is a computer software company that employs 24 extremely bright 18- and 19-year-olds. The manager (Robert/Roberta) is very concerned about a designer drug developed and used by half of the employees that they affectionately call "Sleet." Roberta has hired a social worker to consult with the organization and develop a plan to help employees who are abusing Sleet. The role-play covers the first meeting between the social worker and Robert/Roberta. The social worker's role is to explore the function of Sleet in the company and the potential risks, including physical and psychological dependence, side effects, and social consequences.

**Confidential facts to be read by Robert/Roberta:** The employees using Sleet do not do it on site or during the day, but at home and during off-hours. Most of the employees seem to be able to control when they use it and can stop using it when they want to. They don't appear to suffer any ill effects when they stop using. Employees report that they apply this substance to their foreheads and that it gives them a cool, tingly sensation, followed by a period of exhilaration. Although the employees manufacture this product themselves and say that all the ingredients are legal, they do suffer some ill effects on the downside of intoxication. About an hour after using Sleet, they get headaches, feel tired and grungy, and sometimes get a sense that their skin is crawling. Employees have been using Sleet for about 4 months. Their frequency and amount of use has been increasing, along with the amount of money spent on Sleet. Some employees have been dipping into petty cash to pay for the ingredients. Work productivity and profits have also declined.

**Debriefing (to be read by observers in advance of the role-play so they can take notes during the role-play):** Write down four key questions in which the worker used wording appropriate to this client. Ask the client how she/he felt when asked these questions. Write down two key questions in which the worker used wording that was too technical or contrived. Ask the client how she/he felt when asked these questions. What stage in the continuum of substance use do you think this company was experiencing? How well does this continuum apply to organizations as opposed to individuals?

# Diversity

Different countries have different laws regulating the same substances. To what extent do these differences in laws reflect:

- Different patterns of use?
- Different rates of physical or psychological dependence?
- Different rates of social problems, such as drug-related criminal activity, domestic violence, or absenteeism from the workplace?
- Different belief systems?
- Different attitudes toward substance use and abuse?
- Other differences?

Consider two stereotypes: (1) In Jamaica, people are allowed to use marijuana freely and they do not have problems with it; and (2) the governments of Afghanistan and Pakistan have tolerated, if not encouraged, the production of poppies for heroin trade to the West. What are the actual laws in these countries and how well have these laws been enforced in the last 5 years? What are the actual rates of usage in these countries? What are the differences in the ways that Jamaicans use marijuana, and how Afghanis and Pakistanis use opium, from the ways that Americans use it? Consider how subgroups in each country use these substances (e.g., Rastafarians in Jamaica).

# Ethical Debate: Competence and Professional Turf

All professions value competence in their practice, but many times people from certain professions assume that theirs is the most competent profession for a particular type of presenting problem. Which profession or combination of professions is best suited to work with clients affected by AODAs? Provide your reasoning. If your answer depends on particular factors, what are they?

Complete the following questionnaire to raise your awareness of your attitudes toward competence and professional turf in relation to AODA work.

| | | | | | |
|---|---|---|---|---|---|
| 1. | Social workers do not require extensive education in pharmacology and physiology to practice AODA work.[15] | Strongly Disagree | Disagree | Agree | Strongly Agree |
| 2. | Medical professionals such as doctors and nurses focus too much on physical aspects of AODAs because of their extensive pharmacology and physiology training. | Strongly Disagree | Disagree | Agree | Strongly Agree |
| 3. | Social workers can learn enough pharmacology and physiology in a 10-hour course to be able to practice competently with AODAs. | Strongly Disagree | Disagree | Agree | Strongly Agree |
| 4. | Social workers and medically trained professionals find it difficult to work together because their training provides them with completely different foci for their work. | Strongly Disagree | Disagree | Agree | Strongly Agree |
| 5. | Psychologists are the best professionals for assessing AODA clients because psychologists are trained in psychometric testing. | Strongly Disagree | Disagree | Agree | Strongly Agree |
| 6. | Psychiatrists are the best professionals for conducting community needs assessments pertaining to AODA risks, because psychiatrists are trained to focus on the macro systems level. | Strongly Disagree | Disagree | Agree | Strongly Agree |

---

15. If you are from a profession other than social work, please substitute this profession (e.g., family counselor, psychologist, correctional officer, or nurse practitioner).

As you discuss your answers with people in your class, try to understand the reasons behind the attitudes each classmate is expressing. What additional knowledge do you require in order to make an informed decision on these questions?

# Journaling Exercise

1.  Go into your own medical cabinet, refrigerator, and kitchen cupboards. Identify at least four common foods or medications that you use that contain a psychoactive substance. For each of these foods or medications:
    a.  Categorize the psychoactive substance that it contains.
    b.  Identify the primary intoxication effects of the substance.
    c.  Identify the function(s) that the food or medication serves for you.
    d.  What is your attitude toward the psychoactive substance—e.g., is it a magic pill, a necessary evil, an insignificant part of your life, or something else?
    e.  Describe what your life would be like if you had to stop using this substance today and knew that you could never use it again.

    What has this exercise taught you about yourself?

2.  How comfortable do you feel with your knowledge of the pharmacology of substances? List questions or concerns that you would like some help with—consider taking these questions to a classmate, the instructor, or some other person who has the knowledge and patience to help.

# InfoTrac College Edition

## Key words

◇ Pharmacology
◇ Withdrawal
◇ Tolerance
◇ Stimulant
◇ Depressant
◇ Hallucinogen
◇ Opiate
◇ Inhalant
◇ Cannabis

CHAPTER

# 3

~~∽∿∿∼~~

# Models of Helping Individuals With AODA Problems

Chapter 2 focused on the physiological perspective of AODAs. It is now time to look at a broader range of perspectives. One of the biggest challenges in learning about ways to help people with AODA problems is sorting out the various theories, therapies, and models. For the purposes of this manual, *theory* refers to a conceptual explanation of the nature and cause(s) of particular AODA problems. Some theories have strong empirical support, whereas others are difficult to prove or have not undergone sufficient research to demonstrate their validity. *Therapy* refers to a specific set of strategies, techniques, and skills that are used to help a client system deal with AODA concerns. Some therapies draw from one particular theory (e.g., Psychoanalytic Therapy is based on Psychoanalytic Theory), whereas other therapies are based on more than one theory (e.g., Narrative Family Therapy is based on Social Construction and Cognitive Theory). A model of helping is a notional framework that can be used to guide the intervention process between a social worker and client system, but a model is not as specific as a therapy in terms of guiding the practitioner (e.g., the Biopsychosocial Model suggests that a worker address biological, psychological, and social issues, but does not specify which area to address first and depends on the worker applying other theories and methods of intervention).

The following chart (Figure 3.1) lists a range of theories, therapies, and models of helping, organizing them into a continuum from biological to structural perspectives. The theories, therapies, and models toward the left side of the page suggest that the causes and interventions required for AODAs are related to internal problems (biologically and psychologically). The ones toward the right side of the page suggest that the causes and interventions required for AODAs are related to external problems (family, community, and societal context).[1]

---

1. In other words, this continuum goes from internal to external "locus of responsibility" and from internal to external "locus of control" (Keyson & Janda, 2004).

**FIGURE 3.1**
## Continuum of Theories, Therapies, and Models of Helping

| *Biological* | *Psychological/Spiritual* | *Social/Systems* | *Structural*[2] |
|---|---|---|---|
| Genetic Theory (e.g., physical or psychological traits or predispositions that are inherited) | Psychoanalytic Theory and Therapy | Family Systems Theory and Therapy | Radical Theory and Social Work |
| Physiological Theory | Behavioral Theory and Therapy (e.g., Classical, Operant, and Social Learning; Functional Approach; Substance Refusal Training; Covert Aversion Training; Systematic Desensitization; Contingency Contracting; Coaching) | Adult Children of Alcoholics Theory and Groupwork | Marxist Theory |
| Pharmacological Therapy (e.g., Methadone, Antabuse, Naltrexone, nicotine patch) | Cognitive Theory and Therapy (e.g., Cognitive Restructuring, Psychoeducational Group) | Ecological Model of Social Work | Radical Activism and Advocacy (e.g., civil disobedience) |
| | Trait Theory (e.g., compulsive) | Subculture Theory | |
| | Rational Emotive Behavior Therapy | Supraculture Theory | |
| | Existential Theory and Therapy | Community Reinforcement | |
| | Gestalt Therapy | Criminal Justice Model (e.g., prohibiting possession of certain substances) | |
| | Crisis Intervention | | |
| | Motivational Enhancement Interviewing | | |
| | Reality Therapy | | |
| | Pastoral Counseling | | |
| | Self-efficacy Enhancement | | |

———————————— Solution-Focused Therapy ————————————

———————————— Indigenous Healing and Spirituality ————————————

———————————— Feminist Theory and Social Work ————————————

———————————— Social Construction Theory and Narrative Therapy ————————————

——————— Moral Model ———————

———————————— Medical Model ————————————

——— Public Health Promotion (e.g., use of taxes and regulation to promote health) ———

——— AA/12-Steps Model and Groupwork (including Disease Concept of Addiction) ———

———————— Transtheoretical Model (TTM/Stages of Change) ————————

———————————— Harm Reduction Model ————————————

———————— Generalist Social Work and Biopsychosocial Model of Social Work ————————

2. Includes an analysis of how oppressive systems in society, such as patriarchy, homophobia, racism, ableism, and classism, maintain conditions that cause and perpetuate AODA use and problems.

Some models and therapies extend across more than one perspective. In this chapter, the focus is on helping *individuals*, but even work with individuals must consider social contexts, such as family and community. Chapters 6 and 8 will focus on work with families and communities, respectively.

This chart is not exhaustive of the possible theories, therapies, and models of helping that can be used to assist people with AODA problems. From your readings and classroom discussions, identify at least two other theories, therapies, or models that you want to learn for the purposes of this course (e.g., Resilience Therapy, Relapse Prevention, Empowerment Model). Place these on the continuum, indicating to what extent they focus on biological, psychological, spiritual, social, and structural perspectives. Also, with an asterisk, indicate which of the theories, therapies, and models in the chart are specifically designed for work on AODA problems.

In order to ensure that you have a conceptual understanding of the theories, therapies, and models, use a GSI to help you complete the following chart.[3] There is room for analysis of two theories, therapies, or models. If you want to analyze additional ones, photocopy this page or create your own chart on a word processor. An analysis of Operant Conditioning from Behavioral Theory is provided as an example.

|  | Operant Conditioning | Insert your first example: _____ | Insert your second example: _____ |
|---|---|---|---|
| **Causality**—What is the etiology of AODA problems?[4] | *AOD use or other addictive behaviors are viewed as learned responses, with positive reinforcers encouraging certain behaviors and punishments discouraging certain behaviors.* | | |
| **Interactions**— How do AODAs cause, contribute to, maintain, or alleviate problems?[5] | *Operant Conditioning has a linear view of causality—AODA behaviors can lead to positive consequences or negative consequences (problems).* | | *(continued)* |

---

3. See Chapter 1 for an explanation of Good Sources of Information (GSIs).
4. *Etiology* refers to the understanding of how the phenomenon is caused or generated.
5. Note that some theories, therapies, and models focus on strengths and goals rather than problems or pathologies.

| | Operant Conditioning | Insert your first example: _____ | Insert your second example: _____ |
|---|---|---|---|
| **Symptoms**—Are AODAs viewed as the symptom of a problem or the problem itself? | *AODA behaviors are viewed as a problem, but the negative consequences of AODAs are also viewed as problems.* | | |
| **Intervention**—What type of help is suggested? | *To address AODA behaviors, new patterns of positive and negative reinforcements are required (for example, placing the person in an environment that responds positively when the person does not drink).* | | |
| **Goal**—How is success viewed (e.g., abstinence, moderate use, harm reduction, improved quality of life, improved social functioning in particular areas)? | *Success is determined by a change in behavior as agreed between the social worker and client. The change could be either abstinence or moderated AODA behavior.* | | |

Theories are important because they guide the practitioner's understanding and assessment process. In turn, the practitioner's understanding and assessment of the client's AODA problems guide the process of intervention or helping. To the extent that there is research support for the validity and effectiveness of an intervention, using theories to guide practice ensures that practitioners are using interventions that are known to be effective (Bean, 2003). The choice of theories is complicated by the fact that AODAs are complex social issues, with no single cause or solution that fits all client situations. When applying a single theory, practitioners risk stereotyping or being dogmatic. A theory provides a hypothesis about the nature of a client's AODA problems; this hypothesis needs to be confirmed or rejected during the helping process rather than simply imposing a theory and its consequent intervention on a client.

If one views every problem as a nail, then the solution will always be a hammer. To avoid this type of reductionism or overgeneralization, you should develop your own model of practice, based on your own research and reflections. This does not mean being "eclectic" in the sense of just picking and choosing theories for each client without formal criteria. An integrated, holistic approach requires that you incorporate both knowledge and values into your assessment process. For example, we know that a very "effective" way to stop people from using drugs would be to put them in restraints and lock them up indefinitely. However, this would not be consistent with values such as personal autonomy and respect for all individuals, and principles such as self-determination and use of least restrictive means necessary. Alternatively, we know that a Rogerian (humanistic, client-centered) approach to social work fits with the social work value of self-determination. But do we know how effective a Rogerian approach would be when working with an intoxicated client who is threatening to kill the worker?

In order to develop an integrated model of practice, identify a presenting problem related to AODAs. Explore your understanding of the etiology of this problem, how you define success for working with an individual with such a problem, and specific models of helping that are appropriate and effective for assisting a client with the problem according to your definition of success. The following chart demonstrates how you can summarize this information, with an example relating to a client who says, "I'm too fat," as the presenting problem. As you can see by this example, the manner in which you understand the problem has significant impact on how you view success and the preferred types of help. Be sure to have GSIs to back up your suggestions.

Other presenting problems that you could use include "I was arrested for a DUI (Driving Under the Influence)," "I can't sleep unless I take sleeping pills," or "I have to sell my body for sex in order to support my cocaine habit." You could also use presenting problems from one of the cases in Chapter 1.

| Presenting problem | Usual causes or etiology | Definition of success | Models of helping |
|---|---|---|---|
| Example: "I'm too fat." | 1. Physiological predisposition to above-average weight | 1. Maintains healthy diet and weight level; reduces health risks related to being overweight | 1. Nutrition and exercise education and planning |
| | 2. Psychological compulsion to eat | 2. Deals with underlying cause of compulsion to eat (e.g., response to stress) | 2. Stress reduction and stress management counseling |
| | 3. Response to culturally determined definitions of positive body image | 3. Substitutes unrealistic expectations of body image with more realistic and positive expectations | 3. Narrative Therapy |
| | | | (continued) |

| Presenting problem | Usual causes or etiology | Definition of success | Models of helping |
|---|---|---|---|
|  |  |  |  |
|  |  |  |  |
|  |  |  |  |
|  |  |  |  |

# Distinguishing Different Theories and Approaches

The following multiple-choice questions are designed to help you distinguish between different theories and approaches to AODAs.

1. An abstinence approach to alcoholism refers to:
   a. Encouraging the client to discontinue using alcohol completely, based on the belief that alcoholism can be controlled but not cured.
   b. Discouraging a client from having sexual intercourse because this might stimulate physiological processes that produce cravings for alcohol.
   c. Helping people avoid or minimize the problems associated with alcohol use, even if they choose to continue to use alcohol.
   d. Encouraging people to use more alcohol as a paradoxical intervention.
   e. Praying for salvation from the sins of alcohol addiction.

2. A psychodynamic view of addiction assumes:
   a. Addiction is not a disease but a symptom of an underlying problem, such as an unresolved issue from childhood, weak attachment with a parent, or an expression of hostility.
   b. Addiction is a behavior that is learned through patterns of reinforcements and punishments.
   c. Addiction is part of a compulsive personality trait that is inherited.
   d. Addiction is a social response to pressures from systems in one's social environment.
   e. Addiction develops among people with a well-functioning ego.

3. Sociocultural theories of subtance abuse suggest:
   a. The cause of substance abuse problems within a culture is a genetic defect within the culture.
   b. There are different patterns of use and AOD problems among diverse sociocultural groups or subgroups; for example, people from cultures with high levels of ambivalence toward substance abuse tend to have greater problems with substance abuse.
   c. The subconscious controls urges such as cravings for substances that produce euphoric effects.
   d. Most illicit drug use is caused by lack of punishment by parents of children who use illicit drugs.
   e. Ilicit drug use could be lowered by the use of high levels of chlorine in the water system.

4. Which theoretical perspective or model of helping supports the use of medical detoxification for a person who is dependent on barbiturates?
   a. Physiological.
   b. Pyschoanalytic.
   c. Cognitive.
   d. Radical Social Work.
   e. Transtheoretical.

5. If a social worker is working with an individual client who is in denial about AODA problems, a Family Systems perspective suggests that:
   a. The worker should strip the client down to her emotional core to fight off her defense mechanisms.

b. Involvement of family members might be used to put pressure on the client to admit there is a problem and accept help through intervention with the family.

c. The client will not accept help until she hits bottom on her own.

d. Family members should only be brought into the helping process if they have no problems of their own.

e. The best approach is to offer the client harm reduction rather than abstinence as the ultimate goal.

6. Antabuse is used in pharmacotherapy (treatments that use medications) to help people maintain abstinence from:

a. Valium.

b. Heroin.

c. Alcohol.

d. Cocaine.

e. None of the above.

7. One of the primary criticisms of Psychoanalytic Therapy for AOD problems is that Psychoanalytic Therapy:

a. Focuses too much on the social construction of the AOD problem rather than objective criteria that apply universally.

b. Uses a nondirective approach and tends to focus solely on the client's development of insight into their problems, neglecting the addictive power of AODs.

c. Uses chemical treatments for AODA problems, which runs against the principle of self-determination.

d. Forces clients to give up friends who use AODs and social situations that involve AOD use.

e. Asks the worker to consider biological, social, spiritual, and psychological influences, but does not really direct the worker as to which aspect to focus upon first.

8. Playing pool is a psychological trigger for Kerry to drink beer. This is an example of:

a. Modeling Theory.

b. Operant Conditioning.

c. Classical Conditioning.

d. Cognitive Restructuring.

e. Positive Reinforcement.

9. According to a liberal feminist perspective on AODAs:

a. Women are more likely than men to have AODA problems because they are biologically inferior to men when it comes to how alcohol is metabolized by the body.

b. The male gender is morally inferior to the female gender.

c. Each individual has an independently determined construction or understanding of the way that AODAs fit into their lives, regardless of gender.

d. Inequalities in society between men and women contribute to some of the problems that women have with AODAs.

e. The root cause of AODA problems is related to an overactive Id or dysfunctional Superego.

10. A Biopsychosocial Model suggests that a practitioner should view AODAs as:
    a. An interaction among biological, psychological, and social antecedents and consequences of AOD use or other addictive behaviors.
    b. A self-destructive disease.
    c. A moral defect.
    d. Having single, one-way cause-and-effect relationships that can be proven empirically.
    e. All of the above.
11. Most genetic explanations of AOD addictions suggest that:
    a. Positive reinforcement for substance use will increase the likelihood of compulsive use.
    b. Some people may be predisposed to addiction through inheritance of particular physiological or psychological traits.
    c. Early childhood trauma can cause genetic abnormalities that can cause addiction.
    d. If both of one's parents are alcoholic, then a child is guaranteed to be alcoholic.
    e. People who have Levi genes are more likely to develop alcoholism.
12. A 12-Step Approach to AODAs suggests that:
    a. People can be cured of their addictions only if they accept God into their lives.
    b. People can follow the 12 Steps in any order, since the 12-Steps program is a very individualized approach to treatment.
    c. There is little that a social worker can do for a client who has an AODA problem but does not accept that life has become unmanageable because of an addiction. The client must take the first step in admitting a problem.
    d. People with AODAs can be successful through either abstinence or moderation of their use.
    e. The primary goal of intervention is harm reduction.
13. Carl Rogers's Core Conditions for developing a therapeutic relationship suggest that, regardless of theoretical orientation, an AODA social worker should demonstrate:
    a. Empathic understanding, genuineness, and unconditional positive regard.
    b. Disapproval of AODA behaviors.
    c. Love, peace, and charity.
    d. Willingness to do anything for a client.
    e. Sympathy for the difficulties and losses incurred by the client.
14. Project Match and similar research on matching are designed to:
    a. Study the effects of providing matches instead of lighters to people who smoke cigarettes or cannabis.
    b. Develop research-based criteria to help determine which clients would benefit most from which theoretical frameworks or models of helping.
    c. Create a theoretical basis for the etiology of substance dependence, addiction, and abuse.
    d. Determine whether AODA counselors need to have a history of addiction in order to be effective with clients who have serious AOD problems.
    e. Promote a drug-free lifestyle in the newspapers and other media.
15. A Moral Model of addictions runs contrary to social work ethics because:
    a. Social workers are not allowed by law to have any personal morals.
    b. Clients have a right to confidentiality that might be breached.

c. AOD use is caused by deeply engrained personality disorders that cannot be changed.

d. The Moral Model suggests that people with AOD problems have moral defects, which goes against the social work principle of nonjudgmentalism.

e. Social workers are among the highest users of illicit drugs, so that preaching morality would be inconsistent with the ethical obligation to be honest with clients.

16. A Structural Approach to AODA problems suggests that the Locus of Responsibility for the problems is:

a. Societal, because of issues such as sexism, homophobia, and racism in society.

b. The family, because of social systems effects, including reciprocal relationships.

c. The interaction between a person and social environment, due to lack of goodness of fit.

d. All of the above.

e. None of the above.

17. AA and NA suggest that a person needs to connect with a higher power. A theoretical understanding of this premise could be drawn from:

a. Classical Conditioning Theory.

b. Existential Theory.

c. Psychoanalytic Theory.

d. Personality Theory.

e. Supracultural Theory.

18. From an ecological perspective, success in AODA services should be measured by:

a. The client's ability to achieve her goals, which could include abstinence, controlled use, or harm reduction.

b. How well the client adapts to her social environment.

c. How well the client's environment adapts to meet the needs of the client.

d. Improved social relationships, including ones with family, work, school, and peers.

e. All of the above.

19. From a strengths perspective, the fact that a client uses illicit drugs to block out memories of sexual abuse can be seen as a strength because:

a. The client is avoiding dealing with an underlying problem.

b. The client does not care if he is breaking the law.

c. The client cannot recover until he hits bottom.

d. The client has a disease that cannot be cured, though it can be controlled.

e. The client has learned a method of coping with a problem in order to avoid more severe reactions, such as suicide.

20. According to Developmental Theory, some AOD use among teenagers can be considered normal because:

a. Adolescents have a high level of physical resiliency to AOD use.

b. Experimentation is a part of normal adolescent development.

c. AOD use is learned and is easy to unlearn, regardless of age.

d. Children can use alcohol and illicit drugs as long as they have parental consent.

e. Genetics is the only true predictor of AODA problems.

21. A harm-reduction approach to drug problems refers to:
    a. Prohibiting drug use by criminalizing possession and trafficking.
    b. Promoting abstinence through education.
    c. Helping people avoid or minimize the problems associated with drug use, even if they choose to continue to use drugs.
    d. Encouraging people to use more drugs as a paradoxical intervention.
    e. Praying for salvation from the sins of drug addiction.
22. Naltrexone can be used in pharmacotherapy (drug treatment) to help people who are trying to deal with a physical addiction to:
    a. LSD.
    b. Heroin or alcohol.
    c. Antabuse.
    d. Amphetamines.
    e. Ecstasy.
23. A client has a severe problem with alcoholism, but does not want to stop drinking. The client shows signs of vitamin deficiency and Wernicke-Korsakoff Syndrome. Using a harm reduction approach and starting where the client is, a social worker would:
    a. Declare the client incompetent and obtain a court order to force the person into treatment.
    b. Offer nutritional counseling or information to reduce the risks of malnutrition.
    c. Call the client's boss or significant others to try to put pressure on the client to stop drinking.
    d. Buy wine or beer for the client, or provide access to beer or wine if the client does not have the money.
    e. Have a drink with the client to show that the social worker is not judging the client.
24. *Loss* can be used as a concept in AODA counseling by:
    a. Teaching clients that they have nothing to lose by quitting their AOD use.
    b. Helping clients anticipate the losses that they can expect if they decide to go abstinent, so that they can explore alternatives and grieve the losses.
    c. Asking clients to give up their concept of God or a higher power, so that they will take personal responsibility for their use.
    d. Taking clients out into the wilderness so that they are lost and have to find the way back with no help, so that they will learn how to cope without drugs.
    e. None of the above.
25. The Medical Model for helping people with AODAs suggests that:
    a. Clients are responsible for providing their own diagnosis of the AODA disorder, as well as prescribing the most appropriate treatment.
    b. Clients are responsible for providing the diagnosis of the problem, but expert practitioners are responsible for prescribing treatment.
    c. An expert such as a mental health practitioner is responsible for diagnosing an AODA disorder, as well as prescribing the appropriate form of treatment.
    d. The client and the expert practitioner work together as equals in determining the nature of an AODA problem and the client recommends how they should proceed.
    e. Only a medical doctor can provide treatment for AODAs.

26. Although a Disease Concept is used by many AODA counselors, those who argue against promoting a Disease Concept of alcoholism suggest that:
    a. Some people with alcohol problems might think that because alcoholism is a disease rather than a moral fault, the client has no responsibility for dealing with the problem.
    b. Clients are labeled with a disease that still has stigma attached to it.
    c. Alcoholism may be caused by social factors rather than by a disease that occurs within the individual.
    d. All of the above.
    e. None of the above.
27. Advocates of an abstinence goal for AOD treatment believe:
    a. Moderate use is a viable option for most AOD abusers.
    b. The focus on treatment should be to reduce harm, regardless of use.
    c. The most effective way for people to deal with chronic AOD problems is to stop using AODs altogether.
    d. All of the above.
    e. None of the above.

# Application of Theory

Now that you have learned some general concepts about different theories, the following exercise is designed to help you apply theory to a specific client situation. Identify a theory that you want to learn how to apply, write down at least four key concepts from that theory, and provide explanations of those concepts. Be sure to include concepts that can be used to explain the nature and roles of AODAs. Read the following client history and analyze the dynamics in relation to the theory you have chosen. Using the format provided after the case, apply each of the concepts from the theory to the client facts, demonstrating how this theory explains the nature of the AODA issues raised by the situation.

---

### AQUARIUS

Aquarius is the 35-year-old daughter of flower children, Moonbeam and Sunflower. Moonbeam and Sunflower grew up in an age of liberation. During their adolescent years, they rebelled against what they considered to be restrictive values of their parents' generation. In particular, they shunned many of their parents' taboos against sex and drugs. They saw their parents as real "square" (teetotalers), although Moonbeam's gramps was known to take more than the odd stiff drink.

Sunflower and Moonbeam vowed that their own child would be brought up in an environment of peace and love and openness. In following these vows, they allowed Aqua to make her own choices from a very early age. They did not try to encourage her to toilet train before she expressed her own discomfort with soiled diapers. During grade school, she was allowed to choose if and when she attended school. Moonbeam and Sunflower not only smoked up in front of Aqua, they smoked up with her. Moonbeam and Sunflower smoked pot three, maybe four times a week. They did 'ludes once in a while, and drank the occasional beer. They never got into the hard stuff, but there are a few years back in the early 1970s in which memories are a bit cloudy.

Aqua officially dropped out of school at 16, but she hardly attended school since she was 13. Although she had a happy early childhood, she found school difficult. She had a short attention span in the classroom and did not do well in reading or math. Aqua believed that her teachers and fellow students made her feel stupid. Even when Aqua was at school, she mostly hung out with a couple of other "stoneheads," smoking pot (supplied by her parents) in back of the school gym. A guidance counselor told her she was prone to making poor decisions.

Aqua wanted to be an artist, and she was not without talent. She seemed to have little motivation, however, to develop this talent. Since turning 18, she's lived on her own and with different friends. A job as a sales clerk in a convenience store helps her pay the rent, but little more. She has been busted by the police a few times—caught smoking up in the park. Sometimes the police let her off with a warning. Recently, however, she was put on probation.

As a condition of her probation order, she was supposed to see a substance abuse counselor. The counselor wanted her to set some goals. The only goal Aqua wanted was to stop seeing this [expletive deleted] counselor. She told the counselor she smoked pot virtually daily and that without it she'd be bored. When she really wanted to blow her mind, she'd do acid.

Focusing on Aqua, look at your chosen theory and see how it could be applied to the case. The purpose is not to critique the theories but to see how concepts from each of the theories might help us better understand Aqua and her use of drugs.

| **Example: Functional Theory** | |
| --- | --- |
| Concepts and explanations | Application of concepts to client situation (hypotheses) |
| *Problem versus symptom: AOD use is not a problem, but a symptom of an underlying problem.* | *Marijuana use is not a problem for Aquarius, though it may indicate that she has a problem.* |
| *Function: AOD use serves a positive function (or beneficial purpose) in the person's life, from the person's subjective perspective.* | *Aqua uses pot to relieve boredom.* |
| *Substitution or alleviation: By understanding the function of the AOD use, we can determine the underlying problem and course of intervention. In order to reduce or eliminate AOD use, the intervention can focus on either finding a substitute behavior that can deal with the symptoms in a more functional way, or finding a way to resolve the underlying problem.* | *An intervention with Aqua could focus on identifying better alternatives for dealing with boredom (e.g., what does she like to do, what would give her life meaning or enjoyment). Substitute behaviors (such as watching television) might provide temporary relief from boredom, whereas finding what gives her life real meaning might resolve the underlying problem (e.g., if she found a spiritual connection or a career that gave her a positive sense of contribution to her community).* |

**Theory to Be Applied:** _____

| Concepts and explanations | Application of concepts to client situation (hypotheses) |
|---|---|
|  |  |
|  |  |
|  |  |

# Professional Attitudes, Values, and Ethics

Refer back to the Personal Attitudes questionnaire that you completed in Chapter 1 (page 2). Now that you have had more time to think and reflect upon the causes and effects of AODA problems, answer the questions again (marking your current answers with an *X*), and see how your attitudes have changed. Is your primary attitude toward AODAs reflected by the Moral Model, the Medical Model and Disease Concept, the Ecological Model, the Structural Model, or some other model, namely, _____? (circle one)

## Discussion Question: Is the Moral Model Ethical?

Corey is a social worker who works as a probation officer for people convicted of drug-related offenses. Corey believes that her values are consistent with the six core values of social work as described in the NASW *Code of Ethics* (http://www.naswdc.org):[6] service, social justices, dignity and worth of the person, importance of human relationships, integrity, and competence. Ethel, who has just taken an ethics class, questions Corey's ethics, believing that the criminal justice system is based on the Moral Model because it punishes people for morally weak or sinful behavior. Ethel suggests that being a probation officer for people who have committed drug-related crimes is tantamount to blaming the victim rather than helping people in need. Corey suggests that people must be held responsible for their actions and that without a criminal justice system there would simply be chaos in society. How would you help Corey and Ethel work through these ethical questions?

What, if anything, does the Code of Ethics suggest to social workers regarding whether their practice should be guided by the Moral Model, the Medical Model and Disease Concept, the Ecological Model, or some other model of helping people with AODAs?

## Discussion Question: Does Genetic Predisposition Absolve a Client From Taking Personal Responsibility for an AODA Problem?

Assume that your research on alcoholism convinces you that some people are genetically predisposed to it. How would this information affect your attitude toward a client who is genetically predisposed? Does this mean that the client is not to blame for having alcoholism? Does having a genetic predisposition mean that the client is absolved from taking personal responsibility for dealing with the alcohol problem? Does it matter what is being passed on genetically that predisposes the person to alcoholism—for example, a co-related problem such as a learning disability, a personality trait such as compulsivity, or a physiological problem in how alcohol is metabolized? What do social work values and ethics say about a client's individual responsibility for problems such as alcoholism? Clinically, what attitudes should workers and clients have regarding alcoholism and personal responsibility in order to raise the chances for effective work?

---

6. For students from other professions, see your own professional code of ethics (e.g., psychologists: http://www.apa.org; psychiatrists: http://www.psych.org; nurses: http://www.nursingworld.org; counselors: http://www.counseling.org). See also state or provincial equivalents of these national organizations for your location.

## Role-Play: Providing Informed Consent With Regard to Methadone or Antabuse

The ethical principle of informed consent requires that a client be provided with information about the benefits, risks, and manners of intervention in terms that the client can understand. Then the client can provide consent on a voluntary and knowledgeable basis. In this role-play, a worker named Wanda explains methadone maintenance to a client named Harriet who is physically dependent on heroin. To prepare for this role-play, Wanda should consult a GSI for information about methadone maintenance and write down some key points to share with the client. Harriet's questions include:

1. What is methadone?
2. What are the benefits?
3. What are the risks?
4. What if I want off?
5. How does it work?
6. What do I have to do?

Alternatively, this role-play can be done with a client who has remained abstinent from alcohol for 2 months and the worker suggests Antabuse to help the client maintain sobriety.

**Observing and debriefing:** During the role-play, write down examples showing how the worker responded to each of the six questions. After the role-play, review how well each of the responses answer the questions, taking into account the accuracy of the responses (how well they fit with what you know from your readings) and the appropriateness of language (how well it fits with the client's use of language and level of understanding). How would the worker need to change her approach if the client has significant brain damage resulting from chronic substance abuse?

# Research Question

Why do people with mental illness have higher rates of AOD problems than the general population? A *causative view* suggests that chronic drug use leads to mental illness by producing physiological changes in the individual. A *self-medication view* suggests that individuals choose particular substances to cope with the symptoms of the mental illness (e.g., alcohol for coping with hallucinations or paranoia of schizophrenia; Ritalin for ADHD). Select a particular mental illness—for example, schizophrenia, depression, or attention deficit disorder—that is associated with higher rates of AOD use. Conduct a literature review to critically analyze why people with that mental illness are more likely to have an AOD problem.

# Role-Play Exercise and Assignment

In this section, we focus on the *work phase* of the helping process with individuals.[7] Ordinarily, this phase comes after the engagement and assessment phases, which are presented in Chap-

---

7. For consistency, the steps of the helping process will be referred to as "phases," and the steps of client motivation (described in Chapter 4) will be referred to as "stages."

ters 4 and 5. For learning purposes, gaining a practical understanding of the work phase prior to learning about engagement and assessment will help you solidify your understanding of the various theories, models, and perspectives on AODAs. Before you engage and assess clients, you need to know what you are engaging and assessing them for. You will also have opportunities to practice the work phase after engagement and assessment in the context of family, group, and community work later in this manual. Prior to doing the role-play, read through the additional case facts for your profile, the debriefing notes, and Assignment 3.1, which is based on this role-play. If possible, audiotape or videotape this role-play to assist you with reflection, analysis, and write-up of the assignment.

To prepare for this role-play, the person playing the social worker should refer back to the Case Profile chosen in Chapter 1 and the answers to the first assignment on that Case Profile. Given these answers, select a specific therapeutic framework or model of helping individuals that you want to learn and apply to this case. Using your readings on this framework or model, identify the roles of the worker and 6 to 10 specific strategies and skills that you need to use in order to implement this framework or model. Also, identify 6 to 10 specific behaviors to avoid because they would be counterproductive to implementing your chosen framework or model. The following chart illustrates how to do this, using the example of "Twelve-Step Facilitation Therapy."[8]

**Therapeutic Framework or Model of Helping:** _12-Step Facilitation_

| Roles of the worker | Key strategies and skills | Worker behaviors to avoid |
|---|---|---|
| 1. *Educator—regarding AA view of alcoholism and the 12-Step program* | 1. *Introduce client to the steps of AA* | 1. *Suggest alcoholism is caused by a moral weakness* |
| 2. *Facilitator—encouraging active involvement in AA and progression through the 12 Steps, using client's reports of experiences between sessions* | 2. *Explain concepts such as powerlessness, unmanageability, and denial* | 2. *Insist that client accept a particular notion of higher power (e.g., a Christian view of God)* |
| | 3. *Explore experiences in client's life that illustrate how life has become increasingly unmanageable as a consequence of drinking* | 3. *Imply failure if client has a slip* |
| | 4. *Encourage client to keep a journal of meetings attended, reactions to meetings, discussion of why any meetings were not attended, and reactions to readings* | 4. *Ask client to commit to a lifetime of sobriety* |
| | | *(continued)* |

---

8. Based on the *Twelve Step Facilitation Manual* of the National Institute on Alcohol Abuse and Alcoholism (1999). This manual and similar manuals on Motivational Enhancement Therapy and Cognitive-Behavioral Coping Skills can be obtained through http://www.niaaa.nih.gov.

| Roles of the worker | Key strategies and skills | Worker behaviors to avoid |
|---|---|---|
| | 5. Explore "slips"—where, when, with whom, what the client did about them | 5. Suggest alcoholism is curable |
| | 6. Help client focus on staying sober, one day at a time | 6. Allowing client to deny or rationalize his/her use without exploring the feelings that might underlie the denial or rationalization |
| | 7. Work with client to list ways in which he/she is denying his/her powerlessness and the limitations alcoholism | 7. Pushing client through the 12 Steps too quickly or out of sequence |
| | 8. Suggest readings related to AA | 8. Excusing client from responsibility for drinking or alcoholism because of external pressures or stress |
| | 9. Explore client's notion of a higher power | |

**Therapeutic Framework or Model of Helping:** _____

| Roles of the worker | Key strategies and skills | Worker behaviors to avoid |
|---|---|---|
| | | |

*(continued)*

| Roles of the worker | Key strategies and skills | Worker behaviors to avoid |
| --- | --- | --- |
| | | |

## Profile A: Julia Torres—Work Phase With an Individual

For this role-play, assume that Julia's child protection worker has referred Julia to a social worker who specializes in addiction. During the first session, the social worker engaged Julia and performed a beginning assessment. The social worker and Julia agreed that Julia had a significant physical and psychological dependence on alcohol, which harms her ability to parent and, if not taken care of, could mean that her children would have to be put into alternate care. During today's role-play of the second session, the social worker will implement the theoretical framework or model of helping analyzed in the above chart. Julia will be cooperative with the worker, but may have some ambivalence about how she could possibly live without drinking ever again.

## Profile B: George Favel—Work Phase With an Individual

For this role-play, assume that George is working with his street outreach worker, Kerry, who he has known for 4 months. George tried going to the addictions treatment center that Kerry referred him to, but he said the center looked like a jail to him and he'd prefer to work with Kerry. George's life is still very unstable. He has found temporary living arrangements with a guy he met on the streets, but he still drinks daily and is chronically depressed. At this point,

George is prepared to decrease his drug and alcohol use, but he is not prepared to go "cold turkey" (that is, stop using all AODs immediately).

### Profile C: Randy Lang—Work Phase With an Individual

For this role-play, assume that Randy is seeing the school social worker, Mrs. Schott, and Randy has admitted to using cocaine. He says he only does a few hits a couple of times a week. He is aware that he is starting to mess up at school, and that things with his mother have gotten out of control. He says he is prepared to give up cocaine, but he is still angry with his mother for kicking his father out of the house. He is also feeling stressed about school, as he never seems to do well enough for his teachers or for his parents.

### Profile D: Dionne Thevenin—Work Phase With an Individual

For this role-play, assume that Dionne has agreed to see a social worker, Evan Styles, from the employee assistance program at Evercharge, Dionne's workplace. Dionne is very concerned about her health, which has motivated her to seek help for her heroin use. In some ways, she thinks that she's too old to change. Although she can't afford to continue using heroin, she also thinks she can't afford not to. Heroin and Dionne's faith in God are the only things that Dionne can trust to be there for her. Although Dionne is ready to deal with her AODA issues, she does not want to deal with the possibility that she is HIV-positive at this time.

## Debriefing Role-Play

During the role-plays throughout this manual, the observers should have copies of the chart outlining the worker's role, skills, and strategies to use, and the worker's behaviors to avoid. The observers should give feedback on how well the worker followed the intended role, skills, and strategies, given the theoretical framework or model of helping used by the worker. The observers should also note the extent to which the worker avoided behaviors that are counterproductive to the framework or model of helping. Ask the person playing the worker the following questions:

- What skills and strategies did you think you used effectively, according to your chosen framework or model of helping?
- What would you have liked to do differently to improve upon the way you implemented the framework or model of helping?

Ask the person playing the client:

- What did the worker say or do that you as client found effective?
- As client, what else would you have found useful for the worker to say or do?

Even though there are observers, role-plays should be conducted as if they were private interviews—do not role-play as if the observers were a reflecting team behind a one-way mirror. Role-play for 4 to 10 minutes at a time and debrief for 5 minutes. Then, continue onto the next part of the role-play interview. If you use video or audiotape for feedback, allot extra time for debriefing. You can also rotate who is playing the social worker to give practice time to various members of the class.

# Assignment 3.1: Helping an Individual—Work Phase

For this assignment, prepare an analysis of the role-play including the following information:

1. A process recording that summarizes the role-play and provides a more detailed analysis of some important segments of the role-play (for example, 3 to 5 minutes of the role-play analyzed in detail, with the rest analyzed more generally). The analysis should include a critique of the worker's use of skills and the client's responses, and an appraisal of the extent to which the worker followed the chosen theoretical framework or model of helping, including worker role, skills, and strategies, and behaviors to avoid (referring back to the chart that you created to prepare for this role-play). [4 to 6 pages] See the "Sample Process Recording" below, which illustrates a format that integrates these points using a different case example.

2. Critique of how well the chosen theoretical framework or model of helping fits with the presenting problems of the client and individual client characteristics (including diversity factors such as the client's age, ethnicity, culture, health status, sexual orientation, gender, and socioeconomic status). Refer to a GSI on AODAs and specific diversity issues to assist with this critique. [2 to 3 pages]

3. Reflection on how well the role-play fit or conflicted with the worker's professional and personal values. [1 to 2 pages]

4. Analysis of specific ethical issues that could have arisen from your chosen case:
   a. Julia: Assume that Julia is physically and psychologically dependent on alcohol. Given possible concerns about her two young children's care and safety, would it be ethical (and legal) for a social worker to work on a harm reduction approach with Julia, as opposed to insisting on abstinence? Is controlled use a viable and ethical option?
   b. George: Given George's age, AOD use, and living situation, what are the social worker's ethical responsibilities regarding obtaining parental consent and reporting George to child protection authorities or police? (Remember the worker's agency, YODA, is mandated to help youth who are living on the street, and that most street youth would avoid YODA if they knew they could be turned into police or other authorities.)
   c. Randy: As a school social worker, what are Mrs. Schott's legal and ethical responsibilities regarding Randy's disclosure about cocaine use? Does she need to inform the principal or Randy's parents? Does she need to ask Randy who else in the school is using drugs with him or selling drugs to him? (Check the written policies of a local school or school board to see how it deals with such issues.)
   d. Dionne: What are Evan's ethical responsibilities toward Evercharge regarding information about Dionne's AOD use and HIV status? Does Evercharge have a right to test Dionne for AOD use or HIV? Ethically, do you think Evercharge should have a right to test Dionne for AOD use or HIV? [1 to 2 pages]

5. Social work and interprofessional perspectives: Given your chosen framework or model of helping, what type(s) of professional training is best suited to implement this framework or model: social work, psychology, psychiatry, nursing, medicine, or some other helping profession? What advantages or disadvantages, if any, does a person with social work training and perspectives have when implementing your chosen framework or model? Would it be appropriate for a combination of professionals to work together on implementing your chosen framework or model, and if so, how? [1 to 2 pages]

**Evaluation** will be based on the following criteria: clarity of the summary of the role-play; accuracy of the appraisal of the role-play in conjunction with the roles, skills, strategies, and behaviors to avoid given the chosen framework or model of intervention; originality and level of critical analysis about the appropriateness of the chosen framework or model in reference to the presenting problems and client diversity factors; ability to draw specific, accurate connections between professional values and how the framework or model was implemented; and logic of inquiry concerning the ethical issues. The paper should be 10 to 14 pages, including a bibliography (with at least five scholarly, relevant references), in APA format.

## Sample Process Recording

The following segment provides an example—based on the "All About Eva" case from Chapter 1—for how to do a process recording, which provides a detailed analysis, as below, for key segments of the role-play and summarizes the other parts more generally.

*Process recording: For this role-play, we assumed that this was the second meeting. During the first meeting, the social worker engaged the client, Eva, and obtained agreement to use feminist counseling to help Eva deal with her cocaine-related problems. At the beginning of this role-play, I summarized the first meeting, asked Eva if she was ready to start working, and explained some of the basic tenets of feminist counseling. Eva expressed skepticism about whether feminism had anything to do with her cocaine use, but she said she was willing to learn. The following chart begins at this point in the meeting.*

| Narrative (verbatim) | Observations of client & interpretation | Theory & critique | Skills & alternatives |
|---|---|---|---|
| *Me (social worker): You've told me that you were the only female air traffic controller where you work. What has your experience been like as the only woman there?* | *Eva has been very verbal and has answered questions without hesitation. She seems ready to delve into more difficult areas.* | *A feminist perspective suggests that I should explore any areas of stress related to gender issues, raising the client's consciousness of how sexism might be related to her AODA problems (Spalding, 2003).* | *Summarization of prior client content, plus an open-ended question to help raise client's awareness of issues related to gender.* |
| *Eva (client): It's been sort of tough. I have to be one of the guys. I feel like I have to be perfect or someone will say that women just aren't cut out for this type of work.* | *Eva paused and scratched her head before answering. Her answer was quite stilted. It appears as if she has never really thought about these issues, or at least, never had anyone ask her about them.* | *So far, my use of skills is consistent with the chosen theory.* | *I might have asked, "What is it like to be a woman who uses cocaine? Is it different from being a man who uses cocaine?" This could have raised the issue of how women with AODAs are perceived differently from men with AODAs (Kelly, 2001).*<br><br>*(continued)* |

| Narrative (verbatim) | Observations of client & interpretation | Theory & critique | Skills & alternatives |
|---|---|---|---|
| *Me: So, this pressure to be perfect makes you feel stressed out?* | | *Conflicts somewhat with the feminist principle that women should label their own feelings rather than have the practitioner do this (Justin, 2002).* | *Tuning in and reflecting feelings. Could have used an open-ended question, "Then how does this pressure to be perfect make you feel?"* |
| *Eva: I suppose so. I guess it undermines my self-confidence. I know I can do a good job, but I know it's just time before I mess up.* | *Although Eva agrees, she shrugs in a way that suggests that my reflection of feelings was not really accurate. The issue is self-confidence more so than stress.* | | |
| *Me: Do you think this is an issue that is particular to you, or do other women face similar problems?* | *Eva clenches her hands on the arms of her chair. I am not sure what to make of this, except perhaps she wants to hold onto something for security.* | *Incorporates feminist principle of connecting the "personal with the political" by asking her to consider whether this issue for her personally has a broader context (Pasting, 2003).* | *Asked two closed questions. Could have invited a more open response by use of a query, "I wonder whether women in other occupations have similar concerns to yours."* |
| *Eva: Weren't you listening? I just said that I was the only woman air traffic controller.* <br><br> Etc. [3 to 5 pages] | *Eva's raised voice and whiney tone suggests she's angry with me, thinking that I was asking about women in her workplace.* | *Hypothesis: Eva's quick change in temper may be related to her recent abstinence from cocaine use, which makes client susceptible to overreacting to relatively minor problems (Gage, 2000).* | *Need to use clarification, without putting client on defensive. Perhaps, could also apologize for not being clear enough.* |

*After this exchange, I explored what it was like to be the only woman air traffic controller. Eva began to open up about instances when she was sexually harassed and when she was put down by her peers because she was a woman. Eva said she felt she had to work harder than her male colleagues to prove herself, and that she sometimes felt that perhaps she was not cut out to for the stress of this profession in the same way that the men were. She related her cocaine use to helping her gain confidence to deal with these issues.* [About 1 page summarizing the rest of the session]

# Journaling Exercise

1. Review your assignment based on the role-play with an individual. Place yourself in the situation of the client. Given your own cultural background, personal values, attitudes, and sensitivities, how would you have felt about the theoretical framework or model of helping that was used? What aspects of this framework or model would have been a good fit for you? What aspects might not have been a good fit? Describe why these aspects would be good or not so good fits for you.

2. How comfortable do you feel with your knowledge of the theoretical framework or model of helping that you have chosen to focus on? Identify the areas where you feel quite comfortable, as well as the areas where you would like to learn more (including both conceptual understandings and the ability to put the framework or model into practice). Identify a plan and time frame for how you will fulfill your learning goals.

# InfoTrac College Edition

## Key words

◇ Cognitive Therapy
◇ Behavioral Therapy
◇ Alcoholics Anonymous
◇ Harm Reduction
◇ Motivational Enhancement
◇ Rational Emotive Behavior Therapy

CHAPTER

# 4

~~✳~~

# Techniques of Engagement: Micro–Mezzo–Macro

If a client with an AODA problem comes into your office with a high level of motivation to change, clear goals, a strong support system, a high sense of self-efficacy, and a history of positive experiences with professional helping agents, then engagement will be relatively easy. In practice, clients with AODA problems have varying degrees of ambivalence about changing; their goals may be unclear; they may lack family, friends, work, housing, or other social supports; they may have poor self-images; and they may have had many negative experiences with helping agents (for example, child protection workers, probation officers, welfare workers, or other professionals who clients might have experienced as authoritative, bureaucratic, lacking empathy, or basically unhelpful). This chapter focuses upon how to engage clients when one or more of these challenges exist. This chapter adopts engagement techniques from Motivational Enhancement Counseling (Miller & Rollnick, 2002; NIAAA, 1999, Volume 2; Noonan & Moyers, 2004; Rollnick & Morgan, 1997) and the Transtheoretical Model's first two stages of change, the Precontemplation Stage and the Contemplation Stage (Velicer, Prochaska, Fava, Norman, & Redding, 1998). These models were originally conceived for use with individual clients. Still, they can be used for work with families, groups, and communities, as will be demonstrated in the exercises. Although this chapter isolates engagement as a distinct topic for learning purposes, remember that, in practice, the phases of the helping process (engagement, assessment, intervention, termination, and follow-up) are overlapping and sometimes circular (i.e., you may have to circle back from one phase to an earlier phase as client needs require).[1]

---

1. For clarity and consistency, this book refers to "phases" as the steps of the helping process, and "stages" as the steps of motivation that clients proceed through according to the Transtheoretical Model.

# Motivation to Change

A client's right to self-determination is a central ethical principle for social workers. In order to facilitate client self-determination, a key aspect of engagement is to start where the client is. In other words, identify the presenting problem (the problem as viewed from the client's perspective) and the client's motivation for seeking help at this time. In each of the following scenarios, assume that a worker has asked the client(s), "What has brought you in to see me today?" Your tasks are (1) to identify the presenting problem; and (2) to hypothesize about the client's motivation to change, including whether the motivation is internal to the client or external (e.g., pressure from another person). Hypothesize means to provide your educated opinion or theory about the client's sources of motivation, knowing that you will need to test out your opinion with the client rather than simply assuming it is true. Within a family or other client system, there may be more than one presenting problem and motivating factor for different members of the system.

> Example: An individual client named Cindy responds, "I'm not really sure why I'm here. I suppose I had nowhere else to turn. My husband threatened to divorce me. He thinks I'm hooked on crack. I'm not really. But I'll do whatever my husband wants so I can save the marriage."

> 1. *The presenting problem is that the client's husband has threatened divorce because he believes the client has a problem with crack.*
> 2. *I hypothesize that the client is motivated externally by her concern that her husband might divorce her. At this point in the interview, she has not shown any internal motivation to change her crack use.*

> A. You are facilitating a psychoeducational group for people who have been mandated into treatment because they have been convicted of drug-related crimes. When you ask one member of the group why he decided to join this group, he says, "If I hadn't been caught for break and enter, I probably wouldn't be here. But maybe this was a wake-up call. I knew that heroin was addictive, but I didn't realize how low my life has become. I just don't see myself as a druggie or a criminal."
> 1.

2.

B.   The principal of a high school has hired you to help out with AODA problems in the school. When you ask the principal why she decided to call you in at this particular time, she replies, "There was a school dance last week. We've never really had problems with drugs before, but apparently, some of the guys on the football team gave GHB[2] to one of the cheerleaders so they could have sex with her in the locker room. Things got a bit out of control when a teacher walked in on them. I guess they panicked and hit the teacher with a baseball bat. I wanted to keep this quiet and just deal with the kids who were directly involved, but other parents found out and they've been hounding me to do something to make sure the school is drug free."

1.

---

2. Gamma hydroxybutyric acid—a "date-rape drug" that causes drowsiness and loss of consciousness.

2.

C.   You are working with the Norton family. Mr. and Mrs. Norton are concerned that their daughter, Denise, has some sort of eating addiction. They report that Denise has been gorging herself with food over the past year. They also suspect that she's been using diuretic medications to try to keep her weight down. When you ask why they came for services at this particular time, Mrs. Norton says, "Denise doesn't go out anymore. She has no friends." Mr. Norton adds, "It's just not healthy to eat so much." Denise responds, "Nothing I ever do is good enough for my parents. If I wasn't too fat, then I'd be too thin. Just tell them to leave me alone."

1.

2.

D. The government of your state is considering the decriminalization of marijuana and you are serving on a committee mandated to study this issue. People promoting this change have been motivated by recent research indicating that people with criminal records related to marijuana possession have difficulty obtaining jobs and integrating into society. People opposing this change point to the risks of marijuana use, including cancer, accidental deaths, and a gateway into harder drug use. Others aren't sure which side to believe or support.

1.

2.

# Building Trust

Whereas the last section looked at how to start where the client is, this section looks at other ways of engaging clients. There are a variety of techniques for building trust with clients: demonstrating unconditional positive regard, being genuine or authentic, and demonstrating empathic understanding (i.e., Carl Rogers's core conditions for developing a positive working relationship with clients—1957); using a concrete "here and now" orientation; offering clients the safety of confidentiality so that they do not worry that embarrassing information may be used against them; starting with work that concerns the clients' current interests; clearly explaining your role and how you will be helping the clients with their concerns; and offering realistic hope that they can achieve positive change. The following scenarios present ineffective examples of how to put these techniques into practice. Your task is to provide an example of an effective worker response for each scenario, demonstrating how to put each of the techniques into practice.

### Example—Unconditional positive regard

Client: Last weekend I started to drink and before you knew it I passed out. When I came to the next morning, my baby was screaming and crying. I can't believe what I did. She could have died!

Ineffective worker response: Oh my gosh! That's terrible. What kind of parent is so selfish that drinking takes precedence over the child's needs?

Effective worker response: *I can hear how badly you feel about what happened, but I can also hear that you love your child very much and wouldn't ever want your drinking to put her at risk ever again.*

### 1. Unconditional positive regard

Client in a group setting: I just can't relate to everyone else's stories. It just sounds as if people are sitting around here complaining and blaming everyone else for their troubles.

Ineffective worker response: Here you go again, focusing on everyone else rather than working on your own problems. If you weren't so resistant, you might find this group more helpful.

Effective worker response:

### 2. Genuineness or authenticity

Member of the community participating in the development of a drug prevention program focused on the African American community: What do you know about working with African Americans? Maybe it's not politically correct for me to say this, but you're White.

Ineffective worker response: On the outside, I'm White, but I have had a lot of experiences that help me understand what it's like to be Black. I've taken courses and read textbooks on drug prevention in the African-American community. I think I know where you're coming from.

Effective worker response:

### 3. Empathic understanding

Daughter involved in family counseling: It's like I'm always the bad child and he's always the perfect one. It's not like he's never smoked pot.

Ineffective worker response: So you're saying that you've never smoked up. It sounds as if you and your brother have a good relationship.

Effective worker response:

### 4. Confidentiality

Client: I suppose I'm not sure if it's safe to answer your questions. I don't want to get in trouble with the law or anything.

Ineffective worker response: There aren't really any laws or policies that tell me what I can do or what I can't do. You'll just have to trust me. If you've abused your child or grandparent, it's not as if I'll call the police or anything. I can keep a good secret and half the time my supervisor doesn't even look at my progress notes. The only time I ever had a problem was when I was mouthing off at a party. I didn't know my client's cousin was going to be there. What a mess.

Effective worker response:

## 5. Starting with the client

Client: I know I have to stop using the sleeping pills, but this just isn't the right time. I have my final exams coming up in a few weeks, and the only way I can sleep is to use the pills, sometimes with a brandy chaser.

Ineffective worker response: Abstinence is the first step. Once you stop taking pills, we can start working on the rest of your problems.

Effective worker response:

### 6. Clearly explaining the helping role

Client who is seeking help for a gambling addiction: I've never seen a social worker before. My neighbors had Child Welfare come and scoop their kids right out of their car at the casino. But that's all I know about social work.

Ineffective worker response: My role is to facilitate the therapeutic process through the use of cognitive restructuring to replace your dysfunctional thought patterns concerning your gambling dependency with more functional cognitive processes to help you self-actualize your potential.

Effective worker response:

### 7. Offering realistic hope for positive change

Client who has AIDS and feels despondent: I've been chasing the dragon for over 25 years. Couldn't stop when I was young and healthy. No way I can stop now.

Ineffective worker response: Life is like a bowl of cherries. You just have to pick out some of the bad ones. If you really want it, you can turn back your life to what it was like 25 years ago.

Effective worker response:

# Identifying Stages of Change

Until this point, we have looked at strategies for engagement that can generally be used with any client. In order to individualize your approach for engaging a client, it is important to be able to identify the client's current "Stage of Change."[3] Once you have identified the client's Stage of Change, you can select engagement strategies that fit best with that client's level of motivation. The following exercise focuses on how to identify a client's Stage of Change.

For each of the following scenarios, identify whether the client is at the (a) Precontemplation Stage, (b) Contemplation Stage, (c) Decision Stage, (d) Preparation Stage, (e) Action Stage, or (f) Maintenance and Relapse Prevention Stage. (If you require additional information on Stages of Change, search the Internet or databases for Transtheoretical Model or Prochaska and DiClemente.)

1. During an intake interview with the Highlands Residential Treatment Center, Jack says, "After that last accident, I decided that I'm ready to stop using alcohol. I just need to work out a few details regarding how to take care of my finances and my children while I'm in treatment."
   Jack's Stage of Change: ___

2. Jill was also in a terrible accident. She had just dropped some acid and tumbled down a steep hill. While in the hospital, a social worker helping Jill with discharge plans suggested that Jill consider treatment for her drug problem. Jill responds, "My partner has been telling me that I need help. I know that I've had a couple of accidents since I started using LSD. I'm just not sure whether I want to give it up."
   Jill's Stage of Change: ___

3. Red has been straight and sober for almost one year. As her first anniversary of sobriety is coming up, she is feeling a bit anxious about how she'll deal with the stress. The thrill of her first few months of sobriety has waned since she started wondering again how long before she "falls off the wagon."
   Red's Stage of Change: ___

4. Miss Muffet has been experiencing a number of strange dreams in which spiders are stalking her. She goes to her doctor hoping to get some Valium to help her relax. While taking her medical history, the doctor finds out Miss Muffet has been eating curds laced with hash oil. When the doctor suggests that she cut out the hash oil, Miss Muffet says, "No way! All I need is a little something to help me relax. My eating habits are just fine."
   Miss Muffet's Stage of Change: ___

5. Georgie P. had two eating compulsions: pudding and pie. He decided to go for Cognitive-Behavioral Therapy. During therapy, he identified two situations that seemed to trigger his eating compulsions. The first was girls who cry and the second

---

3. For the Readiness to Change Questionnaire, which can be used to identify a person's stage of change, see http://www.niaaa.nih.gov/publications/rtcq.htm.

was boys who play. Georgie agreed in therapy to try to avoid putting himself in either of these risky situations, hoping this would help control his eating.
Georgie's Stage of Change: ____

6.   Wynkin, Blynkin, and Nod came from a community where everyone used a substance called "crystal." Oddly enough, no one seemed to think this was a problem. Those who used crystal would have incredible hallucinations, going off on great adventures, floating out to sea, and always arriving home safe and sound. When the hallucinations were over, the people of the town would be so exhausted they would just go to sleep.
Community's Stage of Change: ____

Identify the Stage of Change of the client in your role-play from Assignment 3.1 in Chapter 3 and list the observations that led you to this conclusion:

# Support Systems

For people with weak support systems, dealing with AODAs is particularly daunting. Also, support systems can be helpful in encouraging a client to get professional help for AODAs. In order to help someone connect or reconnect with positive support systems, you need to be able to help that person identify possible supports. In the following exercise, begin with yourself: If you were having problems related to cocaine dependency, whom could you turn to for help (consider specific people from your family, school, work, neighborhood, religious or cultural groups, social groups, or helping professions)?

Now, interview a friend or colleague who is from another cultural diversity group. Explore whom she might ask for help if she were addicted to alcohol. List these below and then compare them to your list above:

# Self-Efficacy

If a client has a low sense of self-efficacy, that person may be difficult to engage because he does not feel that positive change is likely. Improving self-efficacy can be a slow process, but there are some techniques that are valuable during the engagement stage: using language that inspires hope, building on strengths, providing positive feedback, and helping the client experience situations outside of the helping relationship that affirm the client's self-efficacy. For each of the following situations, one example is provided for how to foster a higher sense of self-efficacy. Your task is to offer a second alternative for each situation.

1. Peter's girlfriend Ellen left him because she thought he was just a pothead. Peter tells his therapist, "Without Ellen, life sucks. So who cares if I'm a pothead?"
   Example—hopeful language: *The therapist could reframe Peter's last statement as, "It sounds as if you'd like Ellen to come back, and the only way for that to happen would be to kick the pot habit." This example also shows the skill of* immediacy, *moving the client to think about the present and what he can do about it.*
   Alternative:

2.   Barbara tells her social worker that she binges on alcohol whenever she has a tough day at work. She finds her job very disillusioning. Her boss and colleagues are always putting her down. Nothing she does pleases anyone.

Example—building on strengths: *The social worker could ask about times when Barbara felt better about her work. Once Barbara identifies these, the worker could explore what she could take from these experiences so that work could be better.*

Alternative:

3.   Farrah is a survivor of childhood sexual abuse. She slashes her arms and legs, usually after taking barbiturates. Her behavior is self-harmful, but she tells her social worker that she is not out to kill herself.

Example—providing positive feedback: *The social worker could say, "Farrah, you were able to survive years of sexual abuse. You found a number of different ways to cope. That takes a lot of courage and intellect." (The worker might follow this with the skill of* constructive use of silence, *since the client likely needs time to think through her answer and decide what to say.)*

Alternative:

4.   Hans has a heroin addiction. His parents have always treated him as a failure and eventually he began to believe it. He tells you, "Once an addict, always an addict."

Example—affirming experiences: *You ask the client about friends who think more positively about him. You help the client arrange to spend time with these friends so that he will receive more positive feedback from his social environment.*

Alternative:

# Skills of the Transtheoretical Model

The Transtheoretical Model provides strategies and skills that can be used for all phases of the helping process. Because the engagement phase of the helping process is most challenging for clients in the precontemplation and contemplation stages, the following exercises are designed to provide you with practice implementing the skills of the Transtheoretical Model for these two stages.

## Role-Play: Precontemplation Stage

The following role-play involves a person (Gwyn) who is in the precontemplation stage. Although Gwyn is not currently a client, a fellow social worker Kyla will use some skills from the Transtheoretical Model to engage Gwyn in a discussion about her AODA problem. Read the case, take notes, and answer the questions below to prepare for the role-play. Designate one person to play Kyla, one to play Gwyn, and one or two others to play observers (you can re-do the role-play afterward, switching roles).

---

### COWORKER CONFRONTATION

Kyla and a coworker, Gwyn, are community development workers. Both have MSW degrees. Gwyn and Kyla are working together on a project to build support systems for single parents. During a meeting with teachers, parents, and city councilors, Kyla notices that Gwyn smells of alcohol. She is obviously intoxicated. Kyla pulls her aside to speak with her in private. Gwyn says, "I'm not drunk or anything like that. I just had a couple of glasses of wine over lunch. There is nothing to worry about."

This is not the first time that Kyla has suspected that Gwyn has come to work drunk. Kyla is concerned about how Gwyn's drinking is affecting the quality of her work as well as the reputation of the agency and the social work profession. Kyla does not want to get Gwyn into trouble with their agency, but Gwyn does not seem to be responding well when Kyla has expressed concerns to her. Kyla even offered to refer Gwyn to services for her alcohol problem.

---

In order to prepare for the role-play, write down answers to the following questions on a separate piece of paper.

1. What are Kyla's obligations in this situation (a) legally (consider laws that regulate social workers and addiction agencies, including whether the Health Insurance Portability and Accountability Act applies) and (b) ethically (consider the NASW Code of Ethics or another code that applies in your area)?
2. What have you learned about alcohol use in this class and in your readings that may help you understand where Gwyn is coming from?
3. Which Stage of Change best describes Gwyn's current motivational status?
4. Clinically, what do you think is the best way to approach this situation (relate your suggestions to theoretical frameworks discussed earlier in this course)?
5. Refer to the chart below entitled "Constructive Worker Skills Used in the Precontemplation Stage." Have the person role-playing Kyla identify four skills that she wants to practice in this role-play. The observers for this role-play will give Kyla feedback on how well she uses these skills, using the 5-point scale provided in the chart.
6. Refer to the chart below entitled "Counterproductive Worker Behaviors in the Precontemplation Stage." Have the person role-playing Kyla identify three counterproductive behaviors that she wants to learn to *avoid* during the role-play. The observers for this role-play will give Kyla feedback on how well she avoids these behaviors, using the 4-point scale provided in the chart.

---

**Constructive Worker Skills Used in the Precontemplation Stage[4]**

1—Demonstrated this skill at an exceptional level of mastery
2—Demonstrated this skill at an acceptable level of competence
3—Demonstrated this skill at a beginning level of competence
4—Did not demonstrate use of this skill even though it would have been appropriate to use
NA—Use of skill was not applicable in this particular role-play

| | |
|---|---|
| a. Identifies reason for seeing worker (presenting problem) | 1 - 2 - 3 - 4 - NA |
| b. Uses exploration questions to raise awareness of risks and problems with current behavior (e.g., explores stressors, health, work, family relationships, a typical day, etc.) | 1 - 2 - 3 - 4 - NA |
| c. Uses client focus and genuineness to become a client ally (conveys acceptance rather than approval) | 1 - 2 - 3 - 4 - NA |
| d. Demonstrates willingness to work with client on non-AODA goals | 1 - 2 - 3 - 4 - NA |
| e. Demonstrates willingness to let client leave and come back for counseling if and when ready | 1 - 2 - 3 - 4 - NA |
| f. Uses "what if" questions to raise doubt | 1 - 2 - 3 - 4 - NA |
| g. Explores other's perceptions of the client's behaviors | 1 - 2 - 3 - 4 - NA |
| h. Explores the client's understandings of other's reactions to their behavior (depersonalizing) | 1 - 2 - 3 - 4 - NA |

*(continued)*

---

4. These four charts are derived from research published by Barsky & Coleman (2001a).

i. Helps client explore how the behavior is problematic from another's perspective to how it is problematic for them    1 - 2 - 3 - 4 - NA

j. Shows respect for client's choices    1 - 2 - 3 - 4 - NA

k. Gives permission for client to say anything the client wants or needs to say (genuine, nonjudgmental, open)    1 - 2 - 3 - 4 - NA

l. Uses nonjudgmental and neutral language    1 - 2 - 3 - 4 - NA

m. Uses client's terminology    1 - 2 - 3 - 4 - NA

n. Uses consciousness-raising techniques matched to client's learning style and readiness, e.g., journaling, internal dialogue, videotaping, reading, providing experiences, visiting treatment programs (circle ones used)    1 - 2 - 3 - 4 - NA

o. Inquires about good things and not so good things    1 - 2 - 3 - 4 - NA

p. Emphasizes reflective listening versus questioning (demonstrates empathy)    1 - 2 - 3 - 4 - NA

q. Uses primarily open-ended questions    1 - 2 - 3 - 4 - NA

r. Affirms client (demonstrates belief that client will make the right decision)    1 - 2 - 3 - 4 - NA

s. Recognizes and rolls with client resistance    1 - 2 - 3 - 4 - NA

t. Explores inner motivation of client (what client is motivated toward rather than away from, e.g., health, work, finance, fitness)    1 - 2 - 3 - 4 - NA

u. Clarifies discrepancies in client goals or motivations    1 - 2 - 3 - 4 - NA

v. Offers information in a nonpersonal and neutral manner    1 - 2 - 3 - 4 - NA

---

### Counterproductive Worker Behaviors in the Precontemplation Stage

Key:
i—Avoids use of this counterproductive worker behavior throughout interview
ii—Occasionally uses this counterproductive worker behavior
iii—Frequently uses this counterproductive worker behavior
NA—Not applicable: unable to assess during this interview

a. Uses negative labels    i - ii - iii - NA

b. Tries to move client too quickly toward contemplation or action (pacing to fast; uses contemplation or action questions when client has not begun contemplating change)    i - ii - iii - NA

c. Prescribes or directs client    i - ii - iii - NA

d. Tries to convince client (to stay in counseling, to change behavior, etc.)    i - ii - iii - NA

e. Debates client (focuses too much on reasoning)    i - ii - iii - NA

f. Tries to wear client down    i - ii - iii - NA

g. Inundates client with information    i - ii - iii - NA

h. Makes excuses for client    i - ii - iii - NA

i. Declares that the client has an AOD problem    i - ii - iii - NA

*(continued)*

| | |
|---|---|
| j. Implies that the client is the problem | i - ii - iii - NA |
| k. Expresses annoyance with the client | i - ii - iii - NA |
| l. Puts inappropriate restrictions on when a client can seek service | i - ii - iii - NA |
| m. Uses questions geared toward action | i - ii - iii - NA |

Tear out and make photocopies of the charts so that you can use them to provide feedback to others and to monitor your own progress in other role-plays.

## Role-Play: Contemplation Stage

The following case is designed to provide you with practice using skills for counseling clients in the contemplation stage. Read the case, take notes, and answer the questions below to prepare for the role-play. Designate one person to play the group facilitator (Francis), three to play the involuntary clients (Irene, Igor, and Inez),[5] and one or two others to play observers (you can re-do the role-play afterward, switching roles).

### INVOLUNTARY ENGAGEMENT

In this role-play, Francis will be facilitating the first session with a group of clients referred by their probation officers following charges of Driving Under the Influence of alcohol. All three clients are in the contemplation stage. None of them are ready to take steps to deal with their drinking, but they are somewhat motivated to discuss their problems with alcohol in order to satisfy their conditions of probation and avoid further problems with the criminal justice system. Francis should select and use five skills that she wants to practice from the "Constructive Skills Used in the Contemplation Stage" chart (below). She will also select three behaviors from the "Counterproductive Worker Behaviors in the Contemplation Phase" chart that she wants to learn to avoid. After the role-play, the observers will provide her with feedback on these skills and counterproductive behaviors. The clients will read the following confidential facts, which are *not to be read in advance by the person playing Francis.*

**Confidential client facts for Inez only:** Inez presents as very willing to please the worker, but is very cautious about promising to make any changes in her life. She has had three car accidents resulting from her alcohol abuse and is concerned that her license will be suspended. She needs her license in order to work as an ambulance driver. She thinks she can control her drinking and just needs more discipline. She knows that if she could stop drinking, she would feel better, she would not put her job at risk, and she would save money. She can't imagine her life without alcohol, because it has always been like a best friend. When things go bad, alcohol is always there. It never abandons her.

---

5. This role-play can be simplified by turning it into an individual counseling session between Francis and Inez.

**Confidential client facts for Irene only:** Irene is a recent immigrant from Poland. She can't understand why Americans make such a big a deal about alcohol. She used to drink much more when she was living in Krakow. She was charged with Driving Under the Influence when a police officer stopped her because her car was swerving over the center line, but she never had an accident. For Irene, vodka is a social imperative, particularly among her wealthy peers. All her friends drink, and she'd feel like an outsider if she stopped. On the other hand, Irene is thinking of getting pregnant and she has heard that alcohol can cause serious problems for a baby.

**Confidential client facts for Igor only:** Igor knows that alcohol has been his downfall. In addition to the recent criminal charges, his boyfriend Bob has left him and he has lost his job. Bob said he left Igor because Igor became abusive when he was drunk. Igor doesn't remember getting abusive, but there are many things he doesn't remember when he's drinking. Igor lost his job as an airplane mechanic during random drug and alcohol testing. His employer had a zero-tolerance policy on alcohol given the huge risks of an airplane mechanic making an error. In spite of this, Igor is more afraid of a life without beer than a life with beer. He hasn't gone a day without drinking in 12 years.

---

**Constructive Skills Used in the Contemplation Stage**

Key:
1—Demonstrated this skill at an exceptional level of mastery
2—Demonstrated this skill at an acceptable level of competence
3—Demonstrated this skill at a beginning level of competence
4—Did not demonstrate use of this skill even though it would have been appropriate
NA—Use of this skill was not applicable in this particular role-play

| | |
|---|---|
| a. Acknowledges indecisiveness | 1 - 2 - 3 - 4 - NA |
| b. Amplifies discrepancies | 1 - 2 - 3 - 4 - NA |
| c. Amplifies choices with more positive influence | 1 - 2 - 3 - 4 - NA |
| d. Validates the function of the AOD use | 1 - 2 - 3 - 4 - NA |
| e. Helps client explore "normal behavior" (including peer influences) | 1 - 2 - 3 - 4 - NA |
| f. Normalizes ambivalence about change | 1 - 2 - 3 - 4 - NA |
| g. Remains neutral and nonjudgmental | 1 - 2 - 3 - 4 - NA |
| h. Uses client's language (especially descriptions of self or problems) | 1 - 2 - 3 - 4 - NA |
| i. Reinforces client self-efficacy (e.g., looks at past successes in attempts to change; looks at client strengths) | 1 - 2 - 3 - 4 - NA |
| j. Builds on client strengths | 1 - 2 - 3 - 4 - NA |
| k. Explores past changes (what worked, what did not work, what would client do differently) | 1 - 2 - 3 - 4 - NA |
| l. Explores barriers to making changes | 1 - 2 - 3 - 4 - NA |

*(continued)*

m. Instills hope (e.g., identifies signs of movement, relates          1 - 2 - 3 - 4 - NA
   positive experiences with other clients, gives examples of
   how people can and do change; "It's tough, but . . .")

n. Explores client's perceptions and assumptions about AOD use  1 - 2 - 3 - 4 - NA

o. Deals with client's misperceptions about AOD use (e.g.,       1 - 2 - 3 - 4 - NA
   provides information; asks questions to facilitate insight)

p. Accepts client staying in contemplation stage                 1 - 2 - 3 - 4 - NA

q. Obtains client's view about the next step                     1 - 2 - 3 - 4 - NA

r. Treats client as expert in his/her life                       1 - 2 - 3 - 4 - NA

s. Helps client make sense of problems she/he has experienced   1 - 2 - 3 - 4 - NA
   with AODs

t. Completes a decisional matrix (explores disadvantages and     1 - 2 - 3 - 4 - NA
   advantages, long- and short-term; tips balance)

u. Supports client decisions                                     1 - 2 - 3 - 4 - NA

v. Emphasizes client choice                                      1 - 2 - 3 - 4 - NA

---

### Counterproductive Worker Behaviors in the Contemplation Phase

Key:
i—Avoids use of this counterproductive worker behavior throughout interview
ii—Occasionally uses this counterproductive worker behavior
iii—Frequently uses this counterproductive worker behavior
NA—Not applicable: unable to assess during this interview

a. Moves too quickly toward tasks for preparation or action stages    i - ii - iii - NA
   (asks client for behavior changes)

b. Focuses too much on the benefits of moving on                      i - ii - iii - NA

c. Does not permit client to talk about maintaining old behavior      i - ii - iii - NA

d. Demonstrates frustration with client                               i - ii - iii - NA

e. Jumps to conclusions about client's intentions or feelings         i - ii - iii - NA

f. Imposes limits on client (e.g., "You need to let me know by next   i - ii - iii - NA
   week.")

g. Goes into little depth when exploring client thoughts and feelings i - ii - iii - NA

h. Lectures client                                                    i - ii - iii - NA

i. Minimizes client concerns                                          i - ii - iii - NA

j. Speaks over client                                                 i - ii - iii - NA

k. Labels client or client's behavior for him/her                     i - ii - iii - NA

l. Gets caught resisting resistance                                   i - ii - iii - NA

# Assignment 4.1: Engagement Phase

Review the client profile that you selected in Chapter 1, as well as the assignments that you have already completed based on this profile. For this assignment, you will take a couple of steps back from the work phase role-play that you conducted in Chapter 3 and conduct an initial interview that focuses upon engagement with a client who is either in the precontemplation or contemplation stage. Designate someone in your group to play the social worker and someone to play the client. Each person should read only the facts pertaining to his or her own role, and *not the confidential facts of the other person* in the role-play.

During the role-play the worker should try to:

1. Identify the presenting problem(s) and client motivation(s) to change.
2. Explore the client's perceptions of his or her substance use and values toward change.
3. Use appropriate skills and strategies from this chapter to try to connect with the client and build a positive working alliance.
4. Assess whether the worker is the right person to be assessing or working with this client.
5. Assess whether the agency is the appropriate one to be working with the client, given the agency's mandate, resources, and limitations.
6. Instill hope, but do not problem-solve too early or create unrealistic expectations.
7. Apply what you have learned from this chapter about engagement and the Transtheoretical Model.

Write down notes with examples of strategies, skills, questions, and comments that you think could help you during the meeting. Some of these interventions might be riskier than ones that you might do with an actual client. Because this is a role-play, feel free to take a few risks so that you can experiment (and even have some fun) with different types of interventions. See Chapter 3 for the roles of observers and debriefing suggestions.

The written analysis for this assignment should include:

1. A process recording that summarizes the role-play, including an overview of the worker's use of skills and the client's responses and an appraisal of the extent to which the worker followed the Transtheoretical Model of Change and other chosen engagement frameworks, including constructive worker skills and behaviors to avoid (referring back to the charts earlier in this chapter). [4 to 6 pages] See Chapter 3 for a format for process recordings.
2. A critique of how well the Transtheoretical Model fit with the client situation as presented in the role-play (including diversity factors such as the client's age, ethnicity, culture, health status, sexual orientation, gender, and socioeconomic status). Refer to a GSI on the Transtheoretical Model and specific diversity issues to assist with this critique.[6] [2 to 3 pages]
3. A reflection of how well the role-play fit or conflicted with the worker's professional and personal values. [1 to 2 pages]

---

6. See Chapter 1 for an explanation of Good Sources of Information (GSIs).

4. An analysis of specific ethical issues that could have arisen from your chosen case:
    a. Julia: How much time, if any, should the child protection worker give Julia to change her drinking habits, before the worker takes steps to remove the children from Julia's care? Does Julia have a right to know who called child protective services, or does the caller have a right to anonymity?
    b. George: If George were to be caught bringing a substance onto agency premises, what are the ethical responsibilities of the agency staff? Do the obligations differ if it were an illicit substance versus a licit one? If George came high to the agency, what are the ethical responsibilities of the agency staff? Does it matter whether the client is taking drugs because he is depressed?
    c. Randy: Assume Randy accuses the worker of siding with his mother because both of them assume he is using cocaine, even though he hasn't disclosed this to them. How should the social worker respond? Does Randy require a separate worker from his mother's? If Randy's mother is not involved in joint sessions, then what would the social worker work on with Randy, given his denial?
    d. Dionne: What are the social worker's ethical responsibilities if he/she discovered that Dionne was sharing needles with others even though she knew that she was HIV positive? How does the social worker in this situation balance the interests of client confidentiality and protection of others who may be put at risk of contracting HIV? Are the obligations any different if the risk factor was unprotected sexual intercourse? Can an intravenous drug user be trusted if she says she will not put anyone else at risk? Why or why not? [1 to 2 pages]
5. Social work and interprofessional perspectives: Assume the social worker in the role-play wanted to consult with another professional about how to intervene with this client. Identify one other type of professional that the social worker could have consulted and what type of knowledge that professional could have provided to help the social worker with the particular client situation. [1 to 2 pages]

**Evaluation** will be based on the following criteria: clarity of the summary of the role-play; accuracy of the appraisal of the role-play in conjunction with the roles, skills, strategies, and behaviors to avoid given the Transtheoretical Model and other chosen frameworks for engagement; originality and level of critical analysis about the appropriateness of the Transtheoretical Model or other chosen frameworks for engagement in reference to the client situation and diversity factors; ability to draw specific, accurate connections between professional values and how the framework or model was implemented; and logic of inquiry concerning the ethical issues. The paper should be 10 to 14 pages, including a bibliography (with at least four relevant, scholarly references), in APA format.

## Profile A: Julia Torres—Engagement Phase With an Individual[7]

**Julia's confidential facts (client):** In this exercise you will be meeting for the first time with Mr./Ms. Chambers, a child protection worker who has arranged to meet you at

---

7. This case could be played as a family session by adding the fact that the child protection worker arranged to meet with Julia and her sister Maria together. Actually, even without Maria, this situation involves family members DJ and Dominic, though they are only 1 and 3 years old respectively.

your home in response to allegations of child neglect. You suspect that a neighbor reported you, but you are not really sure which one. You already feel a lot of guilt about your alcohol use because you know that your children, DJ and Dominic, both suffer from Fetal Alcohol Effects. Although you love them and would do anything for them, you have not been able to stop drinking. Given that this is your first meeting with the child protection worker, you are not sure if you can trust her. Initially, you are not prepared to admit that you need help with alcohol. You are more prepared to discuss the consequences of your use. The thought of going clean and sober scares you. You have had negative experiences in the past with social workers and may present with mistrust or frustration toward Mr./Ms. Chambers, who you initially view as an unwanted intruder in your life.

Since this meeting will be in your home, feel free to bring props, such as a doll and baby bottle, to enhance the realism of the meeting. The worker is instructed to use the Transtheoretical Model, which you may also want to review. You are at the precontemplation stage, but can be moved into the contemplation stage, depending on the effectiveness of the worker's interventions.

Until recently, you haven't seriously thought about the meaning of alcohol in your life. You may describe alcohol as your best friend—always there when you need her, never talks back, and is part of the good times as well as the bad. On the other hand, you saw how your father's alcohol use led to chaos and fighting in the house (and remember, your role in the family was always the scapegoat). You do not want your children to suffer. If the worker confronts you in a constructive fashion, try to cooperate by showing insight from the confrontation. If you are confronted in a harsh or blaming manner, you may either close down verbally or tell the worker she or he doesn't really know what it's like. You don't think of yourself as an alcoholic—an alcoholic is someone who constantly reeks of alcohol and is living on the street somewhere. You think that you can control your alcohol use if you want to. You do not currently know what your options are.

**Mr./Ms. Chambers's confidential facts (child protection worker):** In this exercise you will play Julia's child protection worker during an initial interview at Julia's house. This interview follows a call from her sister Maria alleging that Julia is not providing her children with proper supervision. Maria said that Julia often drinks to the point of blacking out, and the children are left virtually unattended until the next day when she gains consciousness. From your brief telephone contact with Julia, you suspect that she is in the precontemplation stage, but you will need to assess this further when you meet. Review your materials on the Transtheoretical Model and select five skills that you want to practice, as well as three counterproductive behaviors that you want to avoid. Write down four or five examples of questions or comments that you might use in order to help Julia move toward the next stage of change. Also, select at least two other skills and strategies you have learned and create examples that are relevant to this client profile. For example, if you wanted to *build on client strengths*, you might try:

> In the past, drinking seems to have been something that's helped you cope with [being a single mom/the way your father mistreated you]. But now, drinking seems to be getting in the way of being the good parent that you want to be. I'm wondering what you think.

As part of your preparation, write down point-form answers to the following questions.

1. How will you explain your role as a child protection worker?
2. How will you explain the nature of confidentiality?
3. How will you balance your mandate to ensure the welfare of the children with your ethical obligation of client self-determination, particularly if you assess Julia's drinking to be putting the children at risk of harm?

## Profile B: George Favel—Engagement Phase With an Individual

**George Favel's confidential facts (client):** Your street outreach worker, Kerry, has referred you to a residential facility called True Spirits, which provides temporary assisted living apartments to Native Americans who are trying to make a transition off the streets. You agreed to check out True Spirits because you've needed a place to stay ever since your boyfriend kicked you out of his apartment 8 days ago. You were mugged in the park last night and lost the last $20 you had, so a place that offers safety and free meals seems quite desirable. Your social worker at True Spirits is Tracey. You are not sure if True Spirits is for you, since you've never identified that closely with the Native American community. Also, you are still chronically depressed and huff glue regularly. You will conceal the fact that you are gay unless the worker demonstrates that she or he has a positive attitude toward gay people. Although you need a safe place to live, you want to continue to use glue. It is not illegal, but you are not sure whether it would get you into trouble with True Spirits. In preparation for this role-play, write down four reasons that you would want to continue to use glue and four reasons that you might consider giving up glue. Do not disclose these reasons unless the worker establishes trust and specifically asks for this information. You are more willing to talk about the positives of glue use, and reluctant to talk about the negatives, particularly if that is all the worker starts to focus upon. Also, you are particularly concerned about confidentiality—you don't want the police to know of your whereabouts. Feel free to bring along props, such as a bag that contains an inhalant. Do not disclose what is in the bag unless you feel you can trust Tracey. To prepare for your role-play, study the effects of inhalants and nicotine, as well as signs of depression and skills that contribute to or detract from effective engagement.

**Tracey's confidential facts (a True Spirits social worker):** You are a social worker who does intake interviewing and supportive counseling for True Spirits, an assisted living program for Native Americans transitioning off the streets. If George qualifies as a client, then he can stay for up to 6 months. You know from the referral source, Kerry, that George is a 17-year-old man with Cree ancestry. He has an extensive background of living in foster homes and on the street. You also know that he huffs glue. Your agency does not have a zero-tolerance policy on substance use, provided that illicit substances are not brought onto agency premises and clients are not noticeably intoxicated when they enter the residence. Although your agency does not condone substance abuse, it believes that many people living on the street cannot become completely drug-free until after they have a period of stable living. In this interview, your primary goals are to engage George and to build a relationship of trust. Do not try to problem-solve too early. Try to assess his level of motivation (precontemplation versus contemplation), so that you can use the appropriate skills from the Transtheoretical Model. If he seems to be evasive, try to focus on his positives. Consider how you will deal with diversity issues.

## Profile C: Marge and Randy Lang—Engagement Phase With a Family[8]

**Marge and Randy's confidential facts (clients):** Upon the suggestion of Randy's school social worker, Marge made an appointment for them to see Claire, a counselor at the Family Rehab Center. This agency provides outpatient counseling for individuals and who have AODA problems. Although Randy has admitted "using cocaine socially" to his school social worker, he will not acknowledge this in front of his mother, fearing she will "freak out" on him. During the role-play, Marge will present Randy as a "good boy who has gotten into a bit of trouble by hanging out with the wrong crowd." Marge will sound very distressed. Randy will be embarrassed by his mother's comments and will try to act cool (or whatever the local jargon is for someone who acts dispassionately and as if everything is under control). If the worker builds trust effectively, Marge and Randy will open up. Marge, for example, will talk about the breakup of her marriage and will discuss cocaine use among others in her extended family. Randy will acknowledge that he has had a few bad trips, and may be in over his head (e.g., he owes people money and he has trouble controlling the amount of cocaine he uses once he starts). Throughout the role-play, Randy and Marge will be fidgety, out of nervousness rather than because of AODA related issues. Prepare for this role-play by considering which worker skills will help each of you build trust with Claire and which may cause more barriers.

**Claire's confidential facts (worker):** Mrs. Schott, the social worker at Randy's school, has referred Randy and Marge to you, a counselor at the Family Rehab Center. From a brief telephone intake interview with Marge, all you know is that Randy might be using drugs. You are aware that Randy is likely in the precontemplation or contemplation stage and that, as an adolescent, he may be particularly sensitive to issues of authority. Your primary goal for this interview is to engage both Randy and Marge, using techniques of engagement and skills of the Transtheoretical Model that are relevant to the clients' stages of change. This will be a bit of a balancing act, given that Randy and Marge may be at different stages of change. Supportive comments to one of them may look as if you are siding with that person. Pay attention to various types of client content: cognitive (thoughts/beliefs), behavioral (what the clients have done/plan to do), affective (emotional), and informational.

## Profile D: Dionne Thevenin—Engagement Phase With an Individual

**Dionne's confidential facts (client):** In this role-play, you are seeing Harold, an HIV/AIDS counselor from the clinic that tested you. The clinic has required you to see Harold as part of their follow-up, even though you do not want to see him, or anyone. You are particularly concerned about your confidentiality, not wanting people at work or in church to know anything about your sexual practices, IV drug

---

8. This case could also be played as an individual session with Randy alone.

use, or HIV status. Until Harold can assure you that this is a safe place to talk, you will not be very verbal. You do have some questions about your HIV status and whether your prescription drug use could affect your health. You originally assumed that the sleeping pills prescribed by your doctor were safe, but your sleeping patterns are getting even worse and you're worried. You are ready to make changes regarding your sleeping pills, but you are not ready to make any changes regarding your heroin use. You do not want to have to go through withdrawal. You believe your heroin use is not very risky since you have a safe source (you trust your dealer) and you keep a steady dosage. You are cooperative with the worker when asked about the positive effects of heroin on you; you close down when you are asked about the negative effects, since you do not want to hear any more lectures on the evils of drug use. In order to prepare for this meeting, you may want to read up on the immediate, short-term and long-term effects of heroin and sleeping pills (you can choose which ones). You are not intoxicated at this meeting, but you do present with some of the indicators of long-term heroin use.

If you gain trust in Harold as he uses his engagement strategies and techniques, demonstrate changes in your thinking about the risks of heroin and options for treatment. Your key defense mechanisms will be denial and minimization. If Harold pushes you through these defenses without giving you other means of coping, consider how you might react (go into crisis mode? increase drug use? consider suicide? disengage and terminate?). Prepare some dysfunctional thought patterns that the worker may be able to spot and work with, for example, "It's too late for me to change." Alternatively, you could give the worker some discrepancies that he or she could confront you with, for example, "I can't afford to buy heroin, but I can't afford not to either." Finally, consider how you should dress and what props you might bring to this meeting (e.g., draw tracks on one arm).

**Harold's confidential facts (worker):** You are a counselor at an HIV/AIDS clinic that provides follow-up support for people who have tested positive with HIV. You have not met Dionne before, but you do know that she has been involved in a number of behaviors that put her at risk of contracting HIV. Her file is stamped with two risk factors: "promiscuous sexual behavior" and "intravenous drug user" (though you do not know if she shares needles). If her behaviors are not changed, they could put others at risk. You also know that her drug use might affect her thinking in that she may be more likely to engage in unprotected sex when she is using. You suspect that Dionne is in either the precontemplation or contemplation stage and may have cognitive dissonance (conflicting thought patterns) about her AOD use. Engagement may be particularly challenging because Dionne was told that she needed to see you for follow-up. She did not request to see you and may not be ready to change any of her risky behaviors.

You will need to connect with concerns that motivate her rather than tell her what she needs to do. This is only the first interview, so try not to do too much, too fast. Think about what would be a realistic outcome for this meeting (e.g., to have Dionne leave and decide to go "cold turkey" is too big a jump from where she is at the start of the meeting). In order to prepare for this meeting, you may want to look at literature on the effects of heroin use (immediate, long-term, and short term).

# Journaling Exercise

1. Reflect back on the role-play that you conducted for Assignment 4.1. If you were the client rather than the character in the role-play, what feelings would you be experiencing: prior to the first meeting, during the first meeting, and following the first meeting? Review the Constructive Skills and Counterproductive Behaviors in the charts used in this chapter. As a client, which of the Constructive Skills would have been most important for the worker to demonstrate with you during the engagement phase of work? Which of the Counterproductive Behaviors would have been most troubling for you during this phase? Provide explanations or examples to elaborate on your answers.

2. Review this chapter and your answers to various questions and exercises. List 4 specific things you have learned from this chapter related to engagement with clients affected by AODAs. What questions do you still have outstanding? Consider asking your instructor for help with obtaining answers to the most pressing questions that you have. Which engagement skills are your strengths? Which Counterproductive Behaviors do you need to be particularly aware of so that you can avoid them in practice?

# InfoTrac College Edition

## Key words

◇ Motivational Interviewing
◇ Involuntary Client
◇ Transtheoretical Model (Stages of Change)
◇ Self-Efficacy

CHAPTER

# 5

~~~~~

# Assessment: Micro–Mezzo–Macro

According to the general problem-solving process used by helping professionals, assessment follows the engagement phase. Whereas engagement skills and strategies (Chapter 4) are important in AODA practice because they establish a positive working relationship between practitioner and client, assessment is important because it guides the helping process between the worker and client. This chapter begins with an overview of AODA assessments, followed by exercises that will help you learn about specific types of assessments: brief screenings, comprehensive biopsychosocial-spiritual assessments, ongoing assessments for individuals and families, and needs assessments for communities and organizations. The latter portion of this chapter provides a quiz, role-plays, ethical questions, and journaling exercises designed to help you understand, apply, critique, and reflect upon the assessment processes for people affected by AODAs.

## The What, Who, When, Where, and Why of Assessments

### What Is an Assessment?

I define assessment as "a process in which the social worker and client work toward gaining a better understanding of the client's strengths,[1] needs, and concerns, including but not limited to those directly related to AODAs (for example, substance use, abuse, dependence, discontrol, compulsive behaviors, risks and problems associated with AODAs, and resilience and protective factors)." Your definition of assessment (from other readings and experience) is:

---

1. Including *protective factors* and *resiliency* that help people deal with specific types of stresses, such as growing up in a family affected by AODAs.

_____. These definitions are different in the following ways: _____

_____

_____

## Who Is the Focus of the Assessment?

Social workers conduct AODA assessments with clients in the context of their social environments. A client could be an individual, family, group, organization, or community. Decisions about "who is the client" for the purposes of assessment and intervention should be based upon the following criteria:

1. Who is willing to work with the social worker (taking motivation and voluntariness into account)?
2. Who is required by law to participate in services (e.g., probation, parole, suicidal, and child protection clients under court order)?
3. Which individuals and systems are necessary or desirable for developing and implementing an effective helping strategy?
4. Who needs to participate in the assessment process in order to be eligible for services, including payment for services?
5. Who is the worker competent and able to work with (e.g., a worker who has little training in family work may not be competent to work with families, and an agency that specializes in substance abuse problems may not be able to help a person whose main concern is a gambling addiction)?

Review your Case Profile from Chapter 1 using the questions above. In light of your answers, who do you think is the preferred client for your assessment? Provide your reasons below.

## When Does Assessment Take Place?

Assessment can take place at any time throughout the helping process and could include time-line assessments, in which information is collected over an extended period. Although assessment overlaps with the engagement and work phases of the helping process, this chapter focuses on assessment separately for learning purposes. Different types of assessments can take place at different phases. This chapter covers four types of assessments:

- Brief screening assessments for AODAs or problems associated with use, including risks such as homicidal or suicidal ideation.
- Comprehensive biopsychosocial-spiritual assessments, which include an assessment of AODA risks and problems,[2] but delve into all aspects of the client's life, including strengths and resiliencies.
- Ongoing assessments, in which the social worker and client jointly assess and monitor AODA use, problems, and progress over the course of an intervention.
- Needs assessments, which explore the strengths, needs, and risks related to AODAs within an organization or community.

Brief screening assessments often occur during the beginning phases of the helping process in order to direct the worker and client toward the additional assessments and interventions that might be needed. Screenings also occur throughout the helping process, particularly if the worker has reason to believe that there may be urgent risks such as suicidal ideation, homicidal ideation, or overdosing. Comprehensive assessments are most effective after the worker has engaged the client, though some agencies require such assessments at the initial stages of the helping process. Many intensive AODA treatment programs require comprehensive assessments prior to referral and admission to these programs. Ongoing assessments occur throughout the helping process. Needs assessments typically occur at the beginning phases of the helping process, but can also occur at later phases. Terminal assessments, which this book calls "evaluations," occur at the ending and follow-up phases. Evaluations are covered in Chapter 11.

Using your Case Profile from Chapter 1, describe how each form of assessment might be particularly relevant for the client(s) you have identified. Describe which form of assessment you would begin with and provide your reasoning:

## Where Do We Gather Information for the Assessment?

Assessment can take place on a face-to-face basis in the worker's office, at the client's home, or at another place of convenience. Using telephones, chat rooms, the Internet, or other technology, assessments can also take place when the worker and client are distant from each other

---

2. This could include a DSM diagnosis.

(e.g., for people living in isolated communities, or for people who prefer the relative anonymity of an assessment using information technology). Workers must also determine whether to assess simply by asking questions and interviewing, or whether to supplement this information with direct observations of the client (e.g., in a residential facility); with information from family members, coworkers, or other collateral contacts; with AOD toxicology (e.g., breathalyzer, hair sample, blood, or urine tests for evidence of substances in the person's system); or with assessments and diagnoses from other professionals (e.g., a DSM diagnosis from a psychiatrist). For your Case Profile, describe how you would go about gathering information for your assessment and provide your reasoning for gathering information in this manner. Consider the following factors as part of your reasoning:

1. Which sources are most likely to provide you and the client with the information you need for an effective assessment?
2. Which sources of information and types of information gathering are the clients most likely to accept (taking ethical concerns such as respect, informed consent, and confidentiality into account)?
3. If there are restrictions on the time or costs of conducting an assessment, which ways of conducting the assessment are most feasible and most crucial?
4. How would you work with other professionals (if at all) in order to develop a comprehensive assessment in this case?

## Why Is Assessment Important?

In general, assessment is important because it guides the intervention process based on proven strengths, needs, and concerns. Assessment permits the worker and client to develop a joint understanding of the client's AODAs, helping them work together as a team. Further, assessment allows the client, worker, and agency to monitor progress, make changes as needed, and evaluate what works well and what does not. For a particular client situation, the value of assessment depends on why the client has come for help, for instance:

♦ A client who has presenting problems in areas other than AODAs might come to understand how AODAs are causing or maintaining the problem (e.g., marital discord or inability to keep a job).

- A client who wants AODA help may require assessment as an eligibility requirement for services (e.g., a DSM diagnosis might be required for a client to be able to claim insurance benefits, or a methadone maintenance program will only accept clients who has been physically dependent on heroin for at least 12 months).
- Family members, friends, employers, child welfare, or systems might be pressuring an individual in the precontemplation or contemplation stages to go for an assessment, hoping that an assessment will raise the individual's awareness of AODAs and connect with the individual's motivation to change.

Consider the client in your Case Profile. Why, specifically, might an assessment be important for the client in this situation?

## Assessment Competencies

Refer back to items 7 to 10 in the "Areas of Competence" chart in Chapter 1 (page 15). As you go through this chapter, focus on the areas of competence (regarding assessment) that you have identified as learning priorities. Remember to update the competencies chart as you learn new skills and knowledge and as you identify additional areas that you want to develop.

# Brief Screening Assessments

This section is intended to help you select appropriate AODA screening tools for structured screening assessments, as well as to identify useful questions that you can use as a guide for unstructured or informal screenings. Your choice of screening tools or questions depends on precisely what you want to assess. For each of the following topics, you will be provided with one example of an appropriate assessment instrument and key questions that come from the instrument that you can use whether or not you are using the instrument in a structured way or merely as a guide for an informal screening.[3] Your task is to provide a second example of an appropriate assessment instrument and at least two key questions from that instrument. Also, identify whether that instrument has been designed for use by a client alone as a self-assessment (SA), by a worker and client together (WCT), or either way (SA/WCT).

---

3. An appropriate assessment instrument is one that is "valid" (questions measure what you want it to assess, predictive of risks or need for AODA services) and "reliable" (having been tested with various populations, various raters, test-retest, etc.). See http://www.niaaa.nih.gov/publications/instable.htm for examples available online, but do not restrict yourself to these.

| Focus | Example 1 | Questions | Example 2 | Questions |
|---|---|---|---|---|
| **Risks or resilience related to developing an AODA problem** | *Titus Risk Chart (SA/WCT)* | • *At what age did you begin drinking or using drugs?*<br>• *Do you feel alienated by the community you live in?* | | |
| **Risk of suicide or homicide** | *Hepworth, Farley, & Griffiths, 1995 (WCT)* | • *How hopeful do you feel about the future?*<br>• *Do you feel you can be helped?*<br>• *Are you currently thinking about hurting yourself?* | | |
| **AOD dependence** | *TWEAK[4] (Tolerance, Worry, Eye-opener, Amnesia, Kut down (SA/WCT)* | • *Tolerance: How many drinks does it take to make you feel high?*<br>• *Worry: Have close friends or relatives worried or complained about your drinking in the past year?* | | *(continued)* |

4. Source: Russel, Martier, Sokol, Mudar, Bottoms, Jacopsen, & Jacobsen, 1994. Available without cost or copyright from Marcia Russell, Research Institute on Addictions, 1021 Main Street, Buffalo, NY 14203 (phone: 716-887-2507). Available online at http://www.niaaa.nih.gov/publications/tweak.htm.

| Focus | Example 1 | Questions | Example 2 | Questions |
|---|---|---|---|---|
| | | • *Eye-opener: Do you sometimes have a drink in the morning when you first get up?* | | |
| Determine whether AODA treatment is needed for a child, elderly person, or individual from a specific cultural group | *Problem-Oriented Screening Instrument for Teenagers (POSIT)[5]—also available in Spanish and tested with Hispanic youth (WCT)* | • *Do your friends get bored at parties when alcohol is not served?* <br> • *Have you started using more and more drugs or alcohol to get the effect you want?* <br> • *Does your alcohol or drug use ever make you do something you would not ordinarily do—like breaking rules, missing curfew, breaking the law, or having sex with someone?* <br> • *Do your family or friends ever tell you that you should cut down on your drinking or drug use?* | | |

*(continued)*

---

5. Source: National Clearinghouse for Alcohol and Drug Information, P.O. Box 2345, Rockville, MD 20847-2345 (1-800-729-6686).

| Focus | Example 1 | Questions | Example 2 | Questions |
|-------|-----------|-----------|-----------|-----------|
| Family need for help with an AODA problem | *Are You Troubled by Someone's Drinking (Al-Anon)*[6] *(SA)* | • *Do you make threats, such as, "If you don't stop drinking, I'll leave you?"*<br>• *Do you secretly try to smell the drinker's breath?*<br>• *Are you afraid to upset someone for fear it will set off a drinking bout?* | | |

## Diversity and Biases in Assessment Questions

Some assessment tools have been developed and tested for people from a broad range of backgrounds. Others have been normed for a mainstream population or a specific segment of society (Gopaul-McNicol & Armour-Thomas, 2002). Review the assessment questions listed in the above chart. Identify any questions that have implicit or explicit biases or assumptions related to client diversity factors such as age, sex, sexual orientation, ethnicity, culture, disability, or socioeconomic status. For each question that contains a bias, re-draft the question in a way that corrects the bias and includes people who might otherwise be excluded.

> Example: One question in the Michigan Alcohol Screening Test is: "Does your wife, husband, a parent, or other near relative ever worry or complain about your drinking?" The terms *wife* and *husband* are biased toward heterosexual clients who are married. To correct this bias, the question could be reworded as: "Do any of your close family members (such as a domestic partner, parent, or child) ever worry or complain about your drinking?"

## Critiquing a Screening Interview

Review the following script of a truly awful screening interview and provide your critique of the interview. In particular, identify problems with the social worker's questions, such as being unclear, judgmental, irrelevant, or factually inappropriate. For each problem, provide a more appropriate response that corrects the problem. The first section of the following chart provides an example of how to complete the rest of the chart.

---

6. Source: http://www.al-anon-alateen.org/quiz.html.

| Script of interview | Worker's intention | Problem | More appropriate question |
|---|---|---|---|
| Worker: Have you ever had withdrawal effects after using LSD? | To explore the consequences of client's LSD use. | *Factually inappropriate: LSD does not produce withdrawal effects.* | *How do you usually feel the day after using LSD?* |
| Client: I don't think so. | | | |
| W: You must feel guilty after you've been using, don't you? | To explore client's attitudes toward LSD use. | | |
| C: What do I have to feel guilty about? | | | |
| W: What about accidents? | To determine possible risks associated with LSD use. | | |
| C: I've got a perfect driving record. | | | |
| W: When you shoot LSD do you share needles? | To explore risks associated with administration of LSD. | | |
| C: What needles? I'm no junky. | | | |
| W: When you're seeing sounds or hearing colors, do you ever start to panic? | To explore possible problems related to panic or anxiety. | | |
| C: Are you on drugs or something? | | | |
| W: I'll ask the questions, if you don't mind. Do you experience positive support systems from kinship relation-ships? | To explore possible strengths such as family support. | | |

*(continued)*

| Script of interview | Worker's intention | Problem | More appropriate question |
|---|---|---|---|
| C: I don't have any ships. I can hardly afford a car. | | | |
| W: Why haven't you ever gone for drug treatment in the past? | To explore attitudes toward using professional help. | | |

# Comprehensive Biopsychosocial-Spiritual Assessment

A comprehensive assessment with an individual or family includes a broad exploration of biological, psychological, social, and spiritual aspects of the client's strengths, needs, and concerns. Although this manual focuses on AODAs, a comprehensive assessment is not limited to issues related directly to AODAs, but rather sees AODAs as just one set of factors to consider. The following section introduces you to assessments by asking you to find an assessment form so that you can review its components and analyze its strengths and limitations.

## Critiquing an Assessment Form

Locate an assessment instrument or interview guide. Possible sources include an AODA textbook, an agency that specializes in AODA work, or an AODA Web site (e.g., Addiction Severity Index [ASI], available at http://www.densonline.org/Instrument.htm). Critique this form or instrument according to the following criteria (identifying its strengths, limitations, and needs for improvement). [3 to 6 pages]

1. Client-focused—Includes client's perceptions of strengths, needs, and concerns for help; includes client's attitudes toward AODA behaviors; and includes client-identified goals and challenges to achieving and maintaining positive changes. (In other words, the assessment is not simply driven by the opinions or needs of the worker, the agency, the funding body, the statisticians/researchers, or the insurance company.)

2. Comprehensive—Covers key life areas in the biological, psychological, social, and spiritual spheres, including physical and mental health, intimate partner relationships, nuclear and extended family relationships, education, employment, socioeconomic status, culture, religion, legal issues, recreation and social activities, peer relationships, prior use of professional help, and AODA behaviors and consequences (including both positive and negative impacts of AODAs on the body, mind, social relationships, and spirituality of the client system).

3.  Evidence-based—Conclusions drawn from the assessment are based on knowledge that has a solid research basis (for instance, use of valid and reliable interview formats and diagnostic criteria—cf. Gibbs, 2003).

4.  Purposeful—Topics or questions are purposefully guided by a clear theoretical basis (avoids topics that are irrelevant and intrusive).

5.  Fit with social work—The Assessment Form fits with social work values and perspectives, such as nonjudgmentalism, respect for diversity, competence,[7] person-in-environment, ecosystems and interactive effects,[8] generalist practice, and strengths perspective.

6.  Linked assessment and plans for change—The understanding of the client's strengths, needs, and concerns are closely linked with the plans for change, including the client's responsibilities, the worker's responsibilities, and how others may be brought into the helping process (e.g., the plan includes provisions for continuity of care).

## Beginning With Strengths

Now that you are familiar with at least one comprehensive assessment tool, we will look at some specific strategies for approaching AODA assessments. The following exercise is designed to help you incorporate a strengths perspective in your assessment. Beginning an assessment by focusing on the client's strengths and interests is a useful approach for engaging clients. Typically, people with AODA problems have heard all the reasons not to use and may know them intimately. Be careful about focusing on problems, as you might sound judgmental. Use reflective skills, tuning in, and empathy. Start where the client is. Ask the client for his or her perceptions of AOD use or addictive behaviors. Also ask about his or her attitudes toward change. By assessing strengths with the client, you can then build on these strengths as you develop an intervention strategy. If a client is bright and articulate, for example, then models of helping that require a certain level of intelligence and speaking skills can be used to build on these strengths.

Consider the following scenario and identify at least four potential strengths that the client might possess given the information you have. For each of the four strengths, suggest a question that you could use to help the client gain insight into the fact that he or she has that strength.

You are conducting a psychosocial assessment for a client named Charmaine, an 84-year-old woman who has two children, three grandchildren, and one great-grandchild. Charmaine has suffered from chronic alcoholism since she was in her twenties. Charmaine claims her husband was physically abusive to her and she used alcohol to drown herself in pity. She says, "I stayed with him for 53 years, until he died, because I didn't think I could survive without him. Now that he's gone, it's too late for me to really have my own life." Charmaine's current health situation is poor. She has cirrhosis of the liver and recently broke her hip as a result of a fall while she

---

7. Including the ethical responsibility for social workers to practice only within their areas of expertise and competence.

8. Rather than unidirectional "cause-effect relationships."

was intoxicated. When you ask what she thinks about alcohol, she responds, "It's like I've made a pact with the devil and now I have to live with it for the rest of my sorry days."

Example: *One potential strength is Charmaine's ability to survive. To elicit this strength, I could ask, "How were you able to survive all these years, especially when you had a husband who was abusive?"*

1. Strength:


   Question:


2. Strength:


   Question:


3. Strength:


   Question:


4. Strength:


   Question:


## Ecomap

The above exercise highlights the strengths perspective of social work in the assessment process. The following exercise highlights another important social work approach, the ecological perspective. An ecomap is a useful tool for conducting an assessment from an ecological perspective. From this perspective, AODAs are not problems that arise exclusively within clients or exclusively within their social environments. Rather, AODAs arise because of stresses in the interaction between clients and systems in their social environments. Using the information from the Case Profile you selected in Chapter 1, identify the client (an individual, dyad, or group of family members) and develop an ecomap. Use question marks to identify any missing information that you need to gather from the client or from collateral contacts. See Figure 5.1 for an example that uses the facts from Eva's case in Chapter 1. Once you have developed the ecomap, write a couple of paragraphs to describe the nature of the client's AODA concerns from an ecological perspective. Avoid pathologizing terminology such

**FIGURE 5.1**

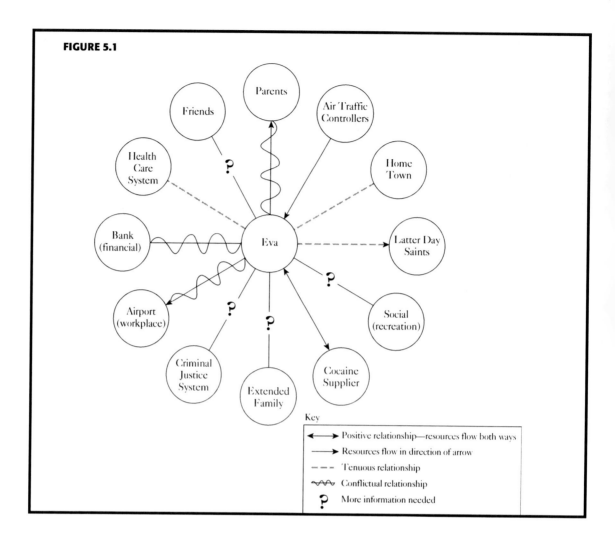

Key

| | |
|---|---|
| ←——→ | Positive relationship—resources flow both ways |
| ——→ | Resources flow in direction of arrow |
| - - - | Tenuous relationship |
| ~~~ | Conflictual relationship |
| ? | More information needed |

as, "The client suffers from an alcohol dependence disorder." Describe concerns or problems as existing in the interactions between systems, for example, "The client describes using alcohol to deal with stress related to being laid off when the factory where he worked was downsized."

## Theoretical Framework to Guide Assessment

An assessment should be guided by the theoretical frameworks that you are using, so that you can focus your questions on issues that are most relevant. The previous two exercises illustrated how the strengths and ecological perspectives could be incorporated into an AODA assessment. Now, we look at an approach to incorporating more specific theories into one's assessment. A theoretically based assessment is vital to ensuring a purposeful connection between your assessment and intervention. If you were using a Cognitive-Behavioral framework, for example, your assessment would explore the relationships between antecedents, behaviors, and consequences (ABCs), as well as the client's thought processes concerning these ABCs. In order to put this framework into practice, you would need to develop questions that elicited this type of information, for instance:

- Antecedents: Tell me about the last time you used cocaine. How were you feeling just before you started to use? What were you thinking about? What activities were you engaged in? Who was with you? Is there anything else that you think might have led to your use?
- Behavior: Please describe how you used the cocaine. Were you snorting, shooting, or smoking it? How much cocaine did you use?
- Consequences: After you used cocaine, how were you feeling? What were you thinking? What were you doing? What were some of the immediate consequences of your use? Over time, what do you see as the benefits of your use? Over time, what do you see as the downsides of your use? How do family members (or friends or co-workers) respond to you when you use cocaine? How does your cocaine use affect the way you look at life generally, and what gives your life meaning?

By having a range of possible questions to ask, you can ensure that your Cognitive-Behavioral assessment is comprehensive, including behavioral, cognitive, emotional, and spiritual antecedents and consequences, as well as both short- and long-term consequences.

In the following exercise, list 5 to 10 questions that you could ask as part of an assessment based on the identified theoretical frameworks (and remember to refer back to these for the role-plays that you will be doing later in this chapter).

- Physiological Theory (especially dependence, tolerance, and withdrawal—for a client who might be addicted to heroin)

- Family Systems Theory (especially enabling behaviors, boundaries, family roles, family rules, disequilibriums—in relation to a family affected by a teen who uses cannabis)

♦ Sociocultural Theory (especially values, attitudes, and beliefs toward use of tobacco—by a Guatemalan man who suffers from emphysema)

## Legal Issues, Confidentiality, and Privilege

We turn now from looking at the theoretical bases of assessments to looking at ethical and legal issues related to assessments. Many clients affected by AODAs are involved in criminal activities, for example, possessing illicit drugs, trafficking in illicit drugs, fraudulently obtaining prescription medications, driving under the influence of alcohol or illicit drugs, breaking and entering or theft while under the influence or to support an AOD habit, and committing acts of domestic violence while under the influence. A comprehensive assessment requires that the worker ask about legal issues, including the history of criminal arrests, charges, and convictions, as well as behaviors that might lead to charges if state authorities knew about them. Consider the following questions (for class discussion or for a written assignment on legal-ethical issues):

1. How can social workers encourage clients to be open and honest about these types of behaviors if there might be a risk that this information could be used against them in a criminal prosecution? Are there any legal or ethical provisions that guarantee that information learned in the course of social work will be protected? Is there a difference for a social worker in general practice versus a social worker who is specifically working in a substance abuse treatment agency?

2. What type of information about a client's criminal activity, if any, should social workers keep in their files? Why?

3. Under what circumstances, if any, does a social worker have a legal or ethical obligation to report a client's drug-related activities to the police or other state authorities?

4. Assume you have offered a client confidentiality, and the client tells you about having obtained Oxycodone illegally by forging a doctor's name on the prescription and taking it to a pharmacy. Subsequently, the police conduct a criminal investigation and press charges against the client for committing this fraud. The state decides to subpoena you and your records, hoping that you will testify that the client has admitted to this criminal act. What are your ethical and legal obligations in this case? How should you (and your agency) respond to the subpoena?

## Ethnoculturally Specific Assessment Tools

Until this point in the chapter, we have focused upon assessment forms and strategies that can be used across different diversity groups. This next exercise asks you to consider whether there are different instruments or approaches to assessment for people from different backgrounds. Conduct a literature search to see if there are any ethnoculturally specific assessment tools for clients from the ethnicity or culture that you have identified for the clients in your Case Profile—for example, the Medicine Wheel is sometimes used by agencies that work with Native American clients. Obtain a copy of your chosen tool and at least one article that explains its use. Critique this tool noting its strengths and limitations, as well as the extent to which it fits or conflicts with social worker perspectives and principles such as person-in-environment, strengths, client self-determination, and nonjudgmentalism.

## What Is Normal?

The above exercise asks us to consider various instruments that are specifically designed for the assessment of people from particular cultural backgrounds. A large part of assessment, however, is not guided by specific and objective assessment tools, but by more open-ended and subjective assessments. We inform our assessments by using our values, knowledge, and experience, including our subjective comparisons between the client's condition and what we perceive as normal. "What is normal?" is a risky question because it is often based on generalizations, stereotypes, and unsubstantiated beliefs. Still, this can be a very useful question for a social worker to consider during assessment in order to raise the social worker's awareness of potential biases during the assessment process. When considering a client situation, workers can ask themselves:

1. My view: What, if anything, about the client's AODA involvement would I consider abnormal?
2. Client's view: From the client's perspective, is this AODA involvement considered abnormal? If the client considers this behavior normal, what explains the difference between our perspectives?
3. Professional view: From my professional knowledge base, is the AODA involvement considered abnormal? If so, why? (As part of your professional knowledge base, consider scholarly literature on diverse populations.)
4. Avoid imposing my biases: How can I ensure that I do not impose my biases on the client (unless the concerns raised involve serious risk to the client, children, or other vulnerable individuals or groups)?

To illustrate this, consider a client who regularly uses 11 different pills. For purposes of this example, let us say that I consider this abnormal, not just because of the large number of pills but also because of the possible side effects of taking so many drugs in combination. To a client who has been taking these pills for the past 2 years, this might seem quite normal. If I understood that the client was taking these pills as part of a prescribed regimen to control the client's AIDS, then I could understand that this was an acceptable use of drugs, at least from the medical profession's perspective. If I believe in homeopathy or folk healing rather than a cocktail of prescription medications, I would need to be aware that this was my bias. I would need to be careful not to impose these beliefs on the client. I might be able to help the client explore different courses of treatment, but I should not make the client feel guilty or pressured about his or her own choice of treatment.

Consider your Case Profile. Identify an example of AODA involvement from the case that you consider "abnormal." Using this example, write down your responses to the above questions.

1.  My view:

2.  Client's view:

3.  Professional view:

4. Avoid imposing my biases:

## Assessment With an Involuntary Client

As the former exercises illustrate, some of the most important aspect of AODA assessments are: avoiding judgment or imposition of biases, building on strengths, explaining the nature and limits of confidentiality, paying attention to client diversity, and using theory to guide your assessments. These lessons are particularly important for assessment with involuntary clients. Because such clients are likely to be in precontemplation or contemplation stages (described in Chapter 4), you will likely need to continue engagement and trust-building strategies throughout the assessment process. The following scenario is designed to provide you with practice in engaging an involuntary client and trying to conduct an assessment during the first interview.

### Facts for Both Dino and the Social Worker

Dino is a 47-year-old male of Italian descent who lives in Delray, Florida. Dino was in a car accident last Saturday night. He was charged with a DUI (Driving Under the Influence of alcohol) and has an upcoming hearing in criminal court. Dino's lawyer told him to see an addictions counselor for an alcoholism assessment because it would look good in court. Dino comes to see you, a counselor who specializes in addictions work. When you ask whether he has a problem with alcohol, he says no. He only wants to see you so you can help him with his court case by telling them that you have no problem with alcohol. You explain that you'll need to go through some questions with him. The following questions come from the CAGE screening tool.

1. Have you ever felt you should *Cut down* on drinking? Dino says no (although you suspect that he got into trouble because he drank too much before he drove).
2. Have people *Annoyed* you by criticizing your drinking? Dino says yes. He talks about the police annoying him, saying that the accident had nothing to do with his drinking. On further exploration, you find out that some of his friends have told him that he drinks too much at parties and becomes abusive. Also, his parents always bug him about his drinking and tell him he's going to wind up a wino on the streets.
3. Have you ever felt bad or *Guilty* about your drinking? Dino denies he has a problem, so why should he feel guilty?
4. Have you ever had a drink first thing in the morning to steady your nerves or get rid of a hangover as an *Eye-opener?* Dino looks a bit nervous and hesitates before he

answers. He says no. He says that all people get hangovers, but it doesn't mean anything, and he has no problem.

Consider the following questions:

a. What is Dino's current stage of change? What are your reasons for identifying him at this stage?

b. Given his stage of change, what strategies would be appropriate for working with him?

c. You suspect that Dino does not trust you, making it difficult for him to be open and honest about his problems with alcohol. Referring back to Chapter 4, what strategies could you use for engaging Dino and building trust in this situation?

d. Select a format for conducting an assessment interview that would be appropriate for working with Dino, given his levels of motivation and trust. Identify strategies for how you will conduct this interview to ensure that you and Dino can work together as effectively as possible.

## Confidential Facts for Dino Only

Because an assessment can cover so many different aspects of the client's life, it is difficult to provide answers to all the possible questions that the social worker might ask: age, family status, job, criminal history, cultural background, prior involvement in treatment services. To simplify things, identify a fictional character that you are familiar with who has an alcohol problem, for example, Nicholas Cage's character (Ben Sanderson) in the movie *Leaving Las Vegas*, Sharon Gless's role (Chris Cagney) in the television series *Cagney & Lacey*, Megan Mullally's character (Karen Walker) in the television show *Will & Grace*, or a character from a novel. Base your portrayal of Dino on that person. Feel free to change the character to a different ethnocultural background or gender (e.g., Dina rather than Dino). Make up facts that you need and write down a few notes to help you prepare your character. During the actual role-play, do not refer back to the notes. Do not disclose the character you are portraying until after the role-play.

## Debriefing After the Role-Play

After the role-play, ask the person playing the social worker to identify which strategies seemed to facilitate trust building and what challenges the worker continued to have difficulty with. Ask the person playing Dino how honest he was in providing answers, and what was going on in his mind as he was deciding what to share and how much detail to provide.

# Ongoing Assessment

Assessment can continue throughout the helping process. The client and social worker monitor their progress toward agreed upon goals and objectives, reevaluating the goals and objectives from time to time, depending on the needs, wishes, and abilities of the client. One method of monitoring progress is *single-system design*. In this method, goals and objectives are specified, including timelines and ways in which the worker and client will know the extent to which goals and objectives are being met (Bloom, Fischer, & Orme, 2003). In the following exercise, you will be provided with examples of broad goals. Your task is to complete the chart by adding feasible and specific objectives, methods of monitoring progress, and timelines for completion of objectives.

Example: A client with a chronic alcohol problem who has been seeing a worker on an outpatient basis agrees to go to a residential treatment program for help.

| Broad goal | Specific objectives | Monitoring methods | Timeline |
|---|---|---|---|
| *Client will be admitted into an appropriate substance abuse treatment program* | • *Worker will prepare a list of programs available for client* | *Client will review this list at the next meeting with worker* | *April 1 (1 week from today)* |
| | • *Client will contact each program and gather information as per checklist* | *Client will follow up with worker by telephone call to discuss progress and challenges* | *April 8 and April 12* |
| | • *Client and worker will review and select the best program* | *Client and worker will use the client's checklist to create "pros and cons" list for each possibility to help make decisions* | *April 15* |
| | • *Client will make suitable arrangements for child care, work, and insurance to be able to go into treatment within 6 weeks* | *Childcare must be approved by client's child protection case manager; client to contact employer regarding arrangements for medical leave; worker to help client submit forms for insurance approval and follow up together* | *April 25* |

Case A: A client who is afraid she might have contracted HIV by sharing needles is considering getting tested for HIV, but is very ambivalent.

| Broad goal | Specific objectives | Monitoring methods | Timeline |
|---|---|---|---|
| Client and worker to jointly decide whether and when client will get tested for HIV | • | | |

(continued)

| Broad goal | Specific objectives | Monitoring methods | Timeline |
|---|---|---|---|
| | • | | |
| | • | | |

Case B: Ms. Graves and Mr. Worth kicked their daughter, Dolores (aged 17), out of their home because they did not approve of her cocaine use, her destruction of property during violent outbursts, and her sexual experiences with a series of different partners. Dolores has been living with various friends. In counseling with a social worker, Dolores and her parents have agreed to work toward a plan where she can come home.

| Broad goal | Specific objectives | Monitoring methods | Timeline |
|---|---|---|---|
| Dolores will move home with a plan that is agreeable to both Dolores and her parents | • | | |

*(continued)*

| Broad goal | Specific objectives | Monitoring methods | Timeline |
|---|---|---|---|
| | • | | |
| | • | | |

Case C: Gayle is facilitating a group of people who are physically and psychologically dependent on heroin. The group is based on a harm reduction approach.

| Broad goal | Specific objectives | Monitoring methods | Timeline |
|---|---|---|---|
| Group members will reduce the risks of social, spiritual, psychological, and physical harm associated with their use of opiates | • | | |

*(continued)*

| Broad goal | Specific objectives | Monitoring methods | Timeline |
|------------|--------------------|--------------------|----------|
|  | • |  |  |
|  | • |  |  |

Case D: A social worker, using a functional approach to counseling,[9] finds that Mr. and Mrs. Clampet tend to smoke pot when they are anxious or bored. They say they would be prepared to give up smoking pot if they could find other ways to cope.

| Broad goal | Specific objectives | Monitoring methods | Timeline |
|------------|--------------------|--------------------|----------|
| To develop alternative ways of coping with anxiety or boredom in order to reduce or eliminate the need to smoke pot | • |  |  |

*(continued)*

---

9. For a comprehensive assessment format based upon a functional approach, see Lewis, Dana, & Blevins, 2002, pp. 245–250.

| Broad goal | Specific objectives | Monitoring methods | Timeline |
|---|---|---|---|
| | • | | |
| | • | | |

# Needs Assessment for an Organization or Community

The first part of this chapter emphasizes assessment with individuals, families, and members of small groups. We now turn to assessment of larger social systems. A "needs assessment" refers to a strategy of gathering information about an organization or community in order to develop a better understanding of its health and social problems and strengths. The purpose of a needs assessment is to develop policies, programs, expenditures of resources, and other methods of intervention to ameliorate the problems or otherwise respond to the identified needs (Brown, 1997). As with a comprehensive assessment for an individual or family, a needs assessment of an organization or community should be holistic. Assessing just the AODA issues would be imprudent given the interactive effects between AODA issues and other health or social problems. The following two sections will help you explore methods of gathering information for a needs assessment, and then provide you with an exercise to practice a needs assessment interview.

# Methods of Gathering Information

Information for needs assessments can be collected through a variety of means, depending on the nature of the needs assessment and the availability of resources to conduct the assessment. For each of the following scenarios, identify appropriate methods of gathering information for a needs assessment, for example, literature reviews, quantitative studies (surveys using probability sampling; direct measures of AODA problems; indirect measures such as social indicator data from criminal justice, social service, workplace, or health care systems), community forums, or ethnographic studies (interviews with key informants, consultation with cultural guides, focus groups, observations, and descriptions) (Brown, 1997). Select methods that will produce information that is valid, reliable, and unbiased, taking financial feasibility into account. Also, consider ways of involving community members, since involvement in a needs assessment can help motivate people to become part of the change process.

*Sample Scenario:* The federal government wants to determine whether additional funding is needed for alcoholism treatment services for people who are deaf.

*The first step in gathering information would be to conduct a review of existing research to see if there are statistics on issues such as the number of deaf people who might benefit from these services, the availability of such services, and whether there is really need for additional services that specifically aid people who are deaf. The Substance Abuse & Mental Health Services Administration and the National Institutes of Health (including NIDA and NIAAA) may be good sources for relevant research, and also may provide funding for research if a nationwide study needs to be conducted.*

*Scenario A:* Parents are outraged at a college football program where two students developed severe health problems as a result of steroid use. The college claims that this was an isolated incident, but agrees under pressure to assess whether steroid use is a systemic problem within the college's sports programs.

***Scenario B:*** The local health department in El Paso is concerned that the working poor cannot afford to purchase medications legally and are resorting to underground sources that may be providing unsafe substances to unwitting customers.

***Scenario C:*** The Jamaican American community in Philadelphia claims that police are using ethnic profiling and entrapment to blame the city's marijuana trafficking on young men from their community. An independent research institute has been hired to study this issue and make recommendations.

***Scenario D:*** Recently, a prenatal care program has noticed a large number of children born with Fetal Alcohol Effects (FAE). The program wants to know more about pregnant women's needs and concerns, so that it can address the problem of FAE prevention more effectively.

## Practicing a Needs Assessment Interview

Select an organization, such as a workplace, a social agency, or your school of social work, where you know someone you can interview. Prepare for and conduct an organizational needs assessment interview with this person. Be sure to explore the following areas:

♦ physical, psychological, social, and spiritual needs
♦ primary issues of concern to people in the organization
♦ risks related to AODAs (e.g., stress, availability of psychoactive substances, overworking, compulsive behaviors, specific unmet needs)
♦ resources if a person has an AODA problem

Write a report based on this needs assessment (even though you only have one person providing the information). Your report should include strengths of the organization, a prioritization of its needs, and risks within the organization related to AODAs (refer to your notes in Chapter 2 for AODA risks; there is a follow-up to this exercise in Chapter 8).

# Assessment Quiz

The following quiz is designed to test your ability to apply what you have learned about assessment to brief client situations. Answers to the quiz can be found in the Appendix.

1. Two parents bring a teenager, kicking and screaming, into your office for a substance abuse assessment. The parents say the teen is "smoking weed." The teen denies use. Of the following, the most appropriate social worker response *initially* would be to:
   a. Ask the teen why she is using pot.
   b. Call the police to advise that a child has been accused of possessing an illegal substance.
   c. Tell the family that there is no purpose in seeing a social worker if they can't agree on whether or not there is a problem.
   d. Demonstrate empathy with each person's view, without agreeing or disagreeing with any of the family members.
   e. Get a court order to commit the child into a psychiatric ward for further assessment.

2. A 15-year-old has been referred to a counselor for an AODA assessment, but the client is reluctant to speak. In order to engage the client by describing confidentiality, the counselor should explain that:
   a. Because the client is under the age of majority, he has no right to confidentiality.
   b. Everything from the assessment will be held confidential, except if the client admits to having committed any drug-related crimes. If the client admits possession of a small amount of pot or driving under the influence of alcohol, for example, the worker has to inform the police.
   c. For the most part, anything they talk about will be treated as a private matter, but the counselor may have to tell others if there are any serious risks to the client or another person.
   d. Parents have a legal right to know everything about their children, so the counselor may have to share everything the child says with the parents.
   e. All of the above.

3. During an assessment, a client expresses uncertainty about his sexual orientation. As an AODA social worker, which of the following is the best way to help the client open up about this issue?
   a. Tell the client that some of your best friends are gay.
   b. Use nonjudgmental language and open-ended questions that invite the client to talk about his sexuality, his uncertainties, or questions about sexuality in general.
   c. Let the client know that homosexuality is one of the root causes of addiction.
   d. Suggest that the client deal with the addiction first and then talk about his sexuality.
   e. Offer to take the client out to a gay bar to see if he is really interested in other men.

4. If a social worker uses CAGE, she should understand that it is an instrument designed to:
   a. Provide an accurate diagnosis of a client's alcohol-related disorders.
   b. Assess a client using a holistic psychosocial framework.
   c. Determine whether a client would suffer withdrawal and needs a medical detox unit.
   d. Measure the level of blood-alcohol in a client.
   e. Screen a client for alcohol problems.

5. In order to increase the likelihood that a client will provide full and honest answers, a social worker would be best advised to:
   a. Assume a position of authority with the client.
   b. Ask nonthreatening questions and provide nonjudgmental responses to the client.
   c. Provide negative consequences for lying, such as refusing to continue to treat the client.
   d. Use an assessment tool with at least 100 questions.
   e. Include parents, employers, or teachers in the session with the client.

6. A social worker reading a client file sees that the psychiatrist on staff has given the client a DSM diagnosis of "Cocaine Abuse." The worker should understand that this diagnosis suggests the client has demonstrated:
   a. A higher intensity and frequency of use than Cocaine Dependence.
   b. Episodes of problematic use, legal difficulties, or neglect of responsibilities.
   c. Evidence of withdrawal and compulsive behavior to avoid withdrawal.
   d. Infrequent dosing to avoid the short half-life of cocaine intoxication.
   e. All of the above.

7. A comprehensive AODA assessment should include discussion about the client's:
   a. Education.
   b. Social supports.
   c. Peer group.
   d. Patterns and effects of drug use.
   e. All of the above.

8. A worker wants to explain the nature of an ecological AODA assessment to a client. Which of the following is the most accurate way to explain this approach?
   a. "To conduct an ecological assessment, I need to explore the trauma and other underlying conflicts from your childhood experiences that have led to your dys-

functional coping, including the use of chemicals and addictive behaviors as an adult."

b. "An ecological assessment identifies the root causes for your disease of addiction, including genetics, physiology, psychopathology, or coexisting mental health disorders."

c. "The basis of an ecological assessment is identifying the psychological processes that have lead to your addictive personality."

d. "An ecological assessment focuses on how the oppressive nature of sexism, racism, and other forms of oppression has caused your addiction."

e. "To conduct an ecological assessment, we need to explore your relationships with family members, peers, friends, and others in your social environment. This will help us determine what contributes to your AODA problems, and what might help you deal with them more effectively."

9. When a social worker speaks with a client about her drug use, it is important for the worker to:

a. Only focus on the negative aspects of drug abuse, so as not to condone that client's drug use.

b. Avoid talking about the possibility of suicide, so that the worker doesn't put bad ideas into her head.

c. Encourage the client to talk about both the positive and negative aspects of her use, to engage with the client, and to get a balanced assessment of her use.

d. Ask about legal drug use only, because if you ask about illicit drug use then you will have to report it to the police.

e. Encourage the client to exaggerate her drug use, so that the client will think that she is having more problems than she actually is having.

10. Using a behavioral approach, an assessment of a client's antecedents to AOD use should include exploration of:

a. Early learning and developmental events.

b. Experiences of withdrawal symptoms.

c. Social pressures.

d. Availability.

e. All of the above.

11. A social worker should screen for suicidal ideation with a client:

a. During the first part of the first meeting.

b. After the client has been engaged in a positive working relationship.

c. During a thorough biopsychosocial assessment.

d. During maintenance and follow-up interviews.

e. All of the above.

12. The Patient Placement Criteria adopted by the American Society of Addiction Medicine identifies factors to consider when determining what type of AODA services are needed. From least intrusive to most intrusive, these five levels are:

a. Cognitive, Psychoanalytic, Family Systems, Jungian, and Humanistic.

b. Level 0.5—Early intervention; Level I—Outpatient Service; Level II—Intensive Outpatient/Partial Hospitalization; Level III—Residential/Inpatient Services; Level IV—Medically Managed Intensive Inpatient Services.

c. Individual, family, group, community, and policy.

d. Engagement, assessment, intervention, termination, and follow-up.

e. Counseling, psychotherapy, pharmacotherapy, restraints, and incarceration.

13. The Patient Placement Criteria suggests that assessment of people affected by AODAs for the purpose of determining services should include consideration of:
    a. Acute intoxication and withdrawal potential.
    b. Treatment acceptance or resistance.
    c. Patient's living environment.
    d. Relapse of continued use potential.
    e. All of the above.

14. Which of the following AOD risks are typically higher for adolescents than for adults?
    a. Liver damage from alcohol use.
    b. Attempted suicide.
    c. Cancer from smoking.
    d. All of the above.
    e. None of the above.

# Assignment 5.1: Assessment

This assignment builds upon the knowledge base you developed in Chapters 1 to 3 concerning the nature of AODAs; theoretical frameworks; diversity perspectives; and information about specific substance use causes, effects, functions, and interactions.[10] Designate someone in your group to play the worker and someone to play the two clients. In developing the assessment, the worker will need to gather information from the client(s) and relate this information to the worker's knowledge base, ensuring that the worker is aware of any personal values and attitudes so these do not bias the assessment. For the purposes of the role-play, assume that you have successfully completed the engagement phase (Chapter 4), and that the client is relatively cooperative. The worker may use structured assessment formats, such as the ones described and critiqued earlier in this chapter, or develop his or her own form of assessment. In either case, the worker will need to provide sound rationale for choosing a particular format.

The write-up for this assignment will include:

1. A written assessment of the client system [4 to 7 pages], using the information you have learned from the assessment interview and linking it to your AODA and social work knowledge bases. Include the worker's analysis of the clients' situation, the clients' understanding and motivation, and the goals that the worker and clients have agreed upon, if any. Ensure that the written assessment is consistent with the type of assessment and theoretical framework(s) you choose, as well as with social work values (e.g., nonjudgmentalism and client self-determination) and the information you have been building on from earlier assignments in this manual. Include the following:
    ◊ How do you define addiction, use, abuse, misuse, relapse, tolerance, and motivation? How did you assess for these in the current case? If any of these terms did not apply, please explain why.

---

10. For example, in Chapter 2, one assignment had you hypothesize about what potential functions were served by the various substances used by characters in your client profile. In the assessment interview, you can test out these hypotheses to see if they fit with the client's experiences.

◇ What are the short- and long-term risks/effects of the AODA behaviors of the client (include positive and negative biological, psychological, social, and spiritual effects)?

◇ What is the nature of the relationship between the addictive or substance-using behavior and the other presenting problems in the case situation?

◇ Choose two or three theories or perspectives that you believe are important to assessing the client system. Provide a rationale for why these perspectives are applicable. Define the key concepts from these theories or perspectives and demonstrate how they apply to the case facts. Also, assess whether there are certain ways in which the case facts are inconsistent with what you know from the literature.

◇ Identify two or three research articles that are related to the client group or presenting problem. What do these articles tell you about the client's vulnerability, risk, and protective factors?

◇ What additional questions or information would you like to have answered that are not accessible in the literature?

2. A critique of the process of assessment, including the following:

◇ What was your rationale for selecting particular assessment tools and theoretical frameworks for this assessment interview? In retrospect, how appropriate were these tools and theoretical frameworks? If they were problematic, what other tools or theoretical frameworks might have been better, and why? [2 to 4 pages]

◇ What were the worker's strengths and limitations in using assessment skills that were appropriate to the client situation (including their diversity), as well as appropriate for the chosen type of assessment and theoretical framework. [2 to 4 pages]

Append any assessment tools and a list of references that you used at the back of the assessment.

**Evaluation** will be based on the following criteria: clarity and accuracy of the assessment; appropriate use of AODA terminology; use of assessment tool(s) that are appropriate to the client's situation; accurate identification of risks of the client's AOD-related behavior; clear and accurate indication of how theory informs the assessment in this case, including diversity issues; and the level of critique of the assessment skills used by the social worker. The paper should be 10 to 14 pages, including bibliography (with at least four relevant, scholarly references), in APA format.

## Profile A: Torres Family—Assessment Phase With a Couple

For this role-play, Ms. or Mr. Smits, the social worker, will be conducting an assessment with Raphael and Teresa Torres (parents of Maria, Julia, Roberto, and Robertito). Mr. Torres has been diagnosed recently with Wernicke-Korsakoff Syndrome (WKS) by his family physician, with early symptoms of dementia related to alcohol use and deficiency of the B vitamin, thiamine. The physician referred Mr. and Mrs. Torres to a social worker who specializes in AODAs for an assessment. Although the Torres's have turned down referrals for alcohol-related problems in the past, the WKS diagnosis acted as a wake-up call and both are anxious to go for the assessment. Prepare for this role-play by reading the prior Case Profiles and your previous notes on this case, which will provide you with family history information. Separate confidential facts are provided below for the clients and the worker. Although this is a first interview, the clients will be relatively easy to engage in the assessment.

**Raphael and Teresa's confidential facts (clients):** To prepare for this case, check out a GSI on Wernicke-Korsakoff Syndrome,[11] so that you can present with some of the typical symptoms and risk factors (e.g., longtime chronic use; dementia and confusion that occurs even when Raphael has not been drinking; general apathy toward drinking, but easily persuaded to drink). Be prepared to answer questions about various life areas (e.g., history and patterns of use, culture, employment, family, physical health, recreation, peer relationships). Note that neither of you have ever gone for AODA treatment before. Both of you feel that you were good parents, raising a family and providing for them throughout their lives, even though you came to America with no money and next to no understanding of the English language. Both of you have continued to work whenever possible, not being able to support yourselves on your pensions. Teresa mostly does bookkeeping and Raphael gets odd jobs in construction. Within the past 3 months, Teresa noticed that Raphael started to forget things and become confused. You were surprised to hear this was related to alcohol use, since Raphael was actually drinking less in the last couple of years, maybe an average of 25 drinks of whiskey per week as compared to 35 or 40 previously. Raphael thinks that his memory problems are not caused by drinking, but by genetics, since two of his older brothers had similar problems.

In terms of criminal history, Raphael had a couple of arrests for assault related to barroom brawls, but was released each time. Teresa had a conviction 10 years ago for a shoplifting misdemeanor and fulfilled her community service as required. Both of you describe yourselves as devout Catholics. Though you were not involved much in church activities when you were raising a family, you have become regular Sunday churchgoers in the past 3 years. You are sad that you have become estranged from your children. You can't understand why Maria turned everyone against you. She seems angry at the world, but she seems to be doing well for herself. You have some contact with Roberto and Julia, but they can hardly keep their own lives together, particularly Julia. You have offered to help raise Julia's children, but she hardly ever brings them around. You describe your relationship with each other as very good. If the social worker builds trust with you, you will disclose other problems, such as Raphael's gambling and Teresa's anger toward Raphael for pushing the children away and wasting so much money on alcohol. If asked, you will deny any physical, emotional, or sexual abuse within the family. Both of you are highly motivated to do something about Raphael's drinking, but you also indicate you're probably too old to change or to recover from all the damage that's already been done.

You respond positively when the worker demonstrates genuine respect. You also attempt to understand the roles of gambling and alcohol in your life (e.g., an anesthetic for painful memories, an escape from current stresses, a way to have some fun). Allow the worker to draw out these insights rather than stating them up front. In presenting yourself, think about what types of attitudes, mannerisms, body language, and so on, you should present. Raphael does not think of himself as an alcoholic, although he has been drinking all his life and he has not considered it a problem. He is not presently intoxicated, though he feels he could use a drink

---

11. See Chapter 1 for an explanation of Good Sources of Information (GSIs).

now. In fact, he might be going through signs of withdrawal. If asked, he would try hard to associate these withdrawal symptoms with his alcohol use. Both Teresa and Raphael present with some signs of depression and have had some past thoughts about suicide, but are not currently in a state of crisis. If your primary text has a chapter on Latin culture, this would be a good time to read it, as you prepare for this exercise.

The purpose of this role-play is to integrate the theory and skills of assessment. As clients, you can prepare by looking at the effects of alcohol and at what functions alcohol might serve. Also, decide whether or not you are physically dependent, psychologically dependent, have a built-up tolerance, etc. Do not use these terms with the worker, but think about how you would answer questions that might elicit information about tolerance and dependence (e.g., how much do you drink, how frequently, when was the last time that you went without drinking, how long was that for, what happened when you were not drinking). Think about the positive and negative effects of alcohol in your life. When you are in the interview, you may have little insight about these issues, but it would be helpful to think about how Teresa and Rafael might answer these types of questions.

In preparation for this role-play, ask the person or people playing the worker which theoretical framework(s) they will be using for their assessment interviews (e.g., a family systems assessment; a functional/behavioral assessment; a developmental assessment; a pharmacological assessment). This will help you to prepare answers for questions. If the approach is based on family systems, for example, think of how you'd describe relationships with each other and your children, as well as with alcohol and gambling; also, consider each of your roles, from your character's perspectives, which may not be overly insightful.

**Ms. or Mr. Smits's confidential facts (social worker):** Think about what type of assessment would be appropriate for this case situation and determine what type of instruments or assessment formats you will use. Refer back to your assignments from Chapter 1 concerning your learning objectives and your initial analysis of this Case Profile. Remember, this role-play is a first meeting. Even if you decide to do a comprehensive assessment, consider what could reasonably be covered in a first interview of 50 to 60 minutes. Think about the theoretical frameworks behind your questions and ensure that your questions have purpose. If you are coming from a feminist perspective, for instance, then what questions are important? If you are going to use a Psychoanalytic Approach or Family Systems Approach, then what questions might you ask? What terminology would be appropriate to the clients and to the perspective? Write down some examples of the questions you would ask. Decide whether you want to gather information using a form that you will be filling in, or whether you will be using a more flexible approach. You may want to audiotape or videotape the interview to help with the write-up of this assignment.

**Debriefing:** After the role-play, debrief using the following questions for each of the role-play participants:

1. Ms./Mr. Smits: What are the strengths of this couple? What are the key challenges that they face? What do you see as the underlying causes or nature of the problems they face? What additional information would you like to have about this couple to complete your assessment? What goals, if any, do you think they would be willing to work on with you at this point?

2. Teresa and Raphael: What did Mr. Smits do that made you feel more comfortable as clients? What additional questions would you have liked him to have asked? What goals would you be willing to work on with Ms./Mr. Smits at this point in the helping process?

## Profile B: George Favel—Assessment Phase With an Individual and His Friend

In this role-play of an assessment interview, George and a close friend, Frank, meet with Tracey, George's social worker at True Spirits. Tracey has informed George that this assessment is required in order for him to continue to stay at True Spirits. George has expressed willingness to cooperate with Tracey.

**George and Frank's confidential facts (clients):** To prepare for this role-play, ask the worker in advance which theoretical perspectives he or she intends to use. Read your notes from previous assignments related to this profile, as well as any sections of your text pertaining to Native American culture or gay men. Review the short- and long-term effects of inhalants, alcohol, and pot. Think about how to present yourselves to the worker (dress, manner, affect), taking into account history of substance abuse, age, and culture. Prepare yourself for questions that the worker might ask in order to determine extent of use, dependence, etc. If you were psychologically addicted to glue, for example, what types of responses would indicate this?

This is the third time George has seen Tracey, but the first time Frank has come along. Frank (19 years old) insisted on coming to this meeting out of concern that George is at risk of committing suicide. At the assessment meeting, George presents in a lethargic, sad, and apathetic manner. He has no immediate plans to commit suicide, but he has had dreams about suffocating himself while huffing a bag of gasoline-soaked rags. He says the dreams did not scare him, because killing himself would finally put him at peace with the world. Frank has rescued George a couple of times already when George was passed out from drinking and huffing glue. If asked, Frank introduces himself as a buddy of George's who he met while working on the streets about 6 months ago. George picked up Frank, not knowing that Frank wanted money for his services. Frank befriended George, taking a protective older brother type of role, since George was so naive about street life. Frank and George are hesitant to talk about their relationship except to describe themselves as the only family that each other has.

George's main reason for agreeing to get help from True Spirits is to have a warm place to sleep. Previously he and Frank were staying at an abandoned house that was at risk of collapsing. Also, George and Frank were beaten and robbed there. Frank continues to live on the streets because he does not want to give up his freedom to do what he wants, when he wants, where he wants (including drinking or blowing a few spliffs).

George and Frank have an upcoming court hearing, as they were charged with soliciting for the purposes of prostitution. They have a lawyer who has suggested that they plead not guilty, but they really have little idea about what is going to happen at the next hearing.

Frank has a talent for writing short stories. George is unable to read them, but enjoys when Frank reads them to him. George is very embarrassed about not being able to read and tries to cover it up. Even Frank is not sure if George can read at all. Frank came from a middle-class home and background. If asked about his culture, he says he doesn't have one or that he's "just plain old American." Frank says he took to the streets when his parents discovered he was gay, just after his high school graduation. His parents just couldn't handle it and told him to "take a hike." He has not spoken with them since. Although Frank recognizes George has a serious problem with glue and alcohol, Frank says his own drug and alcohol use is under control. Frank sees himself as a bit of a loner and is not looking for any serious relationships, though he does care deeply for George.

**Tracey's confidential facts (social worker):** Think about what type of assessment would be appropriate for this case situation and determine what type of instruments or assessment formats you will use. Would you meet with George and Frank together or separately? Refer back to your assignments from Chapter 1 concerning your learning objectives and your initial analysis of this Case Profile. Although your agency, True Spirits, may require certain things to be covered in this assessment, remember to be responsive to issues raised by the clients during the session. If you decide to do a comprehensive assessment, consider what could reasonably be covered in a first interview of 50 to 60 minutes and what you might save for subsequent interviews. Think about the theoretical frameworks behind your questions and ensure that your questions have purpose. If you are coming from a developmental, pharmacological, or a culturally specific perspective, for instance, then what questions are important and what tools could you use? If you are going to use a functional or behavioral approach, then what questions might you ask? What terminology would be appropriate to the clients and to the perspective? Write down specific examples of questions you would ask. Give the people role-playing Frank and George advanced notice of what perspectives you will be using so that they can prepare accordingly. Decide whether you want to gather information using a form that you will be filling in, or whether you will be using a more flexible approach.

You know of an intensive treatment program called Getting off Glue (GOG) that you think might be appropriate for George, but you are not sure if he would be interested in it. GOG accepts 13- to 18-year-olds who have no outstanding criminal charges, who are chronic glue users (more than 12 months), and who have agreed to abstain from all drugs. Prior to admission, the individual must be drug-free for a period of 7 days. You may want to audiotape or videotape the interview to help with the write-up of this assignment.

**Debriefing:** After the role-play, debrief using the following questions for each of the role-play participants:

1. Tracey: Which assessment questions or topics do you think were most useful? What did you learn about Frank and George that you had not anticipated? What potential biases could inhibit a social worker from conducting an effective assessment with George and Frank? At this point, what goals do you think George or Frank would be motivated to work on? In this situation, do you see substance use as a cause, symptom, or effect of the problems facing George and Frank?
2. George and Frank: What did Tracey do that made you feel more comfortable as clients? What additional questions would you have liked Tracey to have asked? What insights did George and Frank learn about themselves from Tracey's assessment process?

# Profile C: Marge and Randy Lang—Assessment Phase With a Youth[12]

This role-play follows directly after the engagement session that Randy and Marge had with Claire, the counselor at Family Rehab Center. Assume that Claire was able to successfully engage Randy, and that he agreed to come back (without his mother) for an assessment.

**Randy's confidential facts (client):** In this exercise, you will begin by asking questions about what information will be shared with your mother, and whether you are free to talk about whatever you want. You have been experimenting with pills (amphetamines) and coke, but you do not believe this is a problem. It's just a way to feel good. While you are often tired or irritable, you do not associate this with your drug use. Unless Claire offers you confidentiality and builds your trust, you would not directly admit drug use to her. You would admit to some drinking (everyone does it), and that some of your friends smoke up or do coke. You want your mom and everyone to get off your back. You would respond most positively if the worker does not sound like your mom or one of your teachers. You would be most likely to disclose your drug use/personal problems if the worker demonstrates empathy and makes you feel you can trust her or him. You sniffle periodically—if the worker asks about it, you say it is just allergies (you know it is from doing coke). While you would not go to the worker while high, think of how else you would present given your developmental stage and background.

The purpose of this role-play is to integrate the theory and skills of assessment. In a real situation Randy might be very difficult to engage. Do not be too difficult, so that the worker can conduct at least a partial assessment. As a client, you can prepare by looking at the effects of alcohol and stimulants, and also what functions these drugs might serve. Decide whether or not you are physically dependent, psychologically dependent, have a built up tolerance, etc. Do not use these terms with the worker, but think about how you would answer questions that would elicit information about tolerance and dependence (e.g., how much do you drink/use drugs, how frequently, when was the last time that you went without drinking, how long was that for, what happened when you were not drinking). Think about the positive functions of drug use in your life. When you are in the interview, you may have little insight about these issues, but it would be helpful to think about how *Randy* might answer these types of questions. Give Claire some signs of violent ideation. When you have run out of money to buy coke, for instance, you have been tempted to rob a store or mug a person on the street. So far, you have not acted on these impulses, though you have purchased a knife.

To prepare for this role-play, review prior notes on this profile. Also, ask the person playing Claire to let you know in advance which theoretical perspectives she is using, so that you can prepare (e.g., if she is going to use a biopsychosocial-spiritual approach, then you will need to be able to answer questions in each of these realms). Finally, look at any sections of your textbook that pertain to Asian culture.

**Claire's confidential facts (worker):** Think about what type of assessment would be appropriate for this case situation and determine what type of instruments or assessment formats you will use. Although you have agreed to meet with Randy alone, what role, if any, would Randy's parents play in the assessment process? Who else might you contact for information? Refer back to your assignments from Chapter 1 concerning your learning objectives and your

---

12. This case could also be played as a family session with Randy and Marge together.

initial analysis of this Case Profile so that you can build upon what you have learned already. Tailor this assignment to your learning objectives. You may use assessment forms from your agencies, forms from your readings, or forms you have developed yourself. Think about the theoretical frameworks behind your questions and ensure that your questions are purposeful. If you are coming from a 12-Steps perspective, for example, then what questions are important? If you are going to use the Transtheoretical Model approach, then what questions might you ask? What terminology would be appropriate to your chosen perspective(s) and to the client's diversity (including culture and developmental stage)? Write down examples of questions you could ask. Decide whether you want to gather information using a form that you will be filling in or whether you will be using a more flexible approach. You may want to audiotape or videotape the interview to help you with the written assignment.

**Debriefing:** After the role-play, debrief using the following questions for each of the role-play participants:

1. Claire: What unexpected challenges did you face in trying to conduct an effective assessment? How did you deal with these challenges? Which theories or models contributed most to your developing an understanding of the role of AODAs in Randy's life? What differences of opinion emerged between you and Randy concerning the nature of the strengths, problems, or goals for work with this client?
2. Randy: What insights did the worker help you gain through her use of assessment skills? What do you see as the cause of the difficulties in your life? At this point in the helping process, what goals would you agree to work on with Claire?

## Profile D: Dionne Thevenin—Assessment Phase With an Adult

This role-play picks up from the role-play in Chapter 4, when Harold (an HIV/AIDS counselor) had a first interview with Dionne and was able to engage her. For this second interview, Dionne has agreed to participate in an assessment interview so that she and Harold can gain a better understanding of her life situation, including AODA problems. Harold has explained that an assessment can help them decide whether Dionne could use a methadone maintenance program, a detoxification and abstinence program, self-help, or some other type of assistance to deal with her heroin use.

**Dionne's confidential facts (client):** To prepare for this role-play, review the Case Profiles and your notes from previous chapters. Ask the person playing Harold which theoretical perspectives he will be using, so that you can think about your answers in advance. The fact situation should remain essentially the same as in the original case study, but you may reveal the following new facts as the worker builds your trust: (a) you are a daily user of heroin; (b) you don't know exactly how much you shoot, but if you do not use heroin, you start to go into withdrawal (do not use the term withdrawal, but look up the indicators of withdrawal so that you can disclose these to the worker, if asked); and (c) you have some symptoms of bulimia (even though you do not know the name for this eating disorder, you have used diuretics to try to lose weight, and you have periodically binged and purged when you felt your weight was getting out of control). Think about the functions that the various substances serve in your life, so that if the worker takes a functional approach to the assessment, you will have some information (e.g., "I use Valium when I feel . . .").

You have no prior mental health or substance abuse treatment history, except for being prescribed sleeping pills and tranquilizers by your family doctor when you complained about anxiety and sleeping problems. You have never been in trouble with the law (although you fear getting stung by police each time you buy heroin). You feel life has passed you by. Without having children or a husband, there is a real void in your heart. Your sister Ruth tried to involve you as a close auntie for her two daughters, Nicole and Jeanne, but this is not the same as being a parent. Nicole and Jeanne are both married and have their own children, but you have not been involved much in their lives. Given your embarrassment over your drug use and now your HIV status, you have kept your distance from family members.

The purpose of this role-play is to integrate the theory and skills of assessment. As a client, you can prepare by looking at the effects of heroin and tranquilizers and at what functions they might serve. Also, decide whether or not you are psychologically dependent or have a built up tolerance. Do not use these terms with the worker, but think about how you would answer questions that would elicit information about tolerance and dependence (e.g., how much do you use, how frequently, when was the last time that you went without using, how long was that for, what happened when you were not using). Think about the positive and negative effects of these substances in your life. When you are in the interview, you (as Dionne) may have little insight about these issues, but it would be helpful to think about how *Dionne* might answer these types of questions.

Since testing positive for HIV, you have been in a state of denial. You have had some thoughts about suicide and really could not deal with acknowledging that you have AIDS. You have no immediate plans to hurt yourself. You are not sure what to tell future sexual partners about your HIV status. You have heard that women cannot give HIV to men, so you think that you will probably just avoid the subject. Review any sections of your textbook relating to African American culture, as well as any sections on HIV/AIDS.

**Harold's confidential facts (HIV/AIDS worker):** Although your specialization is working with clients who have HIV/AIDS, you know that this client could use a comprehensive assessment of issues related to her heroin abuse, as well as other issues that may be troubling her. You understand from prior meetings that Dionne is in a precontemplation stage as far as doing anything about her HIV/AIDS status, so that work with her may be more effective if you talk about areas in which she is prepared to make changes. Because the purpose of this assignment is to help you link the theory and skills of assessment, review your notes from previous chapters on this case, as well as specific information on heroin dependence, risks, and functions. Since this is just a 50-minute assessment session, you may not be able to conduct a complete assessment. Choose areas that you believe are most important and areas that fit with the learning needs that you identified in Chapter 1. Think about the theoretical frameworks behind your questions and ensure that your questions are purposeful. If you are coming from a sociocultural perspective, for example, then what questions are important? If you are going to use the Ecological Model or Family Systems approach, then would you make use of an ecomap or genogram[13] as part of the assessment? What terminology would be appropriate to your chosen perspective(s) and to the client's diversity (including culture and developmental stage)? You

---

13. An example of a genogram (akin to a family tree) is provided in Chapter 6.

may want to assess for physical dependence, psychological dependence, and tolerance (prepare some questions that would elicit the types of information you need to make these assessments). Decide whether you want to gather information using a form that you will be filling in or whether you will be using a more flexible approach. You may want to audiotape or videotape the interview to help with the written assignment.

**Debriefing:** After the role-play, debrief using the following questions for each of the role-play participants:

1. Harold: Which perspective(s) did your assessment of Dionne focus upon—affective (emotions), behavioral (past actions of the client and plans for the future), cognitive (thoughts and beliefs), and/or spiritual? How did each of these areas contribute to your understanding of Dionne? What did you learn about Dionne that may have surprised you or challenged your preconceptions of her?

2. Dionne: Which aspects of your ethnocultural diversity were addressed by Harold in the assessment? What insights did you gain by participating in Harold's assessment interview? At this point in the helping process, what goals would you be willing to work on? What emotional or social barriers might be preventing you from agreeing to work on other problems?

### SAMPLE EXCERPT OF AN ASSESSMENT: *Eva's Case*

The following excerpt shows a possible format for an assessment (building on the Sample Profile in Chapter 1). Your own assessments will have different formats depending on the nature of the case, the agency context, and your individualized learning goals. The facts and articles cited in the example below are fictional. Yours will be real!

**Referral and presenting problem:** *Eva Prior was referred for a substance abuse assessment by her employer, the Federal Aviation Association, which expressed concerns that Eva tested positive for cocaine use during a random drug-testing procedure. Eva contends that she does not have a substance abuse problem and that what she does in her own time is of no concern to her employer, provided that it does not interfere with her work. She also questions the validity of the random drug testing. The FAA has a zero-tolerance policy and has suspended Eva from work pending completion of the assessment process . . .*

**Assessment process:** *Based on the referral information, it was clear that either Eva was not abusing cocaine or she was in the precontemplation stage regarding cocaine abuse (Childress, 2002). I decided to use the Addiction Severity Index (Scrooner, 1996; appended to this assessment) to gain a comprehensive picture of all dimensions of Eva's life. During the assessment, Eva's answers tended to be short and evasive, particularly after questions pertaining to illicit drug use. I decided to switch to a strengths perspective, using Gobel & Staib's (2003) Assessment of Resilience and Protective Factors (ARPF) instrument to guide the interview. Taking the focus away from substance use and abuse seemed to help me engage Eva and she began to open up about other life areas . . .*

**Risks, Resilience, and Protective Factors:** *Results of the interview using the ARPF instrument suggest that Eva's primary risk factors are work-related stress and alienation from her cultural community of origin. Eva's experience of stress as an air traffic controller is consistent with research, which shows that this is one of the most stressful careers and that there is a disproportionately high frequency of AODA problems among this population (Rigors, 2000). Cocaine use, of which Eva is suspected by her* *employer, is not typically the drug of choice among air traffic controllers; alcohol and sedative hypnotics tend to be in far greater use. Cocaine use is frowned upon by the Mormon community generally (Jaxon, Mills, & Forman, 2003) and, as noted in the interview, by Eva's family in particular. Stigmatization for cocaine use within a person's ethno-religious community has been shown to be a deterrent for use, but also acts as a risk factor for those who become dependent upon cocaine, because users tend to lose their familial and peer support systems (Polcek, 1998). This may help explain why it would be particularly difficult for Eva to admit using cocaine. An additional risk factor experienced by Eva was exposure to trauma during childhood. When Eva was 14, she observed her father being killed during an armed robbery at a bank. Eva rated this event as "extremely disturbing" and discussed at length how she had nightmares for years.*

*Eva's ARPF results show that she has three primary sources of resilience: her sense of humor, her positive self-image, and her strong peer relationships . . .*

**Family history:** *Eva describes her family as including her mother, Gerta (61), and her brother, Murray (39).*[14] *Eva does not remember anyone in her family ever drinking alcohol or using illicit drugs. This family history generally suggests low risk for AODA problems (Trouseau, 2001). She describes her parents and grandparents as "teetotalers." Eva reports that her mother has been using antidepressants for the past 3 years, but that she is unaware of any mental illnesses in the family . . .*

**Client motivation:** *Eva says that she has no problem with cocaine, but she is willing to do what is necessary to keep her job. Eva has agreed to participate in drug testing by Salt Lake Toxicology Services over the next 6 weeks, and has signed a confidentiality release form so that results of these tests can be passed on to the FAA. Eva has also agreed to continue counseling to help her work through unresolved issues relating to her father's death. The first part of counseling will include coping-with-stress skills, so that she will have constructive ways of dealing with the anxiety that is likely to surface when the trauma counseling begins (Mendez, 2003) . . .*

**Critique of assessment process:** *During the first part of the interview, my preconceived biases seemed to hinder the assessment process. I assumed that Eva had a problem and that direct questioning about her substance use according to the Addiction Severity Index would lead to an open and honest assessment. My questioning seemed to put Eva on the defensive. Recognizing this, I began to take the focus away from substance use and explore strengths and stresses in her life (Jenkins & Stole, 1968). During debriefing, Eva said that this made her feel more comfortable, as if I was interested in getting to know all about her as a person and not just putting her through an inquisition about cocaine use . . .*

# Ethical Issues for Discussion

Consider each of the following ethical issues and prepare notes to help you discuss them in class. Highlight ethical rules from the NASW Code of Ethics that apply to each situation. Also, identify what additional information you would need to know to make informed opinions and decisions.

---

14. For assignment purposes, a genogram could be attached.

## Torres Family

Mr. Torres has a problem with gambling. Since the state legalizes gambling and receives a share of the profits from gambling, should the state have any special responsibilities to people like Mr. Torres? Should the state ban gambling because of the risks this type of behavior entails? What is the likelihood that Mr. Torres could successfully sue the state for causing his gambling dependency? Would the state have to pay for treatment, for mental and social suffering, or for other damages?

## George Favel

Assume that George comes into your office looking panicked, perspiring, and sounding unintelligible. He smells of gasoline. Upon screening George for suicidal ideation, you find that he is at high risk of committing suicide, having a plan and telling you that he is strongly considering "ending it all." He says his friend Frank dragged him in and is waiting outside. George says he just wants to be left alone. What are your ethical and clinical responsibilities for dealing with this situation?

## Randy and Marge

Assume that you have assessed Randy and believe that the best course of action would be for Randy to participate in the intensive residential program at Family Rehab Center. The fee for this program is $12,000. Marge tells you that she cannot afford it, and that she does not have medical insurance to cover these costs. You know there are other publicly funded services available for people who are "indigent," but you see this family as middle class and are not sure if they would qualify. You also know there are waiting lists for these services and believe that the quality of care is not as good. What are your ethical responsibilities, and what do you say to Randy and Marge?

## Dionne Thevenin

Dionne comes into the office and is bleeding. She tells you that she slashed her wrists. Her eyes look glazed over and she is slurring her speech. When you suggest that she goes to the hospital for medical attention, she tells you that she will not go there because the staff at the hospital looks down on IV drug users, particularly ones who are African American and HIV-positive. She may also have hepatitis. What legal, ethical, and clinical issues does this case raise? What are your responsibilities to the client, to the agency, to society, and to yourself?

# Journaling Exercise

1. Refer back to the Educational Needs Assessment in Chapter 1 (page 13). Describe your present strengths and needs regarding social work assessment with clients affected by substance abuse. Update your professional development plan to include how you will improve upon areas of assessment where you have identified particular needs. Since assessments should be based on data from various sources, compare your self-report (your answers to the above) with the assessment of a classmate or your professor on your strengths and learning needs (in other words, ask them for feedback and check whether their impressions confirm or diverge from your self-report assessment).

2. Reflect upon the role-plays you conducted in this chapter. What types of questions or areas of people's lives did you have the greatest challenge asking about? Which of your own values, beliefs, attitudes, or fears might have made these questions or topics more difficult for you to explore?

# InfoTrac College Edition

## Key words

◇ Risk

◇ Resilience

◇ Suicide Screening

◇ Assessment (alcohol, drug, or biopsychosocial)

CHAPTER

# 6

~~~

# Helping Families Change

This chapter builds on the theoretical frameworks and models identified in Chapter 3, but focuses on helping family units rather than helping one individual at a time. The first subsection, Families With Precontemplaters or Contemplaters, deals with strategies for families in which at least one member is in the precontemplation or contemplation stage. The second subsection, Family Systems and AODAs, focuses on different aspects of Family Systems Theory and intervention: family communication; roles; boundaries, subsystems, and triangular relationships; rules and expectations; family life cycle transitions and adjustments; and Behavior Theory from a family perspective. The last three subsections—Role-Play Exercises and Assignments, Review Questions, and Journaling Exercise—provide role-play exercises for putting family perspectives into practice and questions to help you reflect on and integrate the material covered in this chapter.

Throughout this chapter, the term *family* is used broadly to include not only people related by blood and marriage, but also by other relationships of intimacy; for example, cohabiting couples, extended kinship networks, gay or lesbian couples, and informally adopted families (e.g., youth who live on the street may develop bonds with others on the street who act as surrogate parents or siblings). Using a client-centered approach, the best way to define a client's family is to ask the client who he or she considers to be family.

## Families With Precontemplaters or Contemplaters

### Self-Help for Family Members

Often, the entry point into services for a family affected by AODAs is not through the individual who is abusing substances or has an addiction, but through family members who are concerned about that individual's welfare. If the individual is not ready for help, then a useful strategy may be to refer family members to a particular self-help group (indicated in the chart below in **bold**). For each of the following scenarios, identify the problems with the *Deficient worker response* and write an effective response to family members that: (1) tunes into the feelings and motivations of the client; (2) suggests trying a particular self-help group; and (3) explains the benefits of the group, linking back to the client's motivations. Check out the Web sites for the self-help groups so that you can convey accurate information about each group.

| Client's remarks | Deficient worker response | Effective worker response |
|---|---|---|
| Youth to his school social worker: My mom is back to boozing again. I tried hiding her liquor but she got really mad. I tried making a deal with her, that if she'd cut down on drinking, I'd get a job, quit school, anything . . . | You're not trying hard enough. If only you'd be a better son, your mom could stop drinking. You need to go to **Alateen.** They have medical experts who can tell you how to cure your mom's alcoholism.<br><br>*The problems with this response are that the social worker is blaming the youth and giving advice. The worker is not showing any empathy and is not empowering the client to make his own decisions. The information about Alateen is also inaccurate.* | *Sounds as if you'd do anything to help your mother, but it also sounds as if you know that you can't fix everything by yourself. You might consider checking out Alateen. That's a group of youths like yourself, where everyone comes together to talk about their difficulties, share hope, and learn how to cope with having a parent with alcoholism. They believe you can love someone with alcoholism, but you need to take care of yourself, and only your mom can take responsibility for changing her life. Does this sound like a group that you'd like to learn more about?* |
| Adult daughter to family therapist: Ever since I can remember, I've had to take care of my family, parents included. They know that alcohol pretty much destroyed our childhood. I thought life would be okay once I moved out, but my folks still seem to have control over me. | Feeling sorry for yourself isn't going to help anyone. What you need is a good therapy group. Why don't you try **Adult Children of Alcoholics?** They provide psychoanalysis for people just like you. All your repressed memories will be gone in no time. | |

*(continued)*

| Client's remarks | Deficient worker response | Effective worker response |
|---|---|---|
| Parents to addictions counselor: Our kid is out of control . . . stays up late, smokes pot, hangs out with a bunch of weirdos, and uses language that we wouldn't dare repeat in mixed company. You're the specialist. You fix him. | You poor, poor people. Kids just don't learn any respect these days. You just leave little Johnny here and we'll take care of him for you. You can come back in 4 weeks when he's all fixed. After he's fixed, you can all go to **Nar-Anon,** where they'll teach you how to behave like a normal family. | |
| Client to social worker: My girlfriend does coke now and again, but I think I'm partly to blame. She's just so beautiful. I really don't deserve her. I've told her that I'd leave her if she didn't stop using drugs, but I could never follow through. If you love someone, you have to stay with them, right? | You're right. You don't deserve her. If you want a quick ticket out of her life, you'll get your duff down to the next **Codependents Anonymous** meeting. They're a group of angry spouses of drug addicts who will make sure that you don't keep getting sucked into your girlfriend's disgusting lifestyle. Here's the address. Go! | |

Consider your Case Profile. Which self-help groups, if any, would be appropriate for family members of the individual who is abusing substances or has an addiction? Provide your rationale about whether or not a self-help group would be effective and appropriate for these family members.

How would you react if the family members responded to your suggestion about self-help groups by saying, "But I'm not the one with the problem"?

## Educating Family Members From a Transtheoretical Perspective

Chapter 4 demonstrated how the Transtheoretical Model could be used in the process of helping an individual who was at various stages of change. One approach to helping family members of an individual who is in the precontemplation or contemplation stages is to educate the family members about the Transtheoretical Model, but in lay terms. This will help them understand what the individual is experiencing and what family members can do to support movement of the individual into the next stage of change. It may also free up family members from feeling overly responsible for the individual's AODA predicament.

Consider the following scenario: Mrs. Pringle is concerned that her daughter, Doreen (26 years old), has a sex addiction. Mrs. Pringle goes to a social worker, Stella, pleading for help. Mrs. Pringle explains that Doreen is constantly traveling to different cities to go to sex parties, she frequently leaves work early to hook up with someone for sex, and she has sex in public places. Doreen says she is just having fun and enjoying her sexual liberation. She denies she has a problem even though she has been putting herself in very risky situations, including risk of contracting sexually transmitted diseases, risk of criminal prosecution for having sex in public, and risk of social stigmatization from her friends and family of origin. Mrs. Pringle has tried to help Doreen by covering up for her, by giving her condoms, and by telling her that if she ever gets into trouble, she can always count on her mother to bail her out. Mrs. Pringle asks Stella, "Why can't she see she has a problem? Why can't I make her stop?" In order to help Stella prepare her answer for Mrs. Pringle, write out a sample response to each of the following topics:

1. In plain language, educate Mrs. Pringle about the precontemplation stage and how it might help explain and normalize Doreen's situation.

2. Identify some possible reasons that explain why Doreen is not currently ready to change.

3. Describe at least two possible scenarios that might lead Doreen either to acknowledge she has a problem or, more importantly, to seek out help.

4. Describe some influencing strategies that family members often try to use to help individuals in the precontemplation stage, but are unlikely to work.

5. Describe what Mrs. Pringle might consider doing for herself and for Doreen while Doreen is in the precontemplation stage?

6. Explain how it might be advisable for Mrs. Pringle to withdraw from enabling roles, disengage from Doreen, and work on her own growth and healthy development.

7. Acknowledge what a professional counselor can and cannot do for Doreen while she is in the precontemplation stage.

# Family Intervention

In Chapter 4, we explored different ways to engage clients by building trust and tapping into their motivation. Another way to motivate clients to participate in services for AODA problems is to conduct a "Family Intervention." Family members can be helpful because they love and care for the person. In addition, they have ongoing contact with the person, a vested interest in the person's well-being, and leverage to apply pressure by providing certain types of reinforcements or punishments to encourage certain types of behaviors. To prepare for the exercises below, read one or two GSIs on Family Interventions,[1] sometimes called the "Johnson Intervention" or "Minnesota Model," named for Vernon Johnson who founded the Johnson Institute in Minnesota.

## Planning the Intervention

The following case scenario will be used to help you practice planning a Family Intervention.[2]

---

### BEN'S CASE

Ben (30) is an advertising executive who has been married to Jean (28) for 8 years. They have three children: Cassie (8), Terry (5), and Brian (4). Ben's father was an alcoholic who died 5 years ago from cirrhosis of the liver. He was only 44. Ben's mother, Gramma Helen, was a social drinker for as long as Ben can remember. She now suffers from early stages of Alzheimer's disease. Ben started drinking alcohol in high school, occasionally getting drunk on weekends. Ben and Jean met in high school and decided to marry soon after they found out Jean was pregnant.

In the last 5 years, Ben has been charged with three DWIs (Driving While Impaired). His lawyer is currently fighting the suspension of his driver's license. Ben needs his license so that he can drive to work and meet with clients. In addition

---

1. See Chapter 1 for an explanation of Good Sources of Information (GSIs).
2. If you prefer to use your Case Profile from Chapter 1, you can identify an individual in the scenario who could benefit from a Family Intervention (e.g., Julia or Roberto Torres, George Favel, Randy Lang, or Dionne Thevenin). Assume the individual is still in the precontemplation stage and proceed to the planning questions.

to his dependence on alcohol, Ben is a frequent cocaine user. He is a hard worker, but is having more and more difficulty coping with the pressures at work. He is having problems sleeping and managed to convince his physician to prescribe some tranquilizers. His supervisor, Paul, regards him as one of his most capable and talented employees. He is also aware that Ben's performance and attendance at work can be erratic. Paul often covers for Ben by making excuses to his senior management. Ben recently used cocaine just before an important presentation to a group of clients, believing that he could do this on his own. High on the effects of cocaine, Ben raced through the presentation, inventing facts and making grossly exaggerated claims about the potential impact of the advertising campaign. Ben's continued employment is hanging in the balance.

Ben has become preoccupied with his work and his drug use. Consequently, he is having less and less contact with his family. Jean worries that he is going to injure himself or someone else as a result of his drug use. She never knows what he is going to do next. Working late at home, Ben often has several stiff drinks before falling asleep, and frequently cannot make it to bed. Jean is concerned that the children will see him in that condition. She finds that she is trying to protect them from the knowledge of Ben's unreliable and erratic behavior. Ben has frequently been unable to drive Cassie to her weekend gymnastics class because he has been too drunk or high. Cassie loves her dad so much that she never gets mad at him. In fact, she is very quick to defend him if anyone says anything bad. Recently, other kids at school have teased Brian because they say his dad always has a red nose and puffy eyes, just like a cartoon character named Smudgie. Brian tends to respond by fighting and has been labeled as overly aggressive by his teacher. Terry tends to be very shy and withdrawn. He has an imaginary friend named Garth. Terry describes Garth as "a big mean guy who only likes me and will protect me from bad guys."

Ben has one younger sister, Ruth. They are constantly arguing, primarily about how to care for their ailing mother. Ben says that he wants to share the responsibility for his mother, but frequently he does not follow through when he is using drugs, leaving Ruth to carry on by herself.

One day, Ben gets drunk and forgets to pick up his mother from Ruth's house. Ruth says, "Enough, you need to go for help." She knows he will not go on his own, so she calls Jean and insists that she do something. Jean, somewhat reluctant, calls the employee assistance program at Ben's company and makes an appointment for counseling. Ben refuses to go, so Jean goes alone. During this meeting, the social worker, Ms. Sparrow, helps Jean assess the situation and suggests that they try a Family Intervention. Jean agrees and they begin to plan for a preparatory session.

THE PERSON WHO WILL BE PLAYING BEN SHOULD NOT READ ANY OF THE FOLLOWING MATERIAL AND SHOULD NOT PARTICIPATE IN THE PREPARATION MEETING. The others should answer the following questions to help prepare for this session.

1.   Which family members and other significant people in Ben's life should be invited to the preparatory session for the Family Intervention? What is your reasoning for whom to include and whom not to include? It would be useful to draw a genogram

(family tree) and an ecomap to be able to visualize the people and support systems involved in Ben's life.

2. For each of the participants who you think should be invited to the preparatory meeting, how can Ms. Sparrow engage and mobilize them to be involved in the Family Intervention (identify possible motivations for each of these people)?

3. Prepare a list of questions that the social worker can use in the preparatory meeting to help each participant let Ben know: (a) how much each participant loves, likes, or cares for him; (b) specific behavioral examples or incidents that convey the concerns each participant has about Ben's drug and alcohol use; and (c) what action each participant would be willing to take if Ben refuses treatment. (Assume that they are going to tell Ben that he needs to enter the 60-day Narwood Residential Treatment Center, that they have already received clearance from his health insurance company to cover the costs of this program, and that they have permission for Ben to take sick leave from his job).

Once you have answered these questions, assign roles for each person in the role-play, including Ms. Sparrow and each of the participants that you identified in question 2. Conduct the role-play of the preparatory meeting using what you have learned from this manual and your other readings on the Johnson Intervention. During the role-play, Ms. Sparrow will need to engage the participants, explain the nature of the Johnson Intervention, gain their support for it, assess how they can best motivate Ben using the questions you developed in question 2, and help them prepare for the actual intervention (which you can role-play at a later date).

To debrief after the role-play:

♦ Ask each participant: On a scale of 1 to 10, how prepared do you feel for the actual Family Intervention? What did Ms. Sparrow do that was helpful? What additional concerns could Ms. Sparrow have covered to help you feel one or two points higher on the preparedness scale?

♦ Ask Ms. Sparrow: What did you see as the strengths of your preparation meeting? What challenges do you foresee as you prepare for the actual intervention with Ben? What strategies can you use to deal with these challenges?

## Implementing the Intervention

In this role-play, Ms. Sparrow will facilitate the actual intervention with Ben and the participants who have been prepared in the prior role-play. Ben will prepare by reading the basic facts, but will not know about the specific plans for the intervention. He will begin the role-play denying any problems with AODAs and very clearly in the precontemplation stage. If possible, audiotape or videotape this role-play so that you can review it afterward.

To debrief after the role-play:

♦ Ask Ben the following: Describe your feelings at the beginning of the meeting. How did these feelings change throughout the meeting? What, if anything, made you more likely to accept help for your AODA problems? What, if anything, made you less likely to accept help?

♦ Ask the other participants: How was the actual intervention similar to or different than what you expected from the plans in the earlier role-play? What aspects of the role-plays do you think were either realistic or unrealistic, particularly from your own character's perspective?

♦ Ask Ms. Sparrow: What skills did you use that contributed to the effectiveness of this role-play? How did you feel (personally) about the pressure that was brought to bear on Ben?

### Effectiveness and Ethics of the Family Intervention

This type of Family Intervention is somewhat controversial in the AODA field, as well as within social work. Some people question its effectiveness, believing, for instance, that if the person is not ready to be helped, you cannot force that person into treatment. Further, because this intervention puts the family into disequilibrium, the intervention may actually be causing harm. Others believe external pressure is both necessary and effective to bringing reluctant people with AODAs into treatment. They go further to suggest that an intervention is actually very humane because it "raises the bottom" (referring back to the Jellinek Curve in Chapter 1) by creating a crisis for the person that motivates him or her into treatment without having to hit a natural bottom, which could be much more severe (e.g., experiencing a severe accident or a serious AODA-related disease). Still others suggest that even if this type of confrontational intervention is effective in getting people into treatment, it is unethical because it goes against social work values such as empowerment, self-determination, and respect for the individual (since the individual is blamed for the problem and is deemed responsible for the solution, and the social worker is facilitating a process that is highly coercive).

Conduct a literature review on the ethics and effectiveness of this type of intervention. Write a six-page analysis of the issues, including your assessment of the research and conclusions about whether or when this type of intervention should be used by social workers. Are there any ways to modify the traditional form of this intervention to ensure that it is both ethically sound and effective? Consider how proponents of 12-Step Programs, the Transtheoretical Model, the Harm Reduction Model, and the NASW Code of Ethics would view the ethics and effectiveness of Family Interventions.

### Diversity Perspectives

The Family Intervention with Ben was based on assumptions of having a mainstream, middle-class client family. The scenario and intervention would have been very different if Ben came from another type of background. Consider, for example, if Ben came from a socioeconomic status in which he had a low income, no job security, and no health insurance. The types of leverage that could be used to motivate Ben into treatment would be very different. The risk of losing a job might not be as powerful, since he would have less to lose financially and might even benefit from qualifying for social assistance if he loses his job. In addition, the family members would be faced with the challenge of how to fund Ben's treatment. Narwood might not be an option.

Another aspect of culture to consider is the value base of the family. Mainstream American families, for instance, value individualism—children are raised to be independent, the rights of the individual are more important than the rights of the family or the community, and the use of alcohol or drugs can be seen as an individual choice and responsibility rather than a collective choice or responsibility. In many other cultures, people place a higher value on collectivism, where the rights of the community come first, where individuals are sometimes expected to forgo personal happiness for the good of the community, and where AODA problems are looked at as a community responsibility. Social workers must be careful to understand the relative differences among people from diverse cultures so that they do not impose ethnocentric beliefs, values, or biases (Green, 1999).

Select a diversity group that you are interested in studying further, for example, Native Americans, Asian Americans, Pacific Island Americans, Hispanic Americans, Jewish Americans, African Americans, transgender people, the aged, or people who are deaf. Consult one or two GSIs on your chosen group. Review the materials above and your notes on Ben's case. Write a four-page analysis of the case, deconstructing it from the diversity perspective you have chosen. Your analysis should include answers to the following questions:

1. How might the family dynamics be different if Ben were from your chosen diversity background? (consider communication patterns, values, expectations, and attitudes toward mental health professionals)
2. What aspects of the standard Family Intervention might conflict with the norms, values, attitudes, and needs of the client if Ben were from your chosen diversity group?
3. What recommendations would you give to Ms. Sparrow to ensure that her Family Intervention was appropriate, given the diversity attributes of the client? Or, if a Family Intervention would not be appropriate, even if it were altered, what other model would you suggest as a more appropriate way to engage Ben?

# Family Systems and AODAs

Whereas the previous section explored approaches for helping families that included precontemplators and contemplators, this section provides strategies and skills for working with family members at any stage of change. In particular, we will explore the following Family Systems concepts and how they apply to working with families affected by AODAs: family communication; roles; boundaries, subsystems, and triangular relationships; family rules and expectations; family life cycle transitions and adjustments; and Behavior Theory from a family perspective. Bringing family members or significant others into the helping process can promote positive change for the individuals within the family and the family as a whole (Juhnke, 2002).

## Family Communication

Family communication refers to the patterns of sending and receiving messages among members of the family, including verbal and nonverbal communication. Patterns of communication can be broken down into five categories: **Consonance** (sender's intent closely reflects the impact on the receiver, and the impact is positive or at least neutral); **Condemnation** (criticizing, blaming, judging, or nagging); **Submission** (succumbing to another's will—feeling downtrodden, unworthy); **Intellectualization** (strictly logical, rational, or intellectualized—detached from emotion); **Indifference** (apathy, not caring, avoiding) (Kirst-Ashman & Hull, 2002). Family Systems Theory views Consonance as a functional form of communication, whereas the other forms are considered dysfunctional. Families affected by AODAs often display these latter forms of communication.

For each of the following examples, identify the type of communication pattern that is illustrated. If the pattern is not Consonant, then identify an effective response that a social worker could use in order to help the family members improve their communication. The first example provides a sample answer in italics.

1. Dawn (17) recently ran away from home. To make money, she began running drugs for a guy named Manny. One day, she lost the package she was to deliver, about 8 kilograms of pot. She began to panic. Not knowing what else to do, she called her parents. Dawn's mother responded, "We told you not to get involved with that type of person. When you get home, things are going to be different. No more doing whatever the heck pleases you." Dawn hung up the phone. Her parents decided to see a social worker for help with how to respond if their daughter called back.
   a. Type of communication: *Condemnation*
   b. Effective social worker response:
   *I can hear that you're very upset with Dawn, but also that you care for her very much. Which message do you think Dawn will hear if you say, "We told you not to get involved with that type of person," your anger or how much you love her?[pause for response] How could you express your concern for Dawn so that she hears that your message is coming from a parent who really loves her?*

2. A social worker is working with Salib and his elderly father, Bashar. Salib tells his father, "These sleeping pills are not good for you. I don't care if the doctor pre-scribed them for you. I am going to flush them down the toilet." Bashar nods in agreement, saying nothing.
   a. Type of communication:
   b. Effective social worker response:

3. During a couple's counseling session, the social worker asks Cathy to tell her part-ner Ronda about the impact of Ronda's cocaine use on their relationship. Without any sign of feeling, Cathy turns to Ronda and says, "I've read that people who use cocaine increase their risk of death by heart attack or stroke by at least three times.

Studies of lab rats show that cocaine produces a craving so strong that they will choose to eat cocaine and starve to death because they don't eat their food." Ronda appears unmoved.

a. Type of communication:

b. Effective social worker response:

4. Bob is the 7-year-old son of Mr. Frish. They are being interviewed by a child welfare worker. The worker became involved with the family when someone reported that Mr. Frish leaves Bob unattended all night in a car at the parking lot of a casino while Mr. Frish gambles. During the interview, Mr. Frish asks Bob if he was ever scared or angry with him when he was alone in the car. Bob responds "whatever," while looking blankly into space. Bob responds "whatever" to almost everything Mr. Frish says to him.

a. Type of communication:

b. Effective social worker response:

5. Harold and Maude are seeing a social worker for narrative family counseling. When the worker asks Harold to describe how he would label the problem in the family, Harold says, "Jack Daniels. It's as if Maude is having an affair with Jack Daniels. I don't blame Maude. Jack's a very enticing guy. He seems to make her happy, at least some of the time. I suppose I'd just like a chance to show Maude how much I love

her and how I can provide her with so much more than Jack ever could." A tear rolls down Maude's cheek and she crosses the room to give Harold a big hug.

    a. Type of communication:

    b. Effective social work response:

6.    Werner and his brother Herman are talking to a discharge planner at the hospital. Werner was in a work-related accident when his leg got caught in a piece of machinery and was severed. As they are planning for Werner's return home, Herman turns to Werner and says, "If you weren't such a dumb fool, you wouldn't be such a mess. You know you shouldn't operate machinery when you are taking tranquilizers." Werner responds, "If you weren't always giving me such stress, I wouldn't need the tranquilizers."

    a. Type of communication:

    b. Effective social worker response:

## Roles

Roles refer to the functions or positions that each person plays within the family system. Because a system is a set of interrelated components, the roles and expectations of each person are affected by the roles and expectations of every other person within the family. Accordingly, if one person becomes chemically dependent and cannot carry out his or her usual roles, other members of the system are likely to fill in for those roles. Family Systems Theory and research describe role assignments that tend to be functional as well as those that tend to be problematic. Popular literature, including self-help books on Adult Children of Alcoholics, suggests that the roles people play in their childhood carry through with them into adulthood. This literature suggests roles that may have been adaptive as a child may be dysfunctional for the same person as an adult. Although research does not fully support the claims of this literature, the roles identified in this literature are often used in AODA groups and clinical counseling.

The following list contains the labels that Wegscheider (1981) attributed to the typical members of a chemically dependent family. Match each of these labels with the letter for the best description of each role.

| __ Chemically Dependent Person | A. Typically the youngest child, this person tends to be withdrawn, introspective, or living in a fantasy world. |
|---|---|
| __ Chief Enabler (or Codependent) | B. Typically a middle child, this person diverts attention from the problems in the family by playing the family clown or comic, acting cute or funny, and avoiding seriousness (sometimes viewed as the "immature child"). |
| __ Hero | C. The person who is addicted to alcohol or other drugs; life revolves around this substance to the detriment of the rest of the family. |
| __ Scapegoat | D. Typically the eldest child, this person tends to act like a super-parent, taking care of the younger children and the household, being a perfectionist at school and other activities, and trying to help the family by being the strong one that everyone can lean on (sometimes called the "overachiever"). |
| __ Mascot | E. Typically the second-born child, this person gets into trouble, acts out, and is the focus of blame and negative attention in the family (sometimes called the "delinquent child"). |
| __ Lost Child | F. This person supports, covers up for, and does whatever is necessary to protect the Chemically Dependent Person, working extremely hard to make sure the family is doing well or at least appearing to do well (typically the spouse of the Chemically Dependent Person). |

## Reframing Role Labels

One of the critiques of the types of labels that Wegscheider originally used for the members of a family affected by AODAs is that they are negative and demeaning. The terms *enabler* and *codependent*, for example, have been criticized by feminists and others for blaming women (typically) for "enabling" their partners to be addicted, and pathologizing these women when they are basically just taking care of their partners as best they can. Some theorists suggest reframing *enabler* to *family manager*, which has more positive connotations (this type of reframing could fit with "Cognitive Restructuring" or with a "Narrative Family Therapy" approach to intervention). For each of Wegscheider's other roles, how could your reframe them with more positive language?

Chemically Dependent Person _____

Hero _____

Scapegoat _____

Mascot _____

Lost Child _____

### Diversity Critique of Wegscheider's Labels

Another criticism of Wegscheider's labels is that they only fit a White, western, and individualistic culture. Applying them to people from other cultures could be demeaning and inappropriate. Consider the culture of the family in your primary Case Profile. To what extent are Wegscheider's roles either appropriate or inappropriate for this family? Give examples from the literature that you have read on people from this culture. In particular, consider individualism versus collectivism, role expectations, communication styles, and definitions of family (e.g., nuclear family, extended family, fictive family).

### Applying Role Theory

The following exercise is designed to provide you with practice applying role theory, using Wegscheider's roles or the roles defined by another theorist of your choosing. You can do this exercise based on your Case Profile from Chapter 1, Ben's case (above), or a client family that you have worked with in the past.

1. List each of the people in the family on a separate piece of paper.
2. After each person's name, write a brief description (not a label) explaining the functions that the person plays within the family.
3. Which, if any, of the roles from Wegscheider or your chosen role theory apply to each of the people? Do not try to fit people into roles that they do not fit (one size does not fit all when it comes to family roles). If there is a better term to describe a person's role than the ones from Wegscheider, use that term.
4. Consider the combination of roles within the family. From a Family Systems perspective, why do you think this combination of roles has developed within this particular family (i.e., how do the various roles complement each other)?
5. If the person with the AODA problem were able to overcome this problem, how would this affect the roles that various people play within the family? What roles would some people have to give up? What new roles would they need to assume?
6. What is the relationship between the childhood experiences of adult members of the family and their current strengths and challenges, including their drugs of choice?

### Sculpting Role-Play

Sculpting is an experiential exercise that can be used with families affected by AODAs to help family members gain insight into the roles they play, and how they might want to try playing different roles in the future. Rather than assume that family members play specific roles, as suggested by Wegscheider or others, family members describe their own roles. The person(s) playing the sculptor asks family members to assume specific positions in relation to one another to represent each of the roles that they play within the family. There are many variations of sculpting, so it would be useful to read a couple of GSIs on sculpting before doing the following exercise.

1. Decide whether you want to role-play based on either your primary Case Profile or Ben's case. Assign roles for the social worker and each of the family members that you intend to involve in the sculpture (if you are using Dione's or George's case, you may need to add roles so that there are at least four family members or close friends involved in the sculpting).

2. During the role-play, the social worker will coach one of the family members (not the person with the primary AODA dependence) to be the sculptor: (a) Ask the sculptor to identify a typical situation where the family might be doing something together (e.g., having dinner, going on a vacation); (b) ask the sculptor to recreate this situation by placing each person in a position that represents that person's usual role within the family; (c) have the sculptor describe the scenario, including the meaning of the positions and how they reflect each person's role within the family; (d) debrief with the family, asking each person how it felt to be in the particular role, and whether he or she would like to play a different role in the family; (e) ask each person to give examples of behaviors that were functional when they were growing up but are not serving them well now (that is, how do they need to adapt and change as the family goes through different stages of the life cycle).

If the role-play includes only two people, instead of sculpting you could have the client draw a representation of the family (and prepare by reading about Art Therapy), or have the client represent the family using dolls (and prepare by reading about Play Therapy).


## Boundaries, Subsystems, and Triangular Relationships

Boundaries, subsystems, and triangular relationships are three concepts that come from Family Systems Theory. To test your knowledge of these topics and how they apply to families affected by AODAs, answer the following questions (yes, this is an open-book test, should you desire to check your textbooks):

1. *Boundaries* in Family Systems refer to:

2. In a family affected by AODAs, there might be a very *rigid* boundary around the entire family system because:

3. The boundaries between a person with a severe AODA problem and his or her spouse are often *diffuse* because:

4. A *subsystem* is defined as:

5. In a well-functioning family, the *usual subsystems* include:

6. If a person is involved in a *triangular relationship*, this means that:

7. Families affected by AODAs often *experience triangular relationships* because:

## Application Using a Genogram

Draw a genogram (see Figure 6.1)[3] representing the family in your primary Case Profile (or if you prefer, representing Ben's family from this chapter). Include three generations of family members, if possible, and remember that you can include informally adopted family members

---

3. For more directions on how to develop a genogram see http://genogram.freeservers.com/HTML/geno1.html, or McGoldrick, M., Gerson, R., & Shellenberger, S. (1999). *Genograms: Assessment and intervention* (2nd ed.). New York: Norton (http://www.genogram.org).

**FIGURE 6.1**
**Genogram**

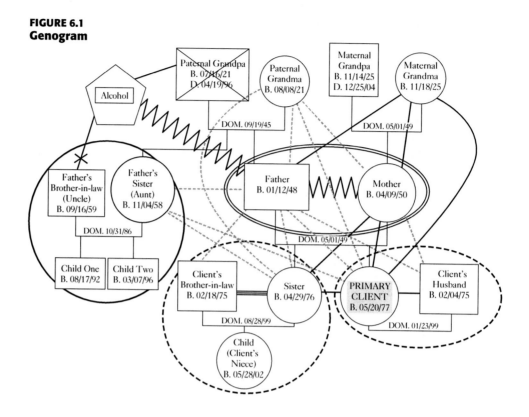

(e.g., members of a street family or intimate friends who are not related by blood or marriage). Use the following key to illustrate the features of the family system:

♦ Squares denote male and circles denote female family members.

♦ Circles around groups of family members denote members of the household.

♦ Double lines denote a rigid boundary, a single line denotes a flexible boundary, and a dashed line denotes diffuse boundaries.

♦ Lines connecting two family members denote key relationships between family members—a single solid line denotes a healthy relationship, a dotted line denotes a distant or weak relationship, a jagged line denotes a conflictual relationship, and a triple line denotes an enmeshed relationship. Where there are three lines connecting three people, this denotes a triangular relationship between them.

♦ Use a pentagon to denote AODs—link the AODs to the person who is abusing or is dependent upon them with a solid line if there is a close relationship, with a jagged line if the relationship is rocky, and with an X through the line if the person has become abstinent from the AODs.

♦ Given the diversity that exists among families from different cultures and even within cultures, feel free to add symbols that represent types of relationships that do not necessarily fit with the basic genogram model (e.g., if a client defines family to include close friends, how would you depict these; if a client views the spirits of deceased family ancestors as part of the current family structure, how could you incorporate them into your genogram?).

Once you have completed the genogram, write a paragraph describing the family dynamics, including the types of boundaries, subsystems, and relationships that exist within this family. Also, provide two or three hypotheses, based on the information you have gathered, about the reasons that certain intergenerational patterns have developed or might affect the next generation. If you prefer, you could conduct a role-play with the family members and ask them to describe the family and what insights they may have gained from the genogram (remember to use plain language with the family rather than jargon such as "triangular relationships" and "diffuse boundaries").

## Family Rules and Expectations

### Starting With Ourselves

Each family constructs its own rules and expectations for the behavior of people within the family. To some extent, these rules are culturally derived. The following exercise is intended to help you gain awareness of some of the rules and expectations within your own family and cultural group, particularly as they relate to AODA issues. Awareness of these issues is important so that you do not unwittingly impose these rules or expectations on clients. First, write down your own answers to each of the following questions. Second, interview a member of your family who is from a different generation than you, asking the same questions and taking notes of the answers. Third, compare and contrast your answers with those of the family member. Finally, write down possible reasons to explain differences between the rules and expectations that you and the other member of your family expressed.

1. At what age do you think that a young person in your family should be able to decide whether or not to try smoking cigarettes?
2. What are the rules in your family concerning when and how it is either appropriate or inappropriate for people in the family to drink beer?
3. If someone in the family were addicted to an illicit drug, would the family rule be "Don't tell anyone, this is a family secret," or would there be another rule?
4. If a person in the family is feeling sad or depressed, would it be appropriate for that person to talk about these emotions, or would the family expect that person to deal with the problems without talking about these emotions?

### Identifying Rules and Expectations Within a Family System

Review the following scenario and identify at least eight rules and expectations that this family subscribes to. Describe how cultural factors might have affected the development of these rules and expectations. Write a hypothesis about how these rules and expectations might contribute to Swan's substance use and obsession with her weight. Finally, consider how the use of different models—moral, disease, ecological, and feminist models—would affect the way that you understand this situation.

---

**VIGNETTE—SWAN**

Swan is a 14-year-old student at the Sea-Cow School for the Performing Arts.[4] Her goal in life is to be a world-acclaimed ballet dancer. She has been dancing ever since

---

4. Names and situations used in this vignette are fictional.

she was 4 years old, when her parents (Rudolph and Karen) enrolled Swan in a Ballet for Tots program. Swan's parents thought she was "oh so cute and talented." As a young girl, Swan had the perfect body for a ballet dancer, slim and flexible. Rudolph is a Jewish man who emigrated from Russia 17 years ago; Karen was born in Florida, of English ancestry.

Within the last year, Swan has become concerned that she is gaining weight. She has heard from friends that smoking cigarettes could help her stay thin. Not knowing exactly why cigarettes might help, she was hesitant at first. She also knew that as much as her parents encouraged her to be "the best darned ballet dancer she could be," they would disapprove of her smoking or using any sort of drugs to enhance her performance.

Eventually, Swan became desperate to control her weight and began smoking. At first she borrowed cigarettes from friends. As she started to smoke more and more, she knew that she needed a stable source of cigarettes. She looked far too young to be able to buy cigarettes from a regular store. She eventually found Snake, an underground supplier in her school. Friends told her that buying from Snake was cheap and safe. Of course, this meant that she had to roll her own cigarettes.

One day, when Swan's father was cleaning her room, he found rolling papers in her drawers. Rudolph and Karen suspected the worst—that is, Swan must be into smoking pot. They confronted Swan, who completely denied ever using pot. Rudolph and Karen were still concerned, so they set up an appointment for the family to meet with the social worker at Swan's school.

Swan knew she was in trouble. She was now smoking almost a pack of cigarettes a day and felt edgy and irritable if she went without smoking for more than a few hours. She thought about what other drugs she might try that would be less obvious—for example, nicotine gum, since it did not have the smell of smoke. She also thought she might be able to try diet pills, barbiturates, or something like that. Most of all, she worried about how she was going to get through the meeting with her parents and the social worker. She hated to let her parents down. Swan even thought it might be better to just run away.

## Reframing Rules and Expectations

Reframing is an approach that is used by cognitive and narrative therapists to help families adapt or reconstruct rules and expectations so that the family functions more effectively. Claudia Black (1981) suggests that children in chemically dependent families learn three rules: don't trust, don't talk, and don't feel. These rules are conveyed in the client statements in the following chart. For each client statement, I provide a deficient worker response. Your task is to provide an effective response, using the technique of reframing as demonstrated in the first example.

| Client's remarks | Deficient worker response | Effective worker response |
|---|---|---|
| Growing up, the house was always chaos. One day, my father was kind and loving. The next day he was drunk and abusive. I learned early on that I couldn't trust other people close to me, even if they seemed to be kind and caring. | *All families are dysfunctional. You just need to get over it, honey. You are doomed to be alone for the rest of your life unless you can start trusting people.* | *It sounds as if "not trusting" was the best way for you to protect yourself when you were growing up. Now that you're an adult and you have more control over your life, I wonder if you might consider a new rule, "Trust in yourself." Perhaps as you gain more confidence in yourself, you will start to feel as if you can take the chance of opening yourself up to the possibility of developing intimate relationships.* |
| Whenever Mom was stressed, she'd pop another tranq. I guess I'm the same way. I'd rather feel nothing than feel anxious or angry or anything bad. | *Feelings, nothing more than feelings . . . It's just like the song. And you don't need drugs just to forget your feelings. Perhaps you could learn how to stuff your feelings deep down and not have to resort to drugs.* | |
| People say that drugs hurt you. In my family, people hurt you. Drugs were the only things you could rely on. Even if it was just for a brief moment of escape, it was worth it. | *You can trust me. I'm here for you. Therapy is like an escape. And it's much better to be addicted to therapy than it is to being addicted to any drug.* | |
| My parents had a tough life, but they never complained. As children, we weren't allowed to complain either. We were just supposed to be grateful for all God's blessings. I still feel ashamed to be coming to you with all these personal issues. | *Shame is a good thing. It means that you have an inner sense of being diminished or insufficient as a person. Paradoxically, it makes you feel strong and forces you to take responsibility for yourself. I hate when people are always whining and not taking responsibility.* | |

# Family Life Cycle Transitions and Adjustments

Literature on the family life cycle and transitions suggests that families experience different stresses as the family moves through various life stages. It also suggests that families have different risk factors and resiliencies toward AODAs depending on the family's particular stage and life course. Refer back to your Case Profile and identify which of the following stages and transitions best represent the current situation for the clients: single adult, couple, family with infant(s), family with young children, family with teenagers, family with children leaving home, family with elder individual(s), family going through separation or divorce, or family experiencing reconstitution (e.g., remarriage). Given the life stages and transitions you have identified, analyze the strengths, resiliencies and stresses, and risk factors as they relate to the AODA concerns in the family [2 to 3 pages]. Make sure that your analysis takes diversity issues into account, including culture, socioeconomic status, and sexual orientation.

*Sample: Referring back to Eva's case in Chapter 1, Eva is a 42-year-old woman who lives on her own. According to traditional family life cycle literature, she would ordinarily be expected to have an intimate partner and children at this stage of her life (Fenwick, 2003). Given societal expectations, she may feel pressured or insecure because she does not have a partner or children. The case facts do not specifically identify whether she has internalized these expectations around having a "family of her own," but this would certainly be a risk factor to consider. In terms of strengths relating to life course issues, at 42, Eva has a well-paying job with a valued status in society. Although she uses cocaine, she has been able to keep her cocaine use from interfering with her job responsibilities. One of Eva's risk factors is being cut off from her family of origin and religious-cultural community, for example, the Mormon community in her hometown (Jospe, 2002). Although alienation from one's community is a key risk factor, she reports that she did not experience this type of isolation during her childhood. Alienation as an adult, while problematic, is not as severe as alienation during childhood (Kinney and Post, 2004). Still, developing a better support system, or even one solid friendship with a mentor, would be useful in order for Eva to be able to deal with current life stresses and her cocaine abuse (Rollinson, 1999). The fact that Eva started using cocaine during adolescence increases her risks of problems in social functioning because early onset cocaine use has been shown to retard development of social skills such as communication and problem solving.*

## Myth or Fact

Although there are common factors that are associated with being at a particular life cycle stage, we must be careful not to stereotype or accept myths as fact. Review each of the following statements, refer to your textbook or other relevant literature, and identify whether each statement is myth (i.e., either factually untrue or unproven) or fact (i.e., supported by research evidence). Provide explanations for each of your answers.

1.  Couples without children have a higher rate of AODA problems than couples with children, because couples without children tend to have a weaker social support system.
    Myth _____ Fact_____ Explanation:

2.  The greatest risk of Fetal Alcohol Syndrome (FAS) or birth defects to a fetus from alcohol use by the mother occurs during the first trimester, often before the mother even knows she is pregnant.
    Myth _____ Fact_____ Explanation:

3.  Women who are chemically dependent tend to find it surprisingly easy to stop using drugs and alcohol when they learn they are pregnant, given that the maternal instinct to care for a child is much stronger than any chemical dependency.
    Myth _____ Fact_____ Explanation:

4.  Children who are permitted by their parents to use illicit drugs as long as the children have adult supervision tend to have fewer problems with drugs than children of parents who strictly prohibit illicit drug use.
    Myth _____ Fact_____ Explanation:

5.  Children model their parents' drinking and drug use *behavior*, regardless of what parents *say* about whether or not it is okay to drink or use drugs.
    Myth _____ Fact_____ Explanation:

6.  Parents with AODA problems who abuse or neglect their children must not really love their children.
    Myth _____ Fact_____ Explanation:

7.  Most teenagers who have problems with AODAs will simply grow out of these problems, regardless of whether they have professional intervention.
    Myth _____ Fact_____ Explanation:

8.  Gay men and lesbians are at greatest risk of having AODA problems if they "come out" during adolescence.
    Myth _____ Fact_____ Explanation:

9.  Men with AODA problems who never marry or enter into a long-term intimate relationship are more likely to refuse treatment because one of the primary motivators for treatment is having a spouse or partner who threatens to leave unless the person gets treatment.
    Myth _____ Fact_____ Explanation:

10. Retirement is a key risk factor for acute AODA-related problems.
    Myth _____ Fact_____ Explanation:

11. Once a person who is physically dependent on alcohol reaches 65 years of age, chances of full recovery are so low that it is not worthwhile to work toward abstinence, though harm reduction should be used.
    Myth _____ Fact_____ Explanation:

12. As elder people addicted to alcohol grow older, their tolerance to alcohol continues to increase, so that the risks related to ongoing alcohol use actually decrease.
    Myth _____ Fact_____ Explanation:

13. After menopause, women tend to have a biochemical Valium deficiency that can be redressed through Alcohol Therapy.
   Myth _____ Fact_____ Explanation:

14. Elder clients who are trying to remain abstinent from alcohol must be careful about using vitamin supplements for the elderly because many of them contain high levels of alcohol.
   Myth _____ Fact_____ Explanation:

15. Elder clients are prone to drug misuse because of problems such as memory loss, visual impairment, and loss of dexterity related to the aging process.
   Myth _____ Fact_____ Explanation:

16. Adults with AODA problems often steal money from their elder parents to pay for their drugs or alcohol.

    Myth _____ Fact_____ Explanation:

## Behavior Theory From a Family Perspective

The above exercises focus on Family Systems concepts such as communication, roles, expectations, boundaries, subsystems, and family life cycle. We now turn to behavior within a family system. Although Behavior Theory originated for work with individuals, it has been adapted for use with families. In terms of associational (or classical) learning, for example, family members can assist the person with the substance abuse or addictive behavior problem by helping that person avoid triggers to the AODA behavior or by helping that person become aware of the triggers and choose alternate behaviors. In terms of operant conditioning, family members can assist by restructuring the responses or consequences to the person, rewarding positive behaviors, and avoiding any positive reinforcement for behaviors that the family wants to discontinue.

Punishing negative behavior is also a behavioral intervention, but punishment tends to encourage avoidance of punishment rather than fostering positive behavior. Further, using punishment goes against the social work values of demonstrating respect for all people and focusing upon strengths. In terms of modeling or social learning, family members can assist by practicing positive behaviors that the individual can emulate. Each of these types of behavior-oriented interventions can help families break the cycle of AODA problems within the family, changing the manner in which the family system interacts and the way each person supports one another. In order to gain practice identifying specific behavioral strategies that can be used within a family helping process, read each of the following scenarios, identify the type of behavioral learning that may be relevant, and offer an intervention strategy that fits with the identified type of behavioral learning. A sample answer is provided for the first scenario.

1. The Grouss family consists of Mr. Grouss, Mrs. Grouss, and their 15-year-old daughter, Zeena. During family counseling, the social worker observes that every time the family broaches topics that are difficult for Zeena, she asks for a smoking break. Mrs. and Mr. Grouss respond by telling her something like, "Go ahead, maybe it will help you cool down dear."

   **Sample Answer:** *One example of behavioral learning within this scenario is operant conditioning. Mr. and Mrs. Grouss offer Zeena positive reinforcement for her smoking behavior.*

*This also reinforces the idea that Zeena can avoid talking about difficult issues by calling for a smoking break. One way the social worker could help the family break this cycle would be to help them identify this pattern. Once they are aware of the pattern, perhaps they could agree that communication would be more effective in the family if they had other strategies to help Zeena deal with stressful conversations. For instance, Mr. and Mrs. Grouss could give Zeena positive feedback each time she responded to difficult content rather than tried to avoid it.*

2. Orlando is the 5-year-old son of Juan Berrios. During Play Therapy, the social worker observes Orlando building tall figures with blocks and then slamming them against the wall so that they break into small pieces. The social worker recalls that when Juan is intoxicated he often has violent episodes where he throws furniture against the wall.

3. Hal Crisp is a 19-year-old young man who likes to dress up in women's clothes and go clubbing. His parents disapprove of this, not only because they are embarrassed that Hal is a cross-dresser, but because they think that the ecstasy and other drugs at the clubs are dangerous. Hal says that he goes clubbing because that's the only place he feels accepted. He says he certainly does not feel accepted by his family.

4. Dierdre Clement is the 72-year-old mother of Melissa. Dierdre was physically and psychologically dependent on barbiturates for 18 years, but is now in her third month of abstinence. During a family session on relapse prevention, the social worker asks Dierdre to identify the most difficult times of the day for her to avoid taking pills. Dierdre says the toughest time is during evenings when Melissa calls to complain about how Dierdre messed her up as a child. Melissa responds by saying her mother is always blaming her for her own problems. An argument of blaming and counter-blaming ensues.

5. Jad and Remmi are brothers who came to the United States as refugees from Burundi, having been victims of torture. When Jad started to have trouble sleeping because of nightmares and flashbacks of the torture, Remmi provided Jad with sleeping pills that Remmi had been prescribed. Both brothers agreed that they wanted to try to forget their experience in Burundi altogether, so they refused to talk about it during counseling.

6. Lydia has two children, Usha (24) and Makua (26). Lydia thinks her daughters are perfect angels. Usha could certainly make her mother proud, but Makua has bulimia, which would be very distressing to Lydia. Usha helps Makua keep her bulimia a secret, making up excuses for Makua to cover up for her; for example, if

Makua has to leave the room during a meal to regurgitate, Usha will say that Makua is vomiting because she must have the flu.

# Role-Play Exercises and Assignments

This exercise is composed of two parts based on your primary Case Profile from Chapter 1: first, a case conference between three professionals, and then, a session with family members incorporating the suggestions made at the case conference. For the purposes of the role-plays in this chapter, read the following additional facts for your case:

## Profile A: The Torres Family

For this chapter, assume that Julia has just completed a 28-day residential treatment program for her alcoholism. Maria was taking care of her children during the program and has agreed to participate in Julia's post-treatment recovery counseling. Julia also wants to bring her parents in for family counseling, but Maria says she does not think that would be appropriate given their own history of alcohol dependence. Julia believes that she cannot change her role in the family unless the others in the family also change their roles and relationships with her. Maria suggests that they just cut their parents out of their lives, pretending they have died and perhaps even have a mourning ritual for their loss. Julia wants to be put on Naltrexone to help her with alcohol cravings.

**Maria's and the social worker's confidential facts (not to be read by Julia or the other professionals):** Unbeknownst to Julia, Maria was sexually abused by her father when she was a teenager. Maria still feels afraid and vulnerable when her father is present or even mentioned. Maria has also been hiding another secret from the family, that she is a regular user of cocaine. She uses cocaine to boost her confidence. Outwardly, Maria always conveys that she is confident and in control. Inside, Maria feels uncertain, confused, and very much out of control. Therapy is scary for Maria because she fears losing what control she currently has of her emotions. She is motivated to participate in therapy to help her little sister, particularly since her sister has done so well by completing residential treatment successfully.

**Julia's and social worker's confidential facts (not to be read by Maria or the other professionals):** Julia is confused about why Maria does not want her parents to participate in therapy. Julia thought Maria would be pleased that the whole family was getting help. Julia has started to participate in AA meetings and strongly believes in abstinence and the Disease Model of alcoholism. She also sees alcoholism as a family disease and believes that her recovery requires family support and participation. Julia is strongly motivated by her desire to break the intergenerational cycle of addiction in the family so that her children will live healthier lives.

## Profile B: George and Frank

For the purposes of the role-plays in this chapter, assume that George has "come out" to the social worker and has said that he would like his partner, Frank, to participate in joint counseling. George and Frank have agreed to a goal of moderate use of alcohol and cannabis, and to abstain from use of glue and all other psychoactive substances. George is still somewhat depressive, but not suicidal. Frank thinks George needs to be put on antidepressants, but the psychiatrist is reluctant to prescribe them while George is still using alcohol. Frank and George have found temporary housing and jobs, so they do not think they need to go into intensive residential treatment. The psychologist has run a battery of tests on George and found that he has moderate levels of cognitive impairment (thinking skills and short-term memory), likely as a result of glue use.

**George's and the social worker's confidential facts:** George has been able to cut down on his substance use, but he still resorts to huffing glue without letting Frank know about it. George feels good that he has been able to come out to his social worker, though he still harbors fears about how others will react to finding out he is gay. George would like to go back to school and get his high school diploma, but he fears he might not be able to succeed. Frank tells him that school is a waste of time, and that trying to go back to school will just make him feel stupid.

**Frank's and the social worker's confidential facts:** Frank does not believe that George should go back to school, partly because Frank never completed school himself. Frank was diagnosed with attention deficit disorder and always had problems with school and jobs. Living on the streets meant that he was accountable to nobody but himself. Now that he's in a relationship with George, Frank does not quite know how to handle the responsibilities that come with this type of relationship. Frank sees himself as caretaker for George, having rescued him from the depths of a suicide attempt and living all alone in the world.

## Profile C: Randy, Marge, and Steve

Assume that Marge and Steve decided that they want to try to reconcile their marriage. Before moving in together, Marge has insisted that they go for family counseling. Steve agreed because he thinks that Randy is still out of control and has a problem with discipline. Randy is not sure what to make of family counseling, but he says he is "willing to go along for the ride." Both parents know that Randy has been experimenting with amphetamines, alcohol, and cocaine, and both strongly disapprove of any experimentation with drugs and alcohol. Randy has learned that it is best not to be around his parents after he has been using, so he makes excuses to stay over at a friend's house or go out of town with friends if he wants to use drugs. Marge suspects that this is what he is doing but does not confront him. The psychologist has assessed Randy as having a learning disability that affects his ability to read and interpret written information. The psychologist does not think these learning problems were caused by Randy's substance abuse. The psychiatrist found no prior substance abuse history in this family, which she found somewhat surprising given her belief that substance abuse is caused primarily by genetic predisposition and social learning within the family.

**Randy's and the social worker's confidential facts:** Randy is not really sure whether his parents should be trying to get together or not, but he does not want to feel responsible if they decide not to get back together. During an interview with the social worker, Randy admitted that he is in trouble with Delta, one of his drug dealers. He owes Delta about $700. Randy thinks he can earn the money back by running drugs for her. Randy does not want to see the psychiatrist again because he thinks psychiatrists are only for crazy people.

**Steve's, Marge's, and the social worker's confidential facts:** Steve and Marge think that getting back together will be the best thing for Randy. Marge feels particularly responsible for Randy's problems at school and with drugs. Steve thinks that if he is around the house, he can impose proper discipline so that Randy will straighten out his life. Both Steve and Marge are embarrassed to be seeing all these different mental health professionals, but they love Randy and will do anything for his benefit.

## Profile D: Dionne and Cousin Vedna

After three months of individual counseling and appointments with her doctor, psychologist, psychiatrist, and social worker, Dionne built up the courage to tell her cousin Vedna that she is HIV-positive and that she probably contracted HIV from IV-heroin use. Dionne felt she could trust Vedna because Vedna was like the matriarch for the whole family. Vedna was the one in the family that everyone could go to for a shoulder to cry on, a warm house to find refuge, or a spiritual encounter when life seemed confusing or without meaning. Vedna responded to Dionne's news with care and compassion, suggesting that they work together with her social worker, as well as with the minister at their church. Dionne says she is not ready to tell anyone at the church. Dionne prefers working with real doctors, such as the psychiatrist, who are professionals that know about HIV, which Dionne sees as primarily a medical issue.

**Dionne's and the social worker's confidential facts:** Dionne appreciates Vedna's support and good intentions, but still feels somewhat judged by Vedna. Dionne does not see how she can live without heroin, but would be willing to try some type of harm reduction approach. Dionne is thinking about moving to San Francisco, far away from relatives and in a much more progressive community, where she thinks she will feel more accepted. She has also heard that there are special programs for Black women with HIV in San Francisco. Dionne has not broached the issue of moving with Vedna, fearing Vedna will just try to talk her out of it.

**Vedna's and the social worker's confidential facts:** Vedna believes that Dionne is a good person but needs to rid her body of "those evil opiates." Vedna says she is willing to support Dionne in whatever way is best, but she believes that Dionne needs to return to the teachings of the church if she wants God's blessings and true healing. Vedna is wary of help from doctors and physicians, feeling that the scientific approach often conflicts with her religious values and beliefs.

## Role-Play of an Interprofessional Case Conference

For the case conference, identify three people in your group to play the professionals—a social worker, a psychologist, and a psychiatrist (you can use your own names, use names from prior role-plays, or make up new names). In preparation for the case conference, each of you will independently prepare your understanding of the client family's situation and your suggestions for intervention based on a different theoretical framework (e.g., designate the social worker to use a Family Systems approach, the psychologist to use a Rational-Emotive-Behavior Therapy approach, and the psychiatrist to use a Pharmacotherapy approach). Refer back to your notes and readings from prior chapters, but be sure to apply this information in a manner that is appropriate to a family context. During the role-play, each of you will present your views and offer suggestions for intervention. The professionals will then try to reach a consensus on how to proceed with the clients. Incorporate principles of interprofessional cooperation, such as respect for one another, value for each other's expertise, and shared goals for the client (see, for example, Geva, Barsky, & Westernoff, 2000). This role-play should last 20 to 30 minutes.

**Debriefing:** To debrief for this role-play, ask each professional:

♦ What were your primary goals and assumptions going into the role-play?
♦ How did these goals and assumptions change as a result of your interaction with the other professionals?
♦ What could you have done differently to improve the nature of the dialogue among all three professionals?

## Assignment 6.1: Write-Up of Case Conference

For this assignment, prepare an analysis of the case conference including the following:

1. A summary of each professional's perspective on the client situation, given his or her professional background, values, and theoretical framework. [2 pages each for a total of 6 pages]
2. A summary of agreed upon goals for the client, if any (e.g., harm reduction; abstinence; controlled use; improved social functioning within the home, school, or work setting; specific changes in behavior; specific changes in attitudes or cognitions; specific changes in emotional response; or functional adaptation to a specific stress). Describe how these goals fit with your theoretical perspective(s), professional values, and assessment of the client's current stage of motivation. [1 to 2 pages]
3. A plan for working with the client based on agreement of the professionals: Which professional will be responsible for what, how will they work together, and specifically, how will the social worker approach the next session with the client? Assume the social worker will take a primary role and will conduct the next session, which will be role-played as described below. Remember that you can use more than one

theoretical approach, as long as the approaches are integrated appropriately and there are no inherent conflicts between the approaches.[5] What are the likely barriers to carrying out your proposed helping process in an ideal manner (e.g., issues personal to the clients; worker challenges, agency challenges, community issues; social policy concerns)? How could you deal with these barriers? [2 to 4 pages]

4.  A critique of the process of the case conference, including conscious use of skills and strategies to communicate effectively and build a consensus on how to proceed with this client. [2 to 3 pages]

**Evaluation** will be based on the following criteria: clarity of the summaries of each professional's original perspective, as well as the collective assessment and suggestions for the client; accuracy of the appraisal of the role-play in conjunction with the roles, skills, strategies, and behaviors to avoid in order to have a constructive interprofessional dialogue; and originality and level of critical analysis about the appropriateness of the agreed upon goals and helping strategies, given the family's presenting problems, motivations, and diversity factors. The paper should be 11 to 16 pages, including a reference list, in APA format.

## Role-Play of a Session With the Family

For this role-play, the social worker will meet with the family members to facilitate a session based on the conclusions from the case conference. The social worker will try to employ the theory or combination of theories from the case conference, using appropriate skills and strategies and remaining responsive to the needs raised by the clients during this session. The clients will be relatively easy to engage, though they will present the social worker with their concerns and issues as described in the original Case Profile and the additional facts raised in this chapter. Regardless of the theoretical framework(s) chosen by the social worker, the social worker will also employ the skills of Motivational Interviewing and avoid counterproductive interviewer behaviors, as listed in the charts below. Provide one or two observers with photocopies of the following two charts, so the observers can provide the social worker with specific feedback on the use of these skills and behaviors during the role-play. This role-play should last 30 to 50 minutes, with extra time taken for breaks, feedback, and suggestions.

---

**Constructive Skills Used in Motivational Interviewing[6]**

Key:
1—Demonstrated this skill at an exceptional level of mastery
2—Demonstrated this skill at an acceptable level of competence
3—Demonstrated this skill at a beginning level of competence
4—Did not demonstrate use of this skill even though it would have been appropriate to use
NA—Use of skill was not applicable in this particular role-play

*(continued)*

---

5. For example, it would be inappropriate for one professional to use a moderate use approach and another to use an abstinence approach with the same individual. On the other hand, it might be appropriate to use Antabuse for pharmacotherapy in combination with Bowenian Family Therapy to help a family affected by alcoholism.
6. These two charts are derived from research published in Barsky & Coleman (2001b). Tear out and make photocopies of the charts so that you can use them to provide feedback to others and to monitor your own progress in other role-plays.

a. Amplifies discrepancies and ambiguities with exploration questions (increases internal dissonance)     1 - 2 - 3 - 4 - NA

b. Uses selective active listening to bring negatives of current behavior forward     1 - 2 - 3 - 4 - NA

c. Conveys faith that client will make right choice for self     1 - 2 - 3 - 4 - NA

d. Does not give advice prematurely (establishes credibility first)     1 - 2 - 3 - 4 - NA

e. Provides clear and compassionate advice to client, without prescribing (gives option to follow or not):     1 - 2 - 3 - 4 - NA
(i) clearly identifies the problem or risk area,
(ii) explains why change is important, and (iii) advocates specific change     1 - 2 - 3 - 4 - NA

f. Helps client identify consequences of his/her behavior     1 - 2 - 3 - 4 - NA

g. Helps client with his/her goals     1 - 2 - 3 - 4 - NA

h. Honest with client about restrictions (e.g., agency policy, client responsibilities)     1 - 2 - 3 - 4 - NA

i. Expresses empathy     1 - 2 - 3 - 4 - NA

j. Supports client self-efficacy     1 - 2 - 3 - 4 - NA

k. Helps client identify barriers to change     1 - 2 - 3 - 4 - NA

l. Helps client overcome barriers (information, resources, support)     1 - 2 - 3 - 4 - NA

m. Offers active help or concrete support for client     1 - 2 - 3 - 4 - NA

---

### Counterproductive Worker Behaviors for Motivational Interviewing

Key:
i—Avoids use of this counterproductive worker behavior throughout interview
ii—Occasionally uses this counterproductive worker behavior
iii—Frequently uses this counterproductive worker behavior
NA—Not applicable: unable to assess during this interview

a. Argues or debates with client     i - ii - iii - NA

b. Attacks client self-image (inappropriate confrontation)     i - ii - iii - NA

c. Uses closed-ended questions during exploration phase of interviewing     i - ii - iii - NA

d. Conveys that the worker is the expert in the helping relationship     i - ii - iii - NA

e. Confronts denial or client resistance with direction or advice     i - ii - iii - NA

f. Labels client     i - ii - iii - NA

g. Focuses on worker's concerns (not client's)     i - ii - iii - NA

h. Blames client for problems or lack of change     i - ii - iii - NA

i. Dictates what client needs to do     i - ii - iii - NA

j. Engages in power struggle with client     i - ii - iii - NA

k. Pushes for change too quickly (ahead of client's pace)     i - ii - iii - NA

l. Defines success in terms of whether the counselor's expected outcomes were met     i - ii - iii - NA

## Debriefing

- ◆ Social worker: How was having a family session different from having an individual session in one of the earlier chapters? What were some examples of how you were able to put the suggestions from the case conference into practice with this family in an effective manner? What were some of the challenges or changes you had to make?
- ◆ Family members: What were some of the differences between the needs or expectations of different individuals within the family? What did the social worker do that was particularly helpful to the family member you portrayed? What would be a challenge for the social worker in the follow-up session?
- ◆ Observers: What were the strengths of the social worker's use of skills with the family, particularly from the perspective of Motivational Interviewing? What types of family boundaries, communication, and roles issues did you see raised within the role-play?

## Assignment 6.2—Write-Up of Family Session

For this assignment, include the following components:

1. Case progress notes—Write notes on this session as if you were writing case progress notes for the agency's files, including: date and type of contact, people present, presenting problem, problem for work, purposes of session, brief assessment, summary of key information from session, plans for next session and rationale for any intervention decisions, description of follow-up (who is responsible for doing what before the next session), description of any ethical issues that arose and how these were handled. [1 to 2 pages]

2. Process recording—Use the same framework as described for Assignment 3.1: Summarize the role-play and provide a more detailed analysis of some important segments of the role-play (for example, 3 to 5 minutes of the role-play analyzed in detail, with the rest analyzed more generally). The analysis should include a critique of the worker's use of skills and the client's responses, and an appraisal of the extent to which the worker followed the Motivational Interviewing approach, including worker's use of constructive skills and counterproductive behaviors as per the chart above. [4 to 6 pages]

3. Critique—Evaluate the overall session with the family, including the extent to which the social worker was able to put theory into practice, the skills that the social worker used well or could have used differently to enhance the helping process, and how well the theoretical frameworks chosen from the case conference fit with the client family's actual presentation of AODA issues. [2 to 3 pages]

4. Ethical analysis—Examine the ethical issue below that relates to your role-play. Describe how you would respond to the issue and provide your rationale, relating your reasoning to specific social work values and ethical rules. [2 to 3 pages]

   a. The Torres family: Assume that Julia brought her two children to counseling and the social worker assessed them as having Fetal Alcohol Effects. Assume further that Julia and Maria refuse to accept this assessment. The social worker suggests that the children could benefit from a special preschool program for children with

FAE, but Julia refuses, saying the children are normal. What clinical, ethical, and legal issues does this situation raise, and how should the social worker respond?

b. George and Frank: Assume that the social worker believes that George's being gay is the cause of many of his AODA problems. What clinical and ethical issues does this raise, and how should the social worker deal with these issues?

c. Marge, Steve, and Randy: Assume that Randy only agrees to participate in counseling because his parents are "on his back." The social worker finds that Randy has no internal motivation to change his substance-using behaviors or to seek help from the social worker. The social worker wonders whether she should terminate work with Randy, given her belief in self-determination and her skepticism about whether working with Randy under these circumstances would be effective.

d. Dionne and Vedna: Assume Dionne and Vedna are matched with a male social worker. During the first session, they say they are uncomfortable with a male, given sensitive issues about sexuality and their religious beliefs about sex as a private matter. How should the worker deal with this situation? Would it be appropriate for the worker to say he'll focus on the issues related to Dionne's heroin use and refer her to a female worker to help her deal with issues related to sexuality?

5. Clinical evaluation: Describe how you will measure the effectiveness of your helping process with the client. Identify specific measures of success, as well as how you will go about measuring success (e.g., qualitative feedback from the client, scaling questions, use of specific quantitative measures, direct observations, feedback from collateral contacts, or single system design). Ensure that your measures for success relate back to the family members' goals and motivation toward change.

**Evaluation** will be based on: comprehensiveness and clarity of the progress notes; level of accurate integration among theory, skills, self-awareness, values, and practice in the process recording and the critique; appropriateness of the intervention plan given the presenting problem and family dynamics; appropriateness and feasibility of the evaluation plan.

# Review Questions

The following questions will help you review Family Systems concepts and how they apply when helping families affected by AODAs.

1. Because children learn about drugs from their family and social context, an appropriate way for an AODA social worker to *begin* work with a child is to:
   a. Educate the child about the dangerous effects of drugs.
   b. Ask the child to voice her understanding of drug abuse.
   c. Advise the child that the American culture disapproves of drug use.
   d. Keep parents and friends out of the treatment process in order to isolate the child from their negative views.
   e. Inform the child that alcoholism is considered to be a disease by the DSM.

2. A 34-year-old client says he has difficulty resisting drugs when offered by family members. An advisable strategy to help the client deal with this issue is to:
   a. Provide skills training, such as role-playing how to speak with his family members. He might not be able to change his family members' drug involvement, but he can change his reactions to their offers.
   b. Tell him to "Just say no." The family will stop making offers.
   c. Advise him to use the drugs so that he will fit in.
   d. Teach him that family members are not important.
   e. Give him a pill that will cause a negative reaction if he is exposed to drugs.

3. Children growing up in families affected by AODAs might have difficulty asking social workers or outsiders for help because:
   a. Children are rarely aware that there are alcohol problems in their family.
   b. Alcoholic families often have rigid boundaries where their parents teach them not to share family secrets or problems with anyone outside of the family.
   c. Children believe that it is fun to grow up in an alcoholic family because they can take on adult roles, such as a hero, and not be accountable to anyone.
   d. Children do not suffer from the problems of their parents until they grow up and are in therapy.
   e. All of the above.

4. Leda grew up in a family where her mother was a compulsive shopper, spending money the family did not have and purchasing many things the family did not need. Leda has modeled her mother's behavior, meaning that Leda:
   a. Has the same "shopping gene" as her mother.
   b. Has developed a reaction formation in which Leda is very careful with her money, to the point of being stingy.
   c. Has learned to pattern her shopping behavior after her mother's.
   d. Likes to build replicas of shopping centers and famous malls.
   e. Is at a high risk for abusing glue.

5. Doris views herself as having a codependent personality, because she derives her self-worth from the feedback she receives from her boyfriend. Using this type of label might be detrimental to Doris because it:
   a. Reinforces a negative self-image rather than helps Doris see her caring for her boyfriend as a positive characteristic.
   b. Says that she is better than her boyfriend.
   c. Suggests that Doris has no role in her boyfriend's life.
   d. Confuses the word dependence with codependence, and Doris is clearly dependent.
   e. Describes Doris as having a personality, whereas codependence or enabling means that she has no personality of her own.

6. Hugo has learned "blaming" as a pattern of communication in his family. Because of this, he may have difficulty:
   a. Telling others that they are at fault.
   b. Seeing problems in people other than himself, given his strong internal locus of control.
   c. Talking about family secrets, such as AODA problems.
   d. Accepting responsibility for his own actions, including using substances that may be detrimental to his well-being.
   e. Using humor to deflect criticism of his family.

7. Using "sculpting" as part of Family Therapy may help family members:
   a. Practice behavioral techniques, such as providing negative reinforcement for unwanted AODA behaviors.
   b. Create a new narrative for the role of violence in the family.
   c. Learn how to use modeling clay as a substitute for compulsive drug use.
   d. Fix a child who is acting out, through a process of direct confrontation and primal screaming.
   e. Gain insight into the roles they play within the family and how each person's role affects and is affected by the roles of others.

8. The Johnson Intervention makes use of the concept of "hitting bottom" by:
   a. Having family members paddle the AOD user's bottom as a fun way to motivate the user into treatment.
   b. Having family members give the AOD user drink after drink until the person finally hits the floor and pleads for help.
   c. Raising the AOD user's bottom (or crisis point) by telling the user that they will withhold their support or impose other consequences if the person refuses to accept the help they are suggesting.
   d. Hiding the AOD user's stash of alcohol or other drugs in the bottom of a septic tank.
   e. Moving the AOD user to the bottom rung of the family ladder, metaphorically speaking.

9. When deciding which family members to involve in family counseling, an AODA social worker should assess:
   a. Prior history of family violence, whether or not it is AODA related.
   b. The stages of change of each family member, since some family members may not be interested in participating in counseling, but others could still benefit.
   c. Who are the important people in the client's life, whether or not they are actually related by blood or marriage.
   d. Who is covered by insurance, who can pay, and who is eligible for services without charge.
   e. All of the above.

10. An example of a Family Systems measure of success is:
    a. Abstinence by the person with the primary AODA problem.
    b. Roles have been restructured so that parents are managing parental responsibilities and children are managing children's responsibilities (as defined by the family).
    c. Cognitive dissonance has been made consonant for the person who felt embarrassed about his AODA problems.
    d. The family counselor feels happy about how things are going.
    e. The agency boasts a 36 percent reduction in AOD use among its clients.

## Journaling Exercise

1. Describe a case situation you have handled involving a family with AODA issues. What theories, skills, and strategies did you use? Given what you know now about helping families, critique your approach with this family.

2.	What was the significance of this chapter's major assignments (Assignment 6.1 and Assignment 6.2) to your own educational objectives for this course?

3.	What roles, patterns of communication, and examples of AOD use did you learn as a child in your family? To what extent have these roles, patterns of communication, and examples of AOD use remained the same for you as an adult?

# InfoTrac College Edition

## Key words

- ◇ Adult Children of Alcoholics
- ◇ Family Systems
- ◇ Genogram
- ◇ Narrative Family Therapy
- ◇ Structured Family Therapy

CHAPTER

# 7

~~~

# Facilitating Change Through Group Work and Treatment Programs

This chapter focuses on helping people with AODA concerns through group interventions and treatment programs. The first subsection will help you explore the full range of AODA services, as well as how to make appropriate and effective referrals given particular presenting problems, stages of change, diversity concerns, values, effectiveness, and other relevant factors. The next two subsections take you through the theories and phases of the intervention process when working with AODA groups. The final three subsections of this chapter take you through ethical issues in group work, review questions, and a journaling exercise. Throughout this chapter, think about how you might react to being a client in various group and treatment program situations, as well as how clients with different beliefs, expectations, and AODA problems might respond similarly or differently.

## Range of Services

The following chart identifies a range of services available for people affected by AODAs. This range notes the *type of service facility* rather than the type of theoretical perspective (as was provided in the Continuum of Theories, Therapies, and Models of Helping chart in Chapter 3). Each type of service facility may have more than one possible theoretical perspective. For example, outpatient services could be based on 12-Steps, Cognitive, Family Systems, or a number of different types of theoretical perspectives. The order of the types of services below goes generally from the least intrusive and least expensive to the most intrusive and most expensive, though not entirely. The order also approximates the order of services that a client could use; for example, assessment services come before detoxification, outpatient, or inpatient services. This range of services for individuals, families, groups, and communities with

AODA problems is not a formal, comprehensive system of care that exists within all communities. Often, a community has only a loose patchwork of services, and one of the social worker's key roles is to help clients negotiate the system by providing information about which service or combination of services will best serve the client. Complete the following chart by identifying the advantages and disadvantages of each type of service and by identifying an agency in or near your community that provides that type of service (including the name, address, phone number, e-mail, and Web address). To identify local services, consult a local directory or Web site of services (e.g., http://www.drug-abuse.com/usa). Sometimes a single agency provides more than one of these services. When considering the advantages and disadvantages of a particular program, consider factors such as:

♦ How does the program measure success?
♦ How effective is the program in relation to its own measures of success?
♦ What risks does the program's form of intervention pose to clients?
♦ How much does the program cost?
♦ How restrictive or intrusive is it for the client?
♦ Does the program provide early intervention?
♦ What are its eligibility requirements?
♦ What level of motivation does the program require?
♦ To what extent does the program ensure access for people with disabilities, different languages, limited financial resources, or other potential barriers to access?
♦ To what extent does the program embrace social-work values?

Examples of advantages and disadvantages have been listed for the first category of service. This chart will provide you with a resource list that you can use to make appropriate referrals for your clients.

| Type of service | Brief description | Advantages | Disadvantages | Local example |
|---|---|---|---|---|
| Prevention[1] | Using community development, targeted prevention programs, outreach, or social policies to ameliorate the conditions that are known to cause AODA problems | • *Can be more cost-effective than intervention* <br> • *Prevents human suffering* <br> • *Empowers the whole community* <br> • *Fits with social-work value of "social justice"* | • *Difficult to know who is at risk and which programs will be most effective at preventing AODAs* <br> • *Sometimes it is more difficult to get funding for prevention than for intervention* | *(continued)* |

1. See Chapter 9 for more information on prevention services and policies.

| Type of service | Brief description | Advantages | Disadvantages | Local example |
|---|---|---|---|---|
| **Natural recovery**[2] | The process by which people with AODA problems overcome these problems without the support of professionals, but rather through their own strengths and skills, and possibly with the help of informal support systems (e.g., family and friends) | | | |
| **Identification** | Professionals who help people identify when they have AODA problems or could use help regarding AODA behaviors (e.g., teachers, doctors, or generalist social workers who are trained to help people identify when they have AODA problems and to refer them to assessment or other services) | | | *(continued)* |

2. See Klingemann & Sobell (2001).

| Type of service | Brief description | Advantages | Disadvantages | Local example |
|---|---|---|---|---|
| Assessment | Professionals or programs that help clients explore the biological, psychological, social, and/or spiritual aspects of their lives, including but not limited to problems related to AODAs | | | |
| Referral | Programs that provide information about AODA services and help link clients with appropriate services (often linked with assessment services; some referral services, such as Web-based listings, provide only referral services) | | | |

*(continued)*

| Type of service | Brief description | Advantages | Disadvantages | Local example |
|---|---|---|---|---|
| Preparation | Services that are offered to clients to help them get ready emotionally, financially, psychologically, and socially for other more intensive AODA services (e.g., while the person is on the wait list for other services, or to help the person deal with problems in the short term, before a more intensive program can help with long-term issues) | | | |
| Self-help | The use of groups, manuals, or Web-based programs that are led by and for people with AODA problems rather than by professionals (e.g., AA, NA, Women for Sobriety, Rational Recovery, SMART Recovery) | | | *(continued)* |

| Type of service | Brief description | Advantages | Disadvantages | Local example |
|---|---|---|---|---|
| Hospital emergency room | Acute care provided for medical crises such as over-dosing, accidents involving severe physical injury, or other acute illnesses related to AODA use | | | |
| Detoxification | Services to help an individual go through physical withdrawal in a safe, monitored environment; depending on the type of substance, an individual may need either a medical detox unit or a non-medical detox unit | | | *(continued)* |

| Type of service | Brief description | Advantages | Disadvantages | Local example |
|---|---|---|---|---|
| Outpatient services (including privately and publicly funded services, insured services, and employee assistance programs) | Individual, family, or group counseling or therapy led by a social worker or other professional, in which the clients continue to live in the community; could be intensive (e.g., day treatment in which clients participate 5 days a week from 9 a.m. to 5 p.m) or non-intensive (e.g., 1 hour per week in the evening or daytime) | | | |
| Institutional services | Hospital-like agencies that provide intensive, in-patient services for people with chronic AODA problems, including dual diagnosis (e.g., people with schizophrenia or depression); usually lasting from 3 to 6 weeks | | | |

*(continued)*

| Type of service | Brief description | Advantages | Disadvantages | Local example |
|---|---|---|---|---|
| **Residential or community-based rehabilitation (including therapeutic communities)** | Longer-term intensive services where the client stays at a house-like facility in the community for a period of 1 month to 1 year (some-times with various stages from inten-sive treatment to minimal support and reintegration into the community) | | | |
| Pharmaco-therapy | Clinics, physicians, or pharmacies that provide medicines to help a person detoxify from AODs or abstain from using them (e.g., using Antabuse, methadone, LAAM, Naltrexone, or clonidine) | | | *(continued)* |

| Type of service | Brief description | Advantages | Disadvantages | Local example |
|---|---|---|---|---|
| Halfway house | A residential facility in the community (similar to a house) that provides some support to people who have completed more intensive residential or outpatient programs and helps the person reintegrate into the community (note that this is a halfway house for AODA clients, not to be confused with halfway houses for people convicted of crimes who are reintegrating into the community after serving time in a prison) | | | |
| Aftercare or relapse prevention | Outpatient services following more intensive services, helping clients maintain their goals and prevent relapse | | | |

*(continued)*

| Type of service | Brief description | Advantages | Disadvantages | Local example |
|---|---|---|---|---|
| Collateral services | Mental health, advocacy, research, and social services that are not specifically AODA treatment services but help clients and communities with related issues (e.g., education-vocational counseling, family therapy, sexual abuse therapy, advocacy for rights of people with AODAs, studying the effectiveness of new interventions) | | | |
| Legal responses | Criminal prosecution for AODA-related offences such as possession, trafficking, or theft to support a drug habit; also, diversion from court to community-based services for rehabilitation, compensation, or punishment | | | |

## Matching Clients With Types of Services[3]

Using the above chart and your course readings, consider each of the following client scenarios and suggest which type of service would be most appropriate for the client at this point in time. As you are making your suggestion, consider factors such as effectiveness, the client's wishes and readiness for different types of services (including the path of least resistance), and the client's needs at this point in the helping process. Explain—using words that you would use with a real client—why you believe this type of service would be most appropriate, as well as why you believe that other possible options would not be as appropriate. The first scenario provides a sample response.

1.    Leda is physically and psychologically addicted to barbiturates. She says she is ready to go into a 28-day intensive institutional program, but the program says that she needs to be abstinent from all psychoactive substances for at least 7 days before she enters.

      *Leda, perhaps you could consider going to a medical detox program. You have said that you are ready to attend an intensive program, but in order to meet their requirement that you be free from any drug use prior to admission, we need to consider a safe place for you to stop using barbiturates. A detox will have medical staff that can monitor your withdrawal and provide you with any medication that is needed to help you withdraw safely and with as little trauma as possible. Once you've successfully detoxed, you will be ready to begin the intensive program. You probably have some questions about a detox, so let's deal with those before making any decisions.*

2.    Fenwick is living on the streets. He uses cocaine and drinks alcohol. He is not ready to give up either, but he would like to control his use, and he would like to have a safe place to stay.

---

3. Remember that matching clients with types of services is different from matching clients with a theoretical approach, as was covered in Chapter 3.

3. Yannick's whole life revolves around sex. He is always thinking about sex and how he can have his next sexual encounter. He has risked his job, his health, and his friendships many times just to have a brief sexual encounter with a stranger. Yannick does not think that he has a problem and resents when anyone even suggests that he go see a mental health professional.

4. Ulli is 18 years old and has just slashed her thighs while high on heroin. She comes in to see her social worker, obviously still intoxicated and bleeding.

5. Shireen admits to her social worker that she has been selling crack to help support her drug habit. Some of Shireen's customers are under the age of 18. Shireen says that she would like to start over in a new town and get away from drugs altogether.

6. Forrest has been alone in the world since his wife of 45 years passed away. He drinks 7 to 8 glasses of whiskey per day, often lulling himself to sleep in a drunken stupor. During a medical checkup, including urinalysis, his doctor discovers that Forrest has severe liver damage. Forrest tells his doctor that he is not willing to give up alcohol, but he would not mind meeting others who have problems with alcohol.

7. Estrella is a refugee from Guatemala, where she escaped severe torture. Estrella self-medicates with a home brew of hallucinogens. She is very afraid to talk to any government official in the United States. She views social workers as government agents. Estrella is currently having flashbacks to her experiences of torture.

8. Noel has been abstinent from opiates for 18 months. This is a huge success, given that he was physically and psychologically dependent on opiates for 14 years. He was able to achieve abstinence through an inpatient, intensive treatment program, which he completed 16 months ago. He has not participated in AODA services

since, but is currently feeling anxious and stressed, which he sees as a warning sign that he is at risk of using again.

9. Billy (4) lives in foster care. His mother was killed in an alcohol-related accident and his father, who also has an alcohol problem, has not been involved in Billy's life since shortly after he was born.

10. Thelma was recently admitted to the hospital for a type of pneumonia related to intravenous drug use. The hospital social worker found an inpatient treatment program for Thelma that is free for people who cannot pay for treatment, but the program has a 3-week waiting list. Thelma wants to know what she is supposed to do while she is on the waiting list since she cannot afford any other type of counseling.

## Assessing Agencies for Possible Referral

Too often, professionals refer clients to services that they do not really know or do not really believe are the best. A useful standard for making referrals is to ask yourself, "Would I feel comfortable referring my parents or someone else that I love to these services?" The following questions can be used as a guide for collecting relevant information about an agency you are considering for referral. You can omit items that do not apply to a particular type of agency or your client's concerns. You may also add questions that are relevant to the client's needs and concerns. Ultimately, you want sufficient information so you feel confident that the referral is appropriate and so you can enable the client to make informed decisions about whether to pursue the referral.

---

**FIGURE 7.1**
**Agency Referral Assessment Guide**

1. What is the name of the agency?
2. What is the contact information for the agency (address, telephone, fax, Web address, e-mail)?
3. Where is the agency located?
4. What is the agency's catchment[4] area?
5. What are the philosophy, purpose, and objectives of this agency? (Identify where you secured this information—from a particular staff member, from the agency's brochure, Web site, or so on.)
6. How does the agency view the etiology or theoretical causations of AODAs?
7. How visible is the agency in the community?
8. Who does this agency view as its target population?
9. What are the eligibility requirements for using this service?

*(continued)*

---

4. Catchment refers to the location from which the agency draws clients, or neighborhood(s) that the agency targets for services.

10. Who is best served by this agency (e.g., what client characteristics [age, sex, culture, or language], presenting problems, and place on the continuum from substance use to dependence; is there research supporting these claims)?
11. What does the referral and admission process require? Who is the contact person?
12. What period of time can a client expect before receiving services? If there is a waiting list, what services, if any, are offered during the waiting list period?
13. Is the agency accessible for clients with disabilities? If so, which types of disabilities do they accommodate—sight, hearing, mobility, cognitive?
14. How is the organization administered and structured?
15. What government statutes or regulations guide the function of the agency?
16. What is the breakdown of funding sources for the program (e.g., what percentage of costs is covered by fee for service; grants; donations; federal, state, or municipal funding; health insurance)?
17. What are the costs to clients for the services provided? Are there any scholarships or sliding scales available for clients who cannot afford to pay full fees for the services?
18. How many clients are served (e.g., beds, clients per group, clients per year)?
19. What is the client to counselor ratio?
20. What are the qualifications of the staff?
21. What types of programs are offered (e.g., residential, outpatient, outreach, research, public education)? What do they consist of?
22. What are the agency's core values? Are these values consistent with your own values, the values of the social work profession, and the values of your client?
23. What theoretical models (e.g., 12-Steps, Cognitive) and methods of intervention (individual, family, group, or community work) are used? What is the agency's rationale for choosing these specific theoretical models and methods of intervention?
24. Does the agency claim a certain success rate? How is success determined/defined? How is data collected? At what points in time is data collected? How is failure defined? (See also Chapter 11 for tips on evaluating programs.)
25. Is there a follow-up, maintenance, or after-care program? What does it consist of?
26. What relationships does the agency have with other agencies?
27. How does the agency see itself differing from other facilities?
28. What are the agency's policies regarding clients who smoke, take medications, or use other drugs during the program?
29. Under what circumstances would a client be asked to leave the program?
30. From your perspective, what are the strengths and limitations of the agency? (Provide your assessment, given what you have heard and seen while researching the agency.)

To practice using this Agency Referral Assessment Guide, consider the clients in your primary Case Profile and the range of services identified at the beginning of this chapter. Identify an actual agency in your community that you think might be able to provide useful services to refer one or more of the clients at the current stage of the helping process (i.e., given the most recent role-plays you have conducted; this agency could provide one of a combination of services that you think would be most appropriate for the clients, so it does not have to provide *all* the services needed by the clients). Prepare for an interview at the agency using the following steps:

a. Check with your instructor to see if this agency is an appropriate agency for the purposes of this assignment (the instructor may know whether the agency is amenable to meeting with students for course assignments, or whether there have been negative experiences in the past; also, the instructor can keep track of which students are going to which agencies in order to avoid duplication of requests to a particular agency).

b. Determine the agency worker who you want to meet in order to get the best information (e.g., program director, community relations worker, clinical supervisor, frontline service provider; this might be determined by their relative availability and the perspectives you want to focus upon).

c. Contact the worker and explain the nature of the assignment, showing appreciation for the person's time and how this interview will help your learning process; request 30 minutes for the interview and a tour of the facilities, if appropriate (some agencies restrict tours to protect client confidentiality). Set up a time to meet that is convenient for the worker.

d. Prepare for the meeting by reviewing the Agency Referral Assessment Guide and highlighting the questions that are most relevant so that your agenda is reasonable. You can gather some information in advance by looking at the agency's Web site, brochure, or information from other referral sources.

e. Dress and present yourself in a professional manner. Bring a paper and pen to take notes (or an audiotape recorder if both of you have agreed to this in advance).

f. Conduct the interview using clear questions to solicit specific information and demonstrating your interest and gratitude for the person's time throughout. Allow the person to refuse to answer any questions if the person prefers not to.

g. After the interview, write an analysis of the program that you can use for helping you decide whether to make referrals for particular clients and to provide you with information that you can pass onto clients to link them to appropriate services [5 to 8 pages]. Provide a thank you letter to the person you interviewed and/or the person's supervisor. Report any problems you experienced to your instructor so that you can jointly decide whether any other follow-up is needed with the agency.

**Evaluation criteria:** Grading for this assignment will be based on the written analysis, including the comprehensiveness of the information provided (in terms of what a referring worker and a potential client would want to know), clarity and accuracy of the information, and level of critical analysis of the agency's strengths and limitations.

## Potential Obstacles to Effective Referrals

Just giving a client the name of an agency or a telephone number to call is not generally sufficient for making an effective referral. To enhance the likelihood that a client will successfully connect with an agency, identify potential obstacles and problem solve with the client about how to deal with these. Literature on resistance, referrals, and the preparation stage can help you identify potential barriers and determine how to help clients overcome them. Obstacles can include practical issues (such as how to pay for services or how to meet eligibility requirements) or emotional issues (such as fears, ambivalence, anxiety, or depression). Review each of the following scenarios, identify potential obstacles, and suggest how you and the client can deal with these in order to raise the likelihood of a successful referral.

1.  Jory has been trying to get admitted to an inpatient program for the past 8 months. Each time he is about to be admitted, something untoward happens. First, he was caught smoking pot by police just 2 days before his first planned admission date. The program would not admit him while he had an outstanding charge, even though it was a minor offence. He went to court and received a suspended sentence because he expressed a willingness to go for treatment. The night before his second planned admission date, Jory decided to have one last blast. Thinking about the prospects of never being able to drink or use pot again, he became anxious and could not sleep, so he decided to drink himself into oblivion. The next day, when he went to the program to be admitted, he was turned away because he was hung over and wreaking of alcohol. They asked him to come back in a month with at least 48 hours of complete sobriety. You are the referring social worker, working with Jory in the community to help him plan for a more successful admission to the program.

2.  You have referred Enid to a day-treatment program for glue huffers. Enid has suffered from severe brain damage as a result of her chronic glue use, affecting her memory and ability to reason.

3.  Macauley loves the party circuit, doing ecstasy and K. He was arrested for possession of drugs at a rave party and agreed to be diverted from court into a weekly therapy group for users of designer drugs. You are the court diversion worker. Macauley tells you that "the group is a joke," and that he will only do what he has to do to stay out of court.

4.  Refer back to Gwyn's case in Chapter 4 (page 103). How severe is Gwyn's problem? Looking at the continuum of AODA services, which type of service do you think is needed? What types of obstacles might inhibit Gwyn from being linked successfully to such services? How do you think that Kyla might be able to help Gwyn overcome these obstacles?

## Making a Referral and Linking Clients With Appropriate Services

Now that you have comprehensive information about an agency and are aware of potential obstacles to making effective referrals, you can use this information to practice making a referral (if you have chosen not to do the previous assignments, you could make up facts about an agency or use information that you already know about a real agency). Prepare for an individual or family session with the client(s) in which you will discuss options for help, provide information about a specific agency that you think would be most appropriate, and try to gain an agreement on who will do what in order to effect the referral. For the purposes of this assignment, the clients will be cooperative (in the planning stage of change), though the clients will demonstrate realistic concerns about the services, not knowing what to expect and having anxiety about their ability to succeed in the program. In order to prepare, write down answers to the following questions, which you can use as a guide for your referral interview.

1.  Identify the clients' primary needs and their motivations to make changes in relation to their AODA concerns.
2.  Summarize the services provided by the agency and how they fit with the clients' motivations and needs. Why do you believe that this type of agency is the best type of agency for the clients?
3.  What are the potential advantages, risks, and disadvantages of the clients' participation in the services of this agency? (Consider the clients' needs and wishes, the agency's definition of success, the level of intrusiveness, the cost effectiveness, the issues of accessibility, and the fit with the clients' values and diversity characteristics.)
4.  What are the eligibility requirements for the agencies (e.g., must clients have a period of abstinence prior to admission)?
5.  What steps must be taken in order to effect a referral and admission into the services? (What forms must be completed? Must clients submit to a physical examination?)
6.  What are the likely challenges or barriers to linking the clients successfully with the services? How can you and the clients preempt or deal with these challenges should they arise?

Conduct a role-play interview (15 to 20 minutes) in which the worker reviews the clients' interests in getting help, asks them to consider services at the chosen agency, and reviews information about the agency with the clients, focusing on questions the clients have about the program. If the clients agree to services, then jointly plan who will be responsible for what in order to increase the likelihood of a successful referral. Discuss any potential challenges or barriers that you identify and try to find solutions for them.

**Confidential facts for clients (not to be read by the worker):** For each of the profiles, the person playing social worker will decide who to include in the session and who to refer for services (e.g., the family or an individual). The following paragraphs give examples of obstacles for each client, though you will only need to role-play the obstacles that are relevant to the clients who are actually being referred to services in the session.

*Profile A:* The Torres family—If Julia is the person being referred to services, then potential obstacles to raise in the role-play include how to obtain child care and how to pay for the services. Julia has no health insurance coverage. If Maria is the person referred, then potential obstacles to raise include Maria's fear of having to disclose childhood traumas (including sexual abuse). She has used drugs to help her avoid talking about her feelings and painful memories, so going for individual, family, or group work would raise a lot of anxiety for her. If Teresa or Raphael Torres were referred, then their issues could include ethnocultural issues, including Raphael's sense of machismo, and their preference to keep family matters private rather than sharing them with other people (read about Latino culture to help you prepare).

*Profile B:* George and Frank—If George is being referred to services, then a potential obstacle would be his depression or malaise about receiving help. Although George has Native American ancestry, he does not retain many of its traditional cultural traits. If George and Frank were being referred together, then a potential obstacle would be that George is more ready to go for help than Frank. Frank still does not fully accept that he has a problem or needs to go for help. Also, both men are concerned about whether they will be judged by the therapist (or group members if it is a referral to a group) because they are gay. George might suggest that he not disclose his sexuality, while Frank suggests that they not be put back into the closet.

*Profile C:* The Lang family—A potential obstacle for Randy is peer pressure. He thinks that if he sees a shrink, friends will think he is "looney" or even worse, a "nerd." As a practical concern, Randy has a learning disability and his level of literacy is low. If he has to write anything during treatment, he would feel very embarrassed and withdraw. For Mr. and Mrs. Lang, consider cultural issues, including their ease with talking about physical issues, but less ease with talking about feelings or individual needs (see literature on Asian culture). Mr. Lang is concerned about the effectiveness of the program, having heard that no treatments have been proven successful.

*Profile D:* Dionne—One potential obstacle for Dionne is her embarrassment about her lifestyle, including her drug use and sexuality. Dionne has strong Christian values and fears how others will react to her, perhaps thinking that she is a hypocrite. She has been very private about these issues, so she fears speaking about them to other people. Dionne also has a fear of public speaking, making participation in a group difficult for her. Finally, she would like a "controlled use" goal rather than an "abstinence" goal.

**Debriefing questions:**

1. Client: What barriers or challenges did you foresee? How were these handled in the interview? What else would have helped you prepare for going to the agency?
2. Worker: How well did your preparation actually prepare you for this interview? What else could you have done to be even better prepared?

## Ethical Issues in Making a Referral

When making referrals, professionals must consider ethical principles such as informed consent, client self-determination, empowerment, professional competence, respect for all individuals, and access to effective services. For each of the following scenarios, identify the ethical issues that arise from the situation. Discuss how you would respond, providing an analysis of the factors that need to be taken into account as part of your ethical decision-making process.

1. Profile A: You have provided Julia with information about various AODA programs that could be helpful, but she does not seem to follow through on any of them. She asks you to select the best program for her and book her a reservation. You explain that she needs to demonstrate motivation and interest, and that you are there to empower her rather than simply do everything for her. Julia tells you she is willing, but she does not have the time or ability to check out programs and make any decisions. She says, "You're the expert. Please just do this for me and it will be easier for both of us."
2. Profile B: You have identified a group that George could attend that seems to be an appropriate and effective program. You have heard from other clients that some of the staff at this program are homophobic. Your community does not have any other programs that seem appropriate for George's needs. Do you refer George? What else should you do from the mezzo and macro perspectives?

3. Profile C: Randy's parents want him to go to services that specialize in work with the Asian community, including using the tenets of Buddhism. Randy says he wants to go to a "regular American" program. How would you handle this situation? Is there any research that you can rely upon to explain whether ethnocultural matching is effective or desirable?

4. Profile D: You refer Dionne to a group, which she attends. Dionne sees Kenneth, a colleague from her workplace, Evercharge, at this meeting. Dionne expresses concerns about her privacy. Although the group leaders told everyone that the meetings are confidential, Dionne fears that there is no way to enforce this. She is a bit concerned because Evercharge has a zero-tolerance policy on the use of illicit drugs. Kenneth only uses alcohol. Further, if Kenneth finds out she is HIV-positive, she fears that they may tell her boss and she will be fired. How do you respond to Dionne? What ethical principles and laws are relevant?

# Theory Behind Group Process

Now that we have considered the range of services and programs, as well as how to refer clients to various types of services and programs, we turn to the various theories that underlie different group processes. We begin by analyzing the theories that inform the 12-Steps Approach. The subsequent sections provide exercises on the effectiveness of group work and how to match clients with groups that adopt different theoretical perspectives.

## Deconstructing the 12-Steps Approach

The most prevalent form of AODA group is the 12-Step group, including AA, NA, Al-Anon, and other self-help groups, as well as professionally led groups that also say they adopt the 12 Steps.[5] Although AODA professionals or theoreticians did not develop the 12 Steps, we could ask, "What psychosocial theories and professional perspectives could be used to explain how various aspects of the 12 Steps contribute to the success of this approach?" The concept of "strict anonymity" in 12-Steps, for example, serves a similar purpose as the professional principle of confidentiality in a meeting with a professional social worker. Both anonymity and confidentiality are intended to create an atmosphere of safety and trust, particularly for people who have been stigmatized for having been affected by AODA problems. Similarly, the 12-Steps principle of "One day at a time" is an example of cognitive restructuring. Whereas overcoming a lifetime of AODA problems seems overwhelming, "One day at a time" reframes the person's task into smaller, more manageable components. The following short essay assignment [3 to 5 pages] is designed to help you deconstruct the 12-Steps Approach and critically analyze its components. For each of the following aspects of the 12-Steps Approach, identify a theoretical or professional explanation for this component. To view the range of possible theories, refer back to Figure 3.1 in Chapter 3 (page 67).

---

5. For alternative self-help groups that do not use the 12 Steps, consider Women for Sobriety, Moderation Management, or Rational Recovery, all of which have detailed Web sites.

1. Reading the 12 Steps
2. Sharing life stories or testimonials
3. Viewing alcoholism or addiction as a disease requiring abstinence
4. Meeting in a group
5. Having sponsors
6. Using slogans such as the Serenity Prayer or "Gratitude is an Attitude"
7. Providing tokens and marking anniversaries of sobriety
8. 90 meetings in 90 days
9. Self-help
10. No cross talk (discouraging people from debating or countering another person's story)
11. Admitting powerlessness
12. Making amends to people whom one has harmed
13. Asking a higher power for help

Given your appreciation of the possible theoretical underpinnings of the 12-Steps Approach, what are some of the theoretical criticisms of this approach? Which theories of AODAs, for example, are not taken into account by the 12-Steps Approach? How well does the 12-Steps Approach take diversity issues into account, particularly for people from the culture, gender, age, and background of the client(s) in your primary Case Profile? What adaptations, if any, should be made to the 12-Steps Approach to better accommodate the diversity of these clients?

## Theory and Effectiveness

In theory, group work is supposed to be an effective method of helping people with AODA problems because:

♦ People can learn from one another's experiences (cognitive learning).
♦ People can model the positive behavior of others who have dealt successfully with their AODA issues (social learning).
♦ People will not feel as isolated if they connect with others who have shared similar experiences (social support as a protective factor).
♦ People can play out some of their interpersonal problems in the safety of the group (experiential learning, skill development, and relational training).

What does the research say about the effectiveness of group work for people affected by AODAs? Is group work more effective than family or individual work for certain types of people or presenting problems? Or is group work a second-rate approach that is used because it is cheaper than providing individual counseling? Or does effectiveness depend on the theoretical perspective that is used by either group or individual helping processes? Review the research and write a 4-page summary of your findings, including myths, facts, and claims that still need more research.

## Theory and Presenting Problems

Consider each of the scenarios below and identify which of the following theoretical approaches or models of group work would provide the best fit for the client given the presenting problem: Psychoeducational, 12-Steps, Harm Reduction, Skills-Based Support, Family Systems, or Rationale-Emotive Therapy. Provide your reasoning for the approach or model you have identified.

1. Yolanda has recently been charged with illegally obtaining a restricted drug, morphine. She is put on probation on the condition that she attends an AODA group. She is clearly an involuntary client in the precontemplation stage of change.

2. Salvador is a devout Catholic. He has problems managing his money and sees himself as a compulsive shopper. Salvador feels a strong sense of remorse, knowing that he is putting his family in dire financial straits by his overspending. He asks if you can refer him to a group that can help him reestablish control over shopping and his life. He does not want family to know he is seeking help.

3.    Kayla and Fritz have been married for 2 years. Almost from the beginning of their marriage, alcohol has been a problem. Neither is physically dependent on alcohol, but both tend to binge when they do drink. Both see alcohol as a social outlet. They like to spend time with friends at the local pub, drinking and gabbing away. Often, they become violent when they are drunk. One time, Fritz pushed Kayla down the stairs while both were intoxicated. Kayla's mother has insisted that they get help. Kayla and Fritz come to you with some ambivalence, knowing that they become irresponsible when they are drinking, but not really convinced that they need to give it up.

4.    Lorraine is a 14-year-old who was recently caught by her parents smoking cigarettes. Lorraine thinks that she is old enough to do whatever she wants. Her parents ask you about a group for Lorraine that will make her stop smoking. When asked why she likes to smoke, Lorraine says it helps her calm down and relax. When you ask about any medication use, her parents say Lorraine was on Ritalin for 2 years, but recently stopped using it because Lorraine did not think she had an attention deficit problem.

5.   Haggar describes herself as a "former cocaine junky and whore." She has been clean and sober for 8 months. She was able to overcome her problem with cocaine through the help of an intensive residential treatment program located in a farm setting. She is now ready to return to the city and would like to attend a group that can help her maintain her sobriety. She does not see her cocaine problem as a disease but as a coping mechanism. She thinks that if she can build a more positive support system and other coping strategies, she can continue to remain clean.

# Phases of Group

The above sections explored how theory informs group practice. The following exercises are designed to give you a sense of the phases of group process that can be applied in groups with various theoretical perspectives.

## Beginning Phase

One of the best ways to supplement the knowledge of AODA groups that you have gained from your readings and classes is to attend an actual group, reflecting on your experiences and observing those of others. Alcoholics Anonymous and other 12-Step groups often have "open meetings" that can be attended by people who are not personally struggling with AODA issues. To learn more about the beginning phase of groups, attend an open meeting of AA or another AODA group. Use the following guide to focus your attention and write a 2 to 3 page summary afterward (do not take notes during one of these meetings as this may distract others and cause concerns about ensuring anonymity).

1. What techniques, if any, did the group use to build trust and rapport between group members?

   ____ Welcome people

   ____ Provide introductions

   ____ Match new people with someone who has attended previous meetings

   ____ Ask people to respect the anonymity or confidentiality of others

   ____ Trust exercise—specify: _____

   ____ Other—specify: _____

2. What rules or norms did the group establish?

   ____ Confidentiality—specify: _____

   ____ Communication—specify: _____

   ____ Use or abstinence—specify: _____

   ____ Topics that were okay or not okay to discuss—specify: _____

   ____ Leadership of the group—specify: _____

   ____ Other—specify: _____

3. How would the group respond to a person who comes to a meeting and is noticeably intoxicated?

   ____ No rule on this was indicated

   ____ Allowed to continue to participate

   ____ Not allowed to participate while intoxicated

   ____ Other—specify: _____

4. Describe the feelings you experienced at the beginning of the meeting.

   ____ Fear

   ____ Anxiety

   ____ Calmness

   ____ Anticipation

   ____ Satisfaction

   ____ Pride

   ____ Support

   ____ Alienation

   ____ Embarrassment

   ____ Other—specify: _____

5. How did these feelings change, if at all, over the course of the meeting?

6.  What, if anything, happened during the meeting to make you feel more welcome, more relaxed, more accepted, or more self-assured?

7.  What could the group members or facilitators have done differently to improve your experience of the group?

8.  How do you think your experience would be similar to and different from the experiences that a person actually affected by AODAs would have had coming to a first group meeting?

# Working Phase

## Designing a Group Session

In order to design a structured session, a group facilitator should consider the following questions:

1. What are the overall goals for the group?
2. How does this session fit into these overall goals for the group and what are the specific objectives of this particular session?
3. What are the possible methods of engaging the group in a manner that will lead to successful completion of these objectives—for example, engaging in large or small group discussion, hearing a presentation by the facilitator or a guest speaker, watching a movie, participating in a role-play or other experiential exercise, or doing a homework assignment? Which method or combination of methods would be the best way to fulfill the objectives?
4. What theoretical perspective(s) will this session be based on?
5. How will success of the session be measured (e.g., specific behavioral observations, informal qualitative feedback, written qualitative feedback, or quantitative survey)?

Consider the work phase of a psychoeducational group for people who have recently tested as being HIV-positive. All members of this group are intravenous drug users and have identified sharing needles as their likely source of contracting HIV. The primary purpose of this group is to provide participants with information about HIV and AIDS so that they can make informed choices about what types of medical, psychological, social, and spiritual supports are available and can best meet their needs. In a previous session, some participants note that they are reluctant to tell their doctors, friends, and family about having HIV for fear of rejection, embarrassment, and being asked about their drug use. Your task is to design a session based on the questions listed above. The following is a truly dreadful example in which the proposal violates social work ethical rules related to self-determination, nonjudgmentalism, and competence. Your example will be clinically and ethically sound, as well as more detailed. [2 to 3 pages including citations for your sources]

> Dreadful example: *The overall group goal is to inoculate group members with information about who to go to for help with their HIV problems. For this particular session, the objectives are: (a) to refer each group member to a particular agency for "the best help" as determined by the facilitator, and (b) to motivate each member to follow through on the referral within 7 days. Some methods that could be used for this session include: showing a videotape called "What You Don't Want to Happen," which will scare people into wanting to go for the prescribed help; having a debate with group members on the pluses and minuses of going to the prescribed services; and role-playing examples of what will happen to them if they do not follow through. I think the last two will work well together in combination. The debate will make people think they have a choice, but the role-play will scare everyone into submission. The theoretical perspective for the debate is primarily Cognitive Theory, as this will get people thinking about the pros and cons of following through with the referrals (Cortez & Thymes, 2002). The theoretical perspective that I will use for the role-plays is behaviorism, particularly the concept of "punishment." If people fear negative consequences, they will avoid behaviors that will bring about*

*punishment (Eagre, 2004). To measure the effectiveness of this session, I will give each person a questionnaire at the end of the session that tests "fear factors" (Molotov, 2003). Any test result of over 75 indicates that the person is likely to behave in a manner that avoids the particular behavior. To be considered successful, at least 12 of the 14 group members should score over 75. I will also request informal, oral feedback, asking the question, "How did you like me during today's group session?"*

## Critically Analyzing a Group Intervention

The following exercise is designed to help you critically analyze a group intervention in the working phase. The material in italics provides abbreviated examples of each step, using Eva's case. Your examples will go into more depth. [3 to 5 pages]

1.  Select a group exercise or intervention from the literature that you think would be potentially useful for one of the clients in your Case Profile. Provide a rationale explaining why you think that this group exercise would be useful for the particular client.

    *In Eva's case, my assessment in Chapter 5 indicated that she was experiencing a high degree of stress and that she may have been using cocaine to help her deal with it, though she was in the precontemplation stage regarding suspected cocaine use. If Eva were participating in a group, a useful exercise would be to provide "Stress Reduction Training," which is not dependant on Eva's admitting she has a problem with cocaine or agreeing to change any substance use behaviors. By hearing others in the group talk about the connection between stress and their substance use behaviors, Eva might be more willing to discuss her cocaine use.*

2.  Find an article or two that explains the group exercise in detail. Write a summary of this exercise including a description of how to facilitate the exercise, the theoretical underpinnings of the exercise, and research findings (if any) on its effectiveness and on how to assess which clients would find this exercise most beneficial.

    *For Eva's group, my write-up would include a description of how the group facilitator would present stress reduction techniques and coach the group members through these techniques (e.g., breathing exercises, body awareness, self-massage). The theoretical underpinnings of these techniques include cognitive-behavioral (becoming aware of stress and developing alternate strategies to substance-using behavior) and Integrative Mind-Body Theory.*

3.  Critique the major tenets and assumptions of the group intervention: Which tenets do you accept, and why? Which tenets do you not accept, and why? Are the assumptions clearly defined and reasonable? Are the tenets and assumptions ethically and socially consistent with my own and social work's assumptions? What does the research say about the effectiveness of this intervention and about client groups that are more likely to benefit from this type of intervention?[6]

    *One of the major assumptions of Stress Reduction techniques is that if people learn to recognize stress early, they can replace substance abusing behavior with more functional and less risky coping strategies. I was not able to find any empirical research that directly confirmed*

---

6. Some of these questions are derived from Mumm and Kersting (1997).

*this, though there has been anecdotal evidence that people with AODA problems find these strategies useful (Krenkowitz, 2004). Most of the research was on alcohol users, and I could not find any research that looked at Stress Reduction with particular ethnocultural groups. Using Stress Reduction fits with the Ecological Model of social work. This suggests that social workers should help people adapt to their social environments, which includes how to deal with stress. However, the Ecological Model also suggests that social workers should not only focus on change for the individual, but change within the social environment. In Eva's case, if her work was very stressful, in addition to helping her cope with stress, it would be helpful to make her workplace less stressful. Ideally, I agree with this, though personally, I think it is often easier to help the individual change than to help larger systems change (particularly in the short term).*

4. How easy or challenging is the group intervention to understand and employ in practice?

    *The literature that I found on Stress Reduction includes very clear and specific directions on how to employ it (Halcyon & Zanacs, 2003). These same authors have also produced a videotape showing how to employ the strategies. The facilitator can follow a script or can vary the directions, depending on his or her comfort level. You do need clients who are willing to participate physically, but the commitment level need not be high to ask people just to try out the techniques during the session. This is less than the commitment that may be needed in an intervention that asks people to open up emotionally.*

5. How applicable is the group intervention across different settings, presenting problems, and client groups (including cultural and ethnic diversity)?

    *I would think his technique is fairly flexible for different settings, problems, and client groups, though there was not a lot of empirical research on this issue (Halcyon & Zanacs, 2003). Stress Reduction has been used for people with various substance abuse and addiction problems, as well as in outpatient and residential settings. Since Eva has rejected spirituality in her life, and since she comes from a background where people did not talk much about their feelings, Stress Reduction might be a good fit in contrast with 12-Steps groups or groups that require high degrees of emotional disclosures or a belief in a higher power.*

### Assignment 7.1: Practicing a Group Exercise

This role-play will bring together clients from all four Case Profiles: Julia, Randy, George, and Dionne. Although they have significantly different backgrounds, stages of change, and AODA issues, they likely have at least one experience in common—loss. People who have problems with AODAs typically experience losses in a range of life realms: physical, psychological, social, and spiritual. The purposes of the loss exercise include: (a) helping clients become aware of the losses they have experienced from AODAs, as well as from deciding to abstain or control their AODAs; (b) reinforcing their motivation to make or maintain positive changes regarding their AODA behaviors; and (c) providing clients with a ritual to grieve their losses, working through feelings of sadness, frustration, emptiness, and so on.

The person playing the social worker will facilitate a group session in the work phase. Assume the clients have been successfully engaged in the beginning phase and are cooperative with the worker. The facilitator will begin with a check-in (asking each member how he or she is feeling at this moment and if they have any issues to discuss) and will then introduce the loss exercise. The facilitator will ask each member of the group to write down answers to the following instructions (you could give these instructions orally, one at a time, or in written form, with room to respond).

1. Identify one substance or behavior in your life that you would like to give up, or have recently given up, because it has caused problems in your life.
2. Describe at least two examples of physical loss in your life that have been caused by using this substance or behavior (e.g., medical problems, accidents, or physical deterioration attributable to the AODA).
3. Describe at least two examples of psychological loss in your life that have been caused by using this substance or behavior (e.g., emotional losses, loss of specific memories, loss of thinking or problem-solving skills, or loss of self-esteem).
4. Describe at least two examples of social losses in your life that have been caused by using this substance or behavior (e.g., loss of family, friends, coworkers, jobs, recreation, or social support systems).
5. Describe at least two examples of spiritual losses that you have experienced as a result of using this substance or behavior (e.g., loss of connection with God or a higher power, loss of a sense of meaning in your life, loss of relationships that gave your life significance, or loss of activities that gave your life meaning).
6. What do you think it is going to be like facing life without using that substance or behavior?
7. Describe what losses (physically, psychologically, socially, and spiritually) you will experience if you abstain from the substance or behavior for the rest of your life.
8. On a scale of 1 to 10 (with 10 being most difficult), how difficult do you think it will be to abstain from or control your substance use or behavior? What do you think might make it more difficult? What do you think might make it less difficult?

Once everyone has had time to write down answers to these questions, the facilitator will engage the clients in a dialogue about their past losses, as well as the possibility of future losses. Rather than ask clients to read their answers, the facilitator will try to engage the clients in a more natural and flowing discussion about these issues. Throughout the discussion, the facilitator should use the following skills:

♦ Open-ended questions to explore the losses each client has experienced or expects to experience in the future
♦ Supportive questions to encourage clients to disclose their thoughts and feelings around their experiences of loss
♦ Demonstrating empathy for these losses through paraphrasing the meaning or reflecting back feelings
♦ Encouraging clients to draw similarities and differences in their experiences of loss through the use of focused questions
♦ Allowing clients to draw their own conclusions about the worth of this exercise for each of them and for them as a group
♦ Staying with the difficult emotions of the clients (e.g., does not try to cheer them up or minimize their losses)

Toward the conclusion of the exercise, the worker will describe how people often find it useful to mark losses with a particular ritual or ceremony, such as a funeral or wake when someone dies or a graduation party when people finish school. The facilitator will ask group members to brainstorm ideas about how they might like to mourn or mark their losses. Once the group comes up with a range of options, the facilitator will ask group members whether they would like to actually follow through on any of these individually or as a group. If they agree to follow through on these, the facilitator will begin to help them plan *how* to follow through.

**Debriefing:**

1. Facilitator: Which of the above skills did you demonstrate well? How could you have improved on the way you facilitated the session and used these skills?
2. Clients: What was the most useful part of this exercise for each of you? What was the most challenging part of this exercise for each of you?
3. Observer: Which skills from the above list did the facilitator use most effectively? How successful was this exercise in achieving the purposes set out above? What could have been done to make this an even more successful exercise?

**Written assignment:** Write up an evaluation of this group role-play, including a critique of the facilitator's use of skills, the appropriateness of this type of session for each of the clients, and links to what you have read about AODAs and loss with the practice experience in this role-play. [4 to 5 pages]

**Evaluation** for this assignment will be based on: degree to which the paper provides specific and accurate examples of the facilitator's use of skills and suggestions for improvement, level of insight into each client's individual experiences—positive and negative—within the group, and extent to which the paper identifies significant moments from the role-play and relates them to relevant readings (include at least four scholarly references).

# Ending Phase

The ending phase of a group process is typically a time when the facilitator helps members deal with feelings of separation, decide how to handle unfinished business, review the group experience, practice for behavioral change, give and receive feedback, determine ways of carrying learning further, and agree to ways to follow up and maintain their progress (see also Chapter 10). Each of the following scenarios relates to the last session or two of a group program that involves AODA concerns. For each, identify "ending phase" issues that a worker needs to address, and suggest ways to address these issues based on your readings on AODAs and group processes.

1. Jenna has been running a support group in a psychiatric facility for people who have recently attempted suicide by trying to overdose on psychotropic medications. The group members were committed involuntarily to the facility and most of them are ready to be released back to the community. Jenna assesses that one client, Obie, is still at moderate risk of overdosing, given his stated wish to simply "go to sleep and

never wake up again." Most of the group members have been prescribed antide-pressants that they will continue to use following release from the hospital.

2. Ginger has been facilitating a group based on the 12-Steps program. Most of the clients have been working through the first five steps. During the final session, two of the clients suggest that 12-Steps does not work. They have still been smoking pot and drinking alcohol. Other group members feel like the disaffected members have attacked them personally.

3.  Penny is in the middle of leading her final session for a group of clients who identify themselves as compulsive gamblers. One of the clients suggests that they keep on meeting for another month. The others agree, saying that they continue to need one another's support, and they need something to do on the weekends other than gamble. Penny has finished going through the psychoeducational material she had planned and believes that the members are ready to proceed without the group. She is concerned that they may be getting too dependent on the group, almost replacing their gambling addiction with a dependence on this group.

4.  Peter is wrapping up a group for clients referred by the probation department for "Driving While Intoxicated" charges. Although Peter feels he is able to provide positive reports for most of the clients, he thinks he will have to advise Harley's probation officer that Harley did not participate verbally during group. He also demonstrated symptoms of glue huffing on at least two of the eight sessions. Peter is not sure whether to say anything to Harley individually or in group during the final session, or simply to provide a report to Harley's probation officer and let the probation officer deal with these problems.

# Ethics in Group Work

Provide an ethical analysis of the issues that arise in the scenario below related to your primary Case Profile or another scenario that interests you. Ensure that you refer to the NASW Code of

Ethics and, if possible, the policies of an agency that you identified in the exercises earlier in this chapter. [3 to 5 pages]

**A. Raphael Torres:** Raphael Torres has been attending a group for elder men with chronic alcohol problems. The group is based on a model of controlled use and all the clients are participating voluntarily. During the second session, Raphael is noticeably intoxicated. As facilitator, you notice that his speech is slurred and he has alcohol on his breath. When you confront Raphael in group about these observations, he says, "So what? You said we were allowed to drink if we want." Others speak up in support of Raphael, saying that he can drink if he wants. You say that your agency has a policy that people cannot come to group sessions while intoxicated, though the policy is not clear on what consequences occur if someone does show up intoxicated. Members of the group say that they never agreed to this rule and maybe the agency needs to change its policy to be more consistent with the "controlled use" approach of the agency. You do not think that Raphael poses any immediate risk to himself or the group, but you are not comfortable with his presence while intoxicated. You also want to honor the group's decisions.

**B. George Favel:** George has been attending your group for glue huffers. After a session, he asks to talk to you privately. George discloses that outside of group other members have been taunting him with racial epithets. He says he wants to leave the group rather than confront the issue within group, as you have offered. You suspect that withdrawal is one of George's defense mechanisms, and you had hoped that group participation would help him through this issue. You cannot force George to stay in the group, but you are thinking of asking the others in the group to leave, as they have broken the ground rule about showing respect for others in the group. You want to ensure the group is safe for everyone.

**C. Randy Lang:** You have been providing individual counseling to Randy for about 3 months. During the previous session, you suggested that Randy explore some groups to help him with family issues related to AODA use. Randy tells you he has found a great program called Enough is Enough. He says that the people there were very welcoming and even offered him a place to stay. From what you have heard of this program, it sounds like a religious cult that uses brainwashing to prey on vulnerable young people with AODA problems. It invites people into their "alternative family," involves them in pagan rituals, and finds them jobs with other cult members. You are particularly concerned about allegations of sexual abuse within the group, though there has never been a criminal conviction. When you relate these concerns to Randy, he says you do not know what you are talking about. He says that Enough is Enough is based on a religion that is just as valid as Christianity or Islam, and that you have no right to put it down or impose your own beliefs on him. How do you respond to Randy? Would your response be any different if Randy said he wanted to go to an NA program and you believed that NA was not an effective or appropriate program? Why or why not?

**D. Dionne Thevenin:** Dionne is attending a group you run for people who are on methadone maintenance. During a session, group members start talking about an HIV-prevention poster on the wall that shows a person shooting up, along with a bleach kit and instructions for cleaning needles. The discussion begins to focus on the different things that group members liked about their own works and rituals around shooting up. You can sense that members are starting to feel excited, even "jonesing." You wonder if the group needs to set ground rules about what issues can be discussed and what images should be shown in the room.

## Review Questions

The following review questions will test your knowledge about various types of AODA treatment services, including the differences among programs and which service types fit best for clients with different presenting problems.

1. "Day treatment" refers to:
   a. Intensive AODA programs where the clients attend group sessions during the day and return home to sleep at night.
   b. Teaching clients to approach life "one day at a time."
   c. Going to 90 AA meetings in 90 days.
   d. Using exposure to daylight as a treatment for alcoholics, helping to alleviate the depressive effects of alcohol.
   e. Providing clients with a daily list of homework, including bibliotherapy and reflective exercises.

2. "Managed care" refers to:
   a. Using educational approaches to teach clients how to manage their lives without drugs.
   b. Putting a price cap on the amount that services can charge clients for AODA services.
   c. Using business management strategies to help clients control their drug use, including management by objectives.
   d. Methods used to control the use of health services, with the intent of providing more efficient and effective use of health care (including AODA services).
   e. None of the above.

3. Early identification of AODA problems is useful because:
   a. If people suffer from negative effects of long-term AODA use before they enter a group or treatment program, their chances of full recovery and good health are lower.
   b. People tend to gather greater financial resources the longer they are abusing AODs, so they are better able to afford AODA treatment.
   c. It is better to provide treatment for someone who has no family support, since family involvement and group treatment are mutually exclusive.
   d. The risks of losing a job or breaking up a committed domestic relationship are NOT significant motivators.
   e. There aren't any group treatment programs for people at risk of AODA problems.

4. A client is not physically addicted to alcohol, but does use it to cope with life stresses, including marital difficulties. He has no prior alcohol treatment history and is ambivalent about giving up alcohol altogether. Based on this information, the most appropriate type of service for him at this stage is probably:
   a. Detoxification.
   b. 28-day inpatient, intensive treatment.
   c. Outpatient, nonintensive counseling.

d. Pharmacotherapy, such as Antabuse.

e. Alcohol use prevention.

5. A client has just overdosed on sedative-hypnotics. The most appropriate type of service at this moment is a:

a. Medical detoxification.

b. Nonmedical detoxification.

c. Residential, long-term treatment.

d. Halfway house.

e. Hospital emergency room.

6. A client has been in an institutional treatment program for 28 days and has been abstinent for more than 5 weeks. The client was homeless prior to treatment. She has no home or family to return to. The most appropriate type of service for this client is:

a. Detoxification.

b. A second 28-day institutional program.

c. A halfway house.

d. Assessment and referral.

e. Self-help.

7. The success of AA programs can be attributed to:

a. A system of sponsorship and social support.

b. A structured series of 12 steps.

c. Positive cognitive messages such as "One day at a time."

d. All of the above and more.

e. None of the above.

8. Al-Anon and Nar-Anon groups are designed specifically for:

a. People who are not sure that they personally have an AODA problem.

b. People who have family members with AODA problems.

c. People who have recovered successfully from an AODA problem.

d. People who have children that they want to prevent from becoming addicted to AODs but do not currently have AOD problems.

e. People who think that they might personally have an AODA problem.

9. Methods typically used in psychoeducational groups for AODA treatment include:

a. Role-plays.

b. Presentation of didactic information.

c. Methadone maintenance.

d. All of the above.

e. Only a and b.

10. Research on AODA treatment effectiveness shows:

a. Minimal effectiveness for any form of treatment.

b. Unequivocal evidence that increased length of stay at a treatment program improves client outcomes.

c. A counselor's interpersonal functioning (including the ability to demonstrate warmth, empathy, and supportiveness) are NOT associated with better client outcomes.

d. Client characteristics, such as socioeconomic status and mental health status, are the strongest predictors of client outcomes.

e. All of the above.

11. The philosophy behind the "court diversion" for people charged with AODA-related crimes is that:
    a. The only way to deter drug crimes is to provide stiff penalties.
    b. People who self-medicate require proper medical attention.
    c. Having to pay for lawyer's fees will deter illicit drug use.
    d. Drug use often reflects a person's difficulty coping with a stressful environment rather than a person who is bad and deserves punishment.
    e. It is cheaper to incarcerate a person than to provide AODA treatment.

12. The role of a case manager for clients with AODAs can be important because:
    a. The case manager can determine which clients should not be allowed into detoxification if they have failed at three or more prior attempts.
    b. The case manager can develop a positive working relationship with clients and walk the clients through the various stages of treatment, from detox to relapse prevention.
    c. The case manager acts as a peer mentor for clients when they complete the intensive residential treatment program.
    d. A case manager is responsible for education about domestic violence, HIV prevention, and public health, in addition to AODA services.
    e. A case manager is responsible for managing the financial resources of a person with AODA problems, so that the person does not spend money irresponsibly on AODAs.

13. Working with homeless people who have AODA problems can be challenging because:
    a. Most emergency housing units and homeless shelters stipulate that a person cannot be using drugs, and it is difficult for a person to stop using drugs while still living on the streets.
    b. They do not have the same types of support networks as individuals living at home, with families, and with stable jobs.
    c. There is often a shortage of beds in publicly funded residential or inpatient programs, resulting in waiting lists for people without insurance who cannot pay for AODA services.
    d. They are not used to the structure that is required in residential or day treatment facilities.
    e. All of the above.

14. A "perinatal addiction program" is designed to provide help for:
    a. Men who have completed detox and now need temporary housing.
    b. Adult children of alcoholics.
    c. Pregnant women with AODA problems.
    d. Elderly clients with chronic natal disorders.
    e. Children born with Fetal Alcohol Effects who have been taken away from their mothers.

15. Therapeutic Communities (TCs) have been found to be:
    a. Ineffective for clients who have been mandated by the court to attend.
    b. More effective for clients who have been legally coerced to attend than for voluntary clients.
    c. Equally effective for clients who have been legally coerced to attend, as for clients who attend voluntarily.
    d. Unsuccessful for any clients.
    e. Successful only during the period of incarceration of clients.

16. In Therapeutic Communities, AODA clients are sometimes asked to wear signs:
    a. To remind them to take their medications.
    b. To ask others to confront them about specific, problematic behaviors.
    c. To indicate their label as an addict or an alcoholic.
    d. To notify police or other authorities to return the person to the locked facility for AODA treatment.
    e. To remind people that these clients pose a risk of violence.
17. Potential drawbacks of having separate groups or treatment programs for gay and nongay clients include:
    a. Reinforcing homophobia in nongay professionals.
    b. Contributing to alienation of gay men and lesbians from the rest of society.
    c. For gay and lesbian clients, facilitation of adjustment to the "real world" includes adjustment to issues between gays and nongays.
    d. Some gay clients will not identify themselves as gay and will go to heterosexual AODA programs where they will not be exposed to other clients who are out of the closet.
    e. All of the above.
18. A "halfway house" refers to:
    a. A hospital-like institution that provides intensive AODA treatment 5 days a week, for 28 to 45 days.
    b. A "crack house" or place where people gather to use crack in the privacy of a home.
    c. A self-help group that typically operates in the basement of a church or community center.
    d. A residential treatment facility that provides some support groups and individual counseling, but also permits clients to reintegrate into the community, through work, schooling, retraining, and so on.
    e. A long-term harm reduction program where clients are provided methadone or other synthetic drugs so they can avoid withdrawal and reduce at least half of the risks related to their drug use.
19. From a therapeutic perspective, group work can be advantageous to AODA clients because:
    a. Group work provides clients with support from others with similar problems and lets them know they are not alone in their challenge with AODAs.
    b. Clients will ridicule one another if they use AODs.
    c. Group work has been proven empirically to be more effective than individual work for AODA clients.
    d. Group work allows the facilitator to strip down the clients' layers of denial and expose all their vulnerabilities to the group.
    e. Clients can make friends with others who know how to obtain illicit substances.
20. Becky tells her social worker that she does not think individual counseling will work for her because the social worker has never had an addiction to cocaine. The social worker might be able to tap into this concern and successfully connect Becky with a group for people addicted to cocaine by explaining to Becky that groups:
    a. Move up the pace of change, providing a more intensive experience.
    b. Remove the facilitator as an expert, as members of the group share common experiences and make use of their expertise.
    c. Provide social support for members outside of the group.
    d. Remove a sense of isolation.
    e. Allow members to confront one another.

# Journaling Exercise

1. Identify a group experience in which you received help from the group (this could be a therapeutic group, a class, a self-help group, or a team that played together for a sport or game). How did you feel about the group the first time it came together? How did your feelings about the group change over time? What contributed to or detracted from the ability of the group to achieve its goals? What can you take from this group experience to help you be an effective facilitator of an AODA group?

2. What have you learned from this chapter about being an AODA group facilitator that you want to remember 5 years from now? What additional group skills or theories do you hope to learn over the next 5 years? What are your plans for developing these new skills and knowledge bases? Write this information down in your calendar, so that you can check up on them 1, 3, and 5 years from now (computerized calendars are ideal for this).

# InfoTrac College Edition

## Key words

◇ Alcoholics Anonymous
◇ Group (drug or alcohol)
◇ Referral
◇ Self-help
◇ Treatment effectiveness

CHAPTER

# 8

~~~

# Helping Communities Change

In this chapter, we explore how to help larger systems change. This chapter defines communities broadly, to include workplaces and other organizational settings, ethnocultural communities, religious communities, neighborhoods, municipalities, and rural districts. The first section looks at how to identify macro issues (community enhancement and social policy development) that require attention, when working with micro systems (individuals and families) affected by AODAs. The second section explores methods of initiating change in a community. The following sections provide exercises on the working phase of the change process: selecting appropriate community development approaches, working with diverse communities, and dealing with ethical issues. The chapter ends with questions for journaling.

## From Micro to Macro

As the ecological perspective of social work suggests, individual and family clients must be considered in the context of their social environment. As with other presenting problems, helping people with AODAs should not be limited to working with individuals and families. Social workers must also identify issues within the community that contribute to problems at the individual and family levels, and they must assist with change at the community level. The first exercise of this chapter asks you to consider the Case Profiles from Chapter 1, as well as additional information you have gathered throughout this course, and identify potential targets of change at the community level. An analysis based on Eva's case is presented below to illustrate how to make these connections between micro and macro issues.

1. Eva

   *Eva's cocaine use seems to be related to stress that she is experiencing in her position as an air traffic controller. As a social worker, I could explore whether this hypothesis is true by assessing the stress of air traffic controllers and by looking at whether there is any research on this issue. Rather than simply help individual air traffic controllers such as Eva cope with stress, I could determine if I could help the community of air traffic controllers and their employers try to improve work conditions so that they are not so stressful.*

*Eva has also told me that she feels alienated from the religion she grew up with, the Church of the Latter Day Saints (LDS). Research indicates that an affiliation with a spiritual community can be a positive support for people with AODA problems and that alienation or rejection by a faith community can be an obstacle (Tyrell, 2005). If I had other AODA clients like Eva who felt alienated from LDS, it might be useful to try to work together with LDS to see if they could develop more support systems within the community for people with AODAs. Alternatively, it might be useful to bring people like Eva together to help them set up a spiritual support system that would fit better with their needs and aspirations.*

2.  The Torres family

3.  George and Frank

4.  The Lang family

5.   Dionne Thevenin

# Initiating Community Change

Refer back to your assignment in Chapter 5 entitled Practicing a Needs Assessment Interview (page 143). Building on this needs assessment, develop a strategy for initiating community change by filling in answers to the following questions:

a.  What is the priority for change?

b.  Why is this a priority? (What is the rationale for focusing on this AODA issue at this time?)

c. Whom can I work with in the community and what resources or expertise do each of these individuals or groups bring to the table (e.g., AODA professional expertise; AODA personal experience; money or physical resources; political clout; compassionate interest; ethical and legal advice; advocacy skills; decision-making responsibility; or business skills such as budgeting, fundraising, management, construction, marketing, and accounting)?

d. What is the best way to approach people to develop a coalition to work on this issue (e.g., individual meetings, large-group meetings, telephone or e-mail contact, or meeting with a few key leaders)?

e. How will this coalition be led (e.g., social worker, psychologist, medical practitioner, elected officials, volunteer committee, paid facilitator)?

f. When and where will the coalition members or leaders meet?

# Community Development Approaches

Social workers who are involved in community development may draw from a broad array of approaches or strategies.

1. Social action—Organizing or empowering members of a community to advocate effectively for the needs of a particular group or for a particular cause (e.g., helping organize petitions, demonstrations, or media campaigns; hiring advocates with specialized expertise in law or public policy formation; or planning civil disobedience to stimulate change).

2. Social support—Organizing or empowering members of a community to develop new or stronger social support systems for all or a segment of the community.

3. Conflict resolution—Helping a community communicate effectively, resolve differences, solve problems, build collaborative relationships, and use conflict in a positive way to produce social change (e.g., by acting as a mediator, consultant, or facilitator).

4. Education—Enhancing the knowledge base of a community by facilitating access to knowledge so that the community can make informed decisions.

5. Fundraising—Helping a community raise money or other resources so that it can enhance social programs.

6. Capacity building—Enhancing the ability of community members to address its needs and goals by teaching skills, providing infrastructure, brokering relationships with people with power, or providing moral support.

7. Raising awareness—Helping a community become aware of current needs or risks that they might wish to address.

8. Program development—Helping create new agencies or build upon existing ones to provide better or more specialized services for people affected by AODAs.

9. Other (specify and provide your definition): _____

_____

For each of the following AODA scenarios, select an approach that you believe would be an appropriate first step for you to take as a community development worker. Provide your reasoning. Consult a GSI to look up any terms or substances that are not familiar to you.[1]

---

1. A GSI is a Good Source of Information, as defined in Chapter 1.

a. You have recently heard through your connections that gamma hydroxybutyrate (GHB) is starting to show up in your community, particularly within the Latino community. You are particularly concerned because when this substance is mixed with alcohol or other drugs, the results can be lethal. You do not think that this issue is getting any attention and do not think it is responsible simply to wait until people start dying so that others will take notice.

b. Police have been arresting women who prostitute in a neighborhood with a high rate of drug dealing. During the booking process, they often confiscate unused needles and bleach kits as evidence of possession of illicit drugs before returning the women to the street. A group of women is outraged because the police seem to be thwarting their efforts to encourage safer drug use within their community. Police contend that they are just enforcing the laws. The women consult you, a harm reduction outreach worker, for help.

c. You are planning to develop a group home for people recovering from AODAs. When neighbors of the group home find out that you are planning to bring "addicts" into their community, they start a campaign to block your plans, contacting city officials, zoning authorities, school administrators, and the taxpayer's association. You do not currently have many organizations supporting your home or responding to the complaints of the "Keep Our Neighborhood Straight and Sober" campaign. Potential clients might support you, but it could be difficult for them to form a coalition given their current AODA problems.

d. A local chapter of Blind Persons, Friends, and Family is concerned that none of the drug treatment programs in the community have any accommodations or materials for Blind clients. They are reluctant to start legal action under the Americans with Disabilities Act and would rather find a collaborative way to help programs make required changes (instead of forcing them into changes through legal action). Typical responses from programs that are asked about access for Blind people include, "We've never had any Blind clients, so it is not a problem," or "We have a limited budget and cannot please everybody."

e. Social workers in Minneapolis have discovered that many of their Somali American clients are using a substance called "khat," a leaf that includes an amphetamine. Some of these clients report that they use it so that they can "talk more easily." The social workers are concerned that khat produces a severe depression, but they do not know what the real dangers are.

# Working With Diverse Communities

Two approaches for gaining knowledge that will raise your competence when working with diverse communities include gleaning knowledge from scholarly literature and gathering knowledge directly from people within the community. Many AODA textbooks now include a section on working with diverse community groups, such as Native Americans, African Americans, Latinos, Asian Americans, women, the elderly, and people with disabilities. These sections should be treated as beginning points for cultural competence rather than comprehensive knowledge bases or complete recipes for how to deal with particular diversity groups. The first exercise below contains review questions to test your knowledge of diversity issues according to information in basic addictions textbooks. The next exercise goes beyond gathering information from textbooks and introduces an ethnographic approach to building a localized diversity knowledge base. It is designed to help you distinguish between popular myths and stereotypes, personal attitudes and beliefs, global empirical information, and localized ethnographic knowledge (Green, 1999).

## Review Questions on Diverse Communities

The following questions are based on reported research on AODA concerns within diverse communities.

1. When designing an AOD prevention program with an African American community, a social worker should consider:
   a. Many African Americans choose to drink because liquor and its distributors are readily available in the community.
   b. There are substantially different attitudes toward drinking among African Americans.
   c. Many African Americans drink out of economic frustration, such as unemployment and economic deprivation.
   d. Alcoholism is often tolerated as a stress reducer for African Americans, given the pain associated with the African American experience.
   e. All of the above.

2. African Americans have twice the rate of cirrhosis as Whites, in spite of the fact that:
   a. The rates of cirrhosis among African Americans have dropped dramatically since World War II.
   b. There are no overall differences in rates of alcohol-related psychiatric disorders.
   c. African Americans have higher rates of substance use disorders than Whites.
   d. African Americans have longer life spans than Whites.
   e. All of the above.
3. Special AOD programs for African Americans have been argued for because:
   a. The experiences of African Americans differ from those of Whites.
   b. Social services controlled by Whites may be viewed as racist.
   c. Generic AOD services that emphasize the here-and-now experience deny African Americans' historical experiences of discrimination.
   d. African Americans may prefer a sense of ownership of their programs.
   e. All of the above.
4. Literature on AOD services for African Americans suggest that intervention should:
   a. Teach clients that alcoholism is a sign of weakness in the African American community, so it needs to be eradicated.
   b. Use the DSM to teach clients that alcoholism is a pathological disease.
   c. Show African Americans that they can be supermen and superwomen who can endure pain without the need for alcohol.
   d. Emphasize strengths rather than deficits.
   e. None of the above.
5. When developing an AOD program for African American males, a social worker should consider:
   a. Discouraging interaction between clients outside of treatment so that they do not create a bad influence on one another.
   b. Using group work to reduce isolation and increase connectedness.
   c. Avoiding cultural language (such as hip-hop expressions), because these are associated with illicit substance abuse and trafficking.
   d. Not using male/female coleaders for groups because this will create sexual anxiety.
   e. None of the above.
6. Some research indicates African Americans tend to be "polar" in their use of alcohol, meaning that:
   a. They tend to either abstain completely or drink heavily.
   b. They only drink when they are manic-depressive.
   c. They tend to drink more alcohol the closer they are to the North or South Pole.
   d. They tend to drink during the week rather than on the weekends for relaxation or celebration.
   e. Going to bars is socially unacceptable within this group.
7. AOD risk factors linked with the African American population include:
   a. Economic deprivation.
   b. Racism.
   c. Stress (including failure to achieve dreams).
   d. Availability of AODs.
   e. All of the above.

8. Absence of alcohol-related problems in the African American population has been positively correlated with:
   a. Good performance in school.
   b. History of multiple criminal arrests.
   c. Early drug experimentation.
   d. Divorce or other instability in family background.
   e. All of the above.

9. When assessing a Native American youth for alcohol-related concerns, it is important for a non-Native social worker to:
   a. Pretend that the Biopsychosocial Model is the same as the Medicine Wheel.
   b. Go into the sweat lodge with the client.
   c. Examine the family's view toward alcoholism.
   d. Pray for the client in accordance with Native American spirituality.
   e. All of the above.

10. A Native American talking circle fits well with the concept of harm reduction philosophy because:
    a. Native American traditions do not allow for an alcohol-free lifestyle.
    b. It provides an opportunity for community members to express their feelings and opinions about how AODAs have affected the community and how to manage AODA problems as a community.
    c. Talking circles discourage the community from trying to reach a consensus.
    d. Native Americans tend to benefit most from individual counseling.
    e. Native Americans are motivated best through direct confrontation by the group.

11. An example of a sociological factor associated with greater risk of AODA problems among Native American youth is:
    a. Lack of spirituality.
    b. Experimental substance use as an expression of age-related rebelliousness.
    c. Poor nutrition.
    d. Genetic predisposition.
    e. Depression.

12. Some Native American groups have being fighting for the right to use peyote (a hallucinogenic drug) legally, so that they can use it:
    a. As a chemical treatment for alcohol dependency.
    b. As part of religious rituals.
    c. To lure non-Natives into submission.
    d. To ease the risk of infant mortality from FAS.
    e. None of the above.

13. A biological explanation for problems with alcoholism within the Native American community is that:
    a. Native Americans were not using alcohol prior to its introduction by Europeans within the last 500 years, so they do not have social norms for use.
    b. On average, Native Americans metabolize alcohol differently from other ethnic groups, although the genetic factors vary significantly within this population.
    c. Native Americans have been exposed to extreme oppression, so that alcoholism is a normal reaction.
    d. Alcoholism is learned as a behavior from early childhood.
    e. All of the above.

14. People living with AIDS must be careful about AOD use because:
    a. Using AODs might lead them to engage in unsafe sexual practices.
    b. Sharing needles for AOD use is a high-risk behavior.
    c. If a person has HIV, AOD use might further depress the immune system.
    d. All of the above.
    e. None of the above.
15. Higher rates of suicide attempts and certain types of problem drug use among some groups of gay men and lesbians are correlated with:
    a. Genetic weaknesses that are more common to homosexuals.
    b. Moral deviance among gay men and lesbians.
    c. Coping with stress in a society that discriminates against gay men and lesbians.
    d. Greater creativity among gay men and lesbians.
    e. The fact that homosexuality is a disease.
16. One of the primary problems with studies that explore the incidence of AODAs among lesbians and gay men is:
    a. Incidence studies serve no purpose because AODA prevention programs should target all people, regardless of sexual orientation.
    b. There are no control groups.
    c. The number of gays and lesbians is too small to study.
    d. Use of AODs among lesbians and gays is too small to study.
    e. Samples are often drawn from gay or lesbian associations, bars, or other social settings that may not represent the entire gay and lesbian population.
17. Research comparing the incidence of AOD use among lesbians, bisexuals, and gay men (LBGs) with that of heterosexuals indicates:
    a. AOD use among LBGs is similar to that of heterosexuals.
    b. AOD use among LBGs is greater than that of heterosexuals.
    c. AOD use among LBGs is lower than that of heterosexuals.
    d. AOD use is higher among gay men, but lower for lesbians than heterosexuals.
    e. More conclusive research is needed, though numbers of LBG clients seeking help for AOD problems is sufficiently high enough to warrant knowledge of LBG populations for all addictions professionals.
18. A lesbian client comes to you for help with an alcohol problem. Using a functional approach with her, you:
    a. Tell her the risks of alcohol abuse.
    b. Focus on reducing the harms related to alcohol abuse.
    c. Explain how her metabolism is different from that of a heterosexual woman.
    d. Ask about the positive uses of alcohol (e.g., whether it reduces her anxieties associated with coping with homophobia).
    e. Invite her to talk about the traumatic events in her life.
19. Studies on the relationship between "outness" and AOD problems suggest:
    a. Gays and lesbians need to be out before they can become sober.
    b. Becoming sober helps gays and lesbians accept their sexual orientation.
    c. The more out a gay man or lesbian is, the more severe the AOD problem.
    d. Internalizing an alcoholic identity is inconsistent with identifying as gay or lesbian.
    e. None of the above.

20. When doing AOD work with gays or lesbians, it is important to ask about culture because:
    a. All cultures stigmatize gays and lesbians.
    b. All religions say that homosexuality is an abomination.
    c. Cultural communities are always a positive source of support.
    d. Different cultures have different views on sexual orientation that can either contribute to or help alleviate AOD problems.
    e. All of the above.

21. A lesbian client who is physically dependent on alcohol presents in a state of crisis, thinking that her parents might have found out she is lesbian. She is very concerned about their reaction, believing that they will reject her. By the end of the meeting, you assess that she is at low risk of suicide, but want to ensure that she is safe. In order to ensure her safety:
    a. You advise her to avoid being a lesbian for the next 24 hours.
    b. You suggest that she come out to her family so that they can keep an eye on her.
    c. You have a legal obligation to commit her to a psychiatric facility because lesbians have a high rate of suicide.
    d. You help her identify a support system, which may include friends from the lesbian community who can be with her through the period of crisis.
    e. You refer her to a physician who can prescribe her Antabuse.

22. Incidence studies comparing drug use among different ethnocultural and religious groups suggest that:
    a. Jewish people have a higher rate of illicit drug abuse than the general population.
    b. Jewish people have a higher rate of alcohol abuse than the general population.
    c. Jewish people have a higher rate of prescription drug abuse than the general population.
    d. Jewish people have a higher rate of inhalant abuse than the general population.
    e. None of the above.

23. When working with religious Jews, AODA programs should consider:
    a. Scheduling meetings so that they do not conflict with the Sabbath or holidays.
    b. Offering kosher meals.
    c. Holding self-help groups in synagogues.
    d. Emphasizing that surrendering power in AA need not be associated with the Holocaust and that surrender is to God or to oneself.
    e. All of the above.

24. Research suggests that the following factors may help Jews, particularly Orthodox Jews, avoid alcohol problems:
    a. Jews tend to believe that they are not susceptible to alcohol problems.
    b. Jews tend to drink moderately, mostly while eating, and teach these practices to their children.
    c. Jews include ritualistic drinking during religious observances.
    d. Rather than rationalize excessive drinking, Jews tend to avoid drinking too much by practices such as nursing a single drink at a party.
    e. All of the above.

25. Regardless of ethnic groups, women:
    a. Use more alcohol than men.
    b. Who abuse alcohol tend to be stigmatized more than men who abuse alcohol.
    c. Have higher rates of completed suicides than men.

d. Use more illicit drugs than men.

e. All of the above.

26. A structuralist or radical feminist explanation of drug abuse among minority groups (including women) suggests that:

a. AOD use among politicians contributes to the high level of fraud in government.

b. Minorities have a genetic predisposition to drug use.

c. The majority makes drugs available to minority groups to make them more powerless.

d. Minorities with addictions are responsible for their social condition and need to take responsibility for making changes.

e. Women have a certain personality type that makes them less prone to AOD addiction.

27. Although Latin Americans are reported to underutilize health and mental health services, Mexican Americans have been found to use alcoholism services at higher rates than their representation in the population. This can be explained by the fact that:

a. Mexican Americans have fewer stigmas about treatment than other Latin Americans.

b. More of the Mexican Americans in alcohol programs have been admitted involuntarily.

c. Mexican Americans who have alcohol problems are less likely to have depression or other mental health problems.

d. Mexican Americans are entitled to free alcoholism services under a U.S.-Mexico treaty.

e. All of the above.

28. Some experts suggest that psychoeducational groups for Latin American clients be offered for men and women together. The reason for this is that:

a. Men might perceive women-only groups as a threat to family cohesion.

b. Women can learn a sense of respect (*respeto*) from the men.

c. Women are more likely to vent anger when men are present.

d. Punishment and wearing signs is more effective when both sexes are present.

e. All of the above.

29. Growing up in Catholic communities, some Latin American women are encouraged to emulate the Virgin Mary through self-sacrifice and suffering. If an AODA social worker thinks that this type of belief is causing the client to suffer, the social worker should:

a. Show that she or he values the client's religion by reinforcing the need for the client to accept suffering.

b. Advise the client that research has shown that self-sacrifice contributes to substance abuse, low self-esteem, and potentially suicide.

c. Reframe carefully, encouraging the client to see Mary in a feminist light that emphasizes her strengths and independent characteristics.

d. Tell the client to accept that she is powerless.

e. All of the above.

30. You are designing an AODA treatment program for Latin American men. One of the main challenges that you will need to address is:

a. Public disclosure of personal problems is generally unacceptable for Latin men and can result in feelings of emasculation.

b. Latin men tend to take a passive role.

c. Latin men believe that abstinence is the only way to express machismo.

d. Latin men view the staggering drunk (*borrachero*) as a positive role model.

e. None of the above.

31. AODA risk factors common to Latin Americans include:
    a. Stresses of acculturation.
    b. Language barriers.
    c. Dropping out of school.
    d. Exposure to AODAs among family members.
    e. All of the above.

32. When working with Latin AODA clients, involving extended family in the helping process is often desirable because:
    a. The goal of treatment with Latin clients is to increase their codependency.
    b. Family support is important with Latin clients, and family members may resist individual changes, particularly if they are not involved in the therapeutic process.
    c. The social worker can educate the whole family about how to give up their old Latin ways and take on the more appropriate ways of mainstream American culture.
    d. Latin families tend to have higher rates of depression after an individual has gone for AODA treatment.
    e. All of the above.

33. Within Asian cultures where there is a strong sense of shame, access to AODA services can be improved by setting up services in a manner that allow clients to:
    a. Ridicule others.
    b. Save face.
    c. Challenge their parents or other authority figures.
    d. Reject their cultural traditions.
    e. Display their AODA behavior in front of a public audience.

34. A Japanese American man brings his mother in to see a social worker because she is addicted to Valium. If the mother has traditional Japanese values, the mother is most likely to:
    a. Express pride that her son is looking out for her mental health.
    b. Feel angry that her son has betrayed her.
    c. Share her emotions by yelling or hitting her son in front of the social worker.
    d. Ask for a quick fix, such as a prescription for marijuana as a replacement for Valium.
    e. Confront the social worker by questioning the social worker's credentials.

35. Culturally based models of AODA treatment for Asian-Pacific Islanders include:
    a. Using elders or native healers.
    b. Acupuncture.
    c. Affirmation of cultural identity and differences.
    d. All of the above.
    e. None of the above.

36. Asian American youth may be at particular risk of AODA problems when they experience anomie, which tends to occur as a result of:
    a. Breakdown of the traditional family structure when the children challenge the obedience that is expected by their parents.
    b. Complying with traditional authoritarian family structures.
    c. Holding onto traditional Buddhist, Islamic, or Hindu beliefs.

    d. Learning English.

    e. All of the above.

37. In Cambodia, Cambodians tend to use alcohol, herbs, and drugs in moderation. Cambodian immigrants to America tend to have greater problems with these substances if they have experienced:

    a. Stress from war, persecution, or torture.

    b. Smooth adjustment processes when they adapted to American culture.

    c. Medically prescribed drugs in their country of origin.

    d. All of the above.

    e. None of the above.

38. Some AODA scholars argue that the effects of being in a particular ethnocultural group cannot be separated from the effects of social class. An example illustrating this point would be:

    a. Deviant behavior is higher among the White population than the Asian population, so one would expect higher AODA rates among Whites.

    b. Higher rates of certain AODA problems in the African American population could be attributed to a higher percentage of the population living in poverty, which is not simply a race issue.

    c. Crack is more available in poor communities than in rich communities.

    d. Racial injustice leads to stress, which leads to substance abuse.

    e. Immigrants who integrate well into society tend to have fewer AODA problems.

39. When considering differences in AOD use and abuse patterns in different cultural groups, it is important for social workers to remember that:

    a. Patterns within the groups may vary depending on the level of acculturation.

    b. Patterns within the groups may vary depending on diversity factors, such as socioeconomic status, gender, age, or sexual orientation.

    c. Patterns within the groups may vary depending on individual differences.

    d. As social workers, we must be aware of our own culturally determined attitudes, as we look at other cultures through our own cultural lenses.

    e. All of the above.

# An Ethnographic Approach to Working With Diverse Communities

The quiz above focuses on information from research and textbooks. Although such information can be useful, social workers must be careful about how to use this information because it may not apply to specific communities or individuals within those communities. The following exercise will help you practice an ethnographic approach that can be used to identify the unique characteristics of specific communities and individuals within those communities. Use the following steps to guide you through a process of ethnographic interviewing. This will help you develop a localized knowledge base concerning a particular diversity group and its relationship with AODAs (for more information about this approach, see Green, 1999).

1. **Identify a specific sociocultural community or subgroup** from your region about which you would like to learn more (e.g., Orthodox Jewish, Pakistani Moslem, Irish Catholic, Haitian, Navajo, Korean, Texan, Deaf, transgender, lesbian, or economically destitute people).

2. Write down your **first impressions** of how you think this community deals with AODAs (do not think, just write what quickly comes to mind).

3. What **stereotypes** regarding AODAs exist for this community (consider images portrayed in popular media such as movies, novels, television shows, advertising, Web sites, and newspapers)?

4. What do your primary textbook and at least one other scholarly article or chapter report about this group's experiences with AODAs? Summarize key themes under each of the following headings:
   ◇    Strengths/resiliencies of the group

   ◇    Cultural attitudes toward AOD use and addictions

   ◇    Special concerns regarding AODAs within this group

◇     Suggestions for social workers working with this community on AODA issues

5.     Identify a cultural guide or interpreter who can provide you with local information about this group and its experiences with AODAs (that is, a person who has in-depth experience with the group, such as a social worker who specializes in working with the group and perhaps is a member of this group). Ask for permission to interview this person and take notes or tape-record the meeting. Use the following techniques of ethnographic interviewing:
   ◇     Demonstrating interest in learning and care for improving your ability to serve this community (acting as an "appreciative learner" or an "ignorant but concerned professional").
   ◇     Inquiring about the strengths and resiliencies of the group in relation to AODAs.
   ◇     Asking open-ended questions to explore AODA attitudes or the meaning that this community gives to issues such as alcohol and drug use, addiction, recovery, and use of professional help.
   ◇     Asking open-ended questions to explore special concerns or problems faced by the community in relation to AODAs.
   ◇     Asking open-ended questions to solicit suggestions for you as a social worker if you wanted to help this community in relation to AODAs.
   ◇     Checking out possible myths, biases, or stereotypes from your personal beliefs, popular stereotypes, or the scholarly literature you have read.
6.     Write up your findings, including similarities and differences among what you learned from comparing your own attitudes with popular stereotypes, information from scholarly literature, and your ethnographic interview. [6 to 8 pages]

**Evaluation** will be based on: selection of relevant, scholarly literature; identification of specific diversity characteristics and how they relate to AODA problems within a particular community; and identification of specific similarities and differences between what you learned from the ethnographic interview and what you identified as your own attitudes, popular stereotypes, and information from the literature.

# Applying AODA Knowledge to Community Situations

Although community workers make use of knowledge from community members, they should also make sure that they apply knowledge from research and scholarly literature. Review each of the vignettes presented below and draw from your knowledge of AODAs to answer the following questions:

1. Looking at AODA literature, what are the key risks raised by the type of AOD use described in the vignette?
2. Based on what you have learned this term, how would you explain the root causes of this pattern of alcohol use in the community? How would you analyze the causes from a Moral Model? A Psychological Model? An Ecological Model? A Sociocultural Model?
3. What does each of these models suggest in terms of appropriate forms of prevention or intervention? Of these approaches, which approach would you suggest to the community group? What are your reasons for favoring this approach? Consider: If the strategy is aimed at prohibiting alcohol, what might happen to other types of substance abuse in the community?

## Vignette 1—Tampona Beach Spring Break

Over the last 3 years, Tampona Beach has become known for "spring break," a time when university students from all over the country descend upon this otherwise dowdy town for a week of partying, drinking, loud music, and letting loose. During spring break, bars are filled to capacity, tax revenues from liquor sales escalate 90 percent over the annual average, professional prostitutes from all over North America set up shop in Tampona, and hotel revenues double. While some townsfolk are thrilled with the economic prosperity and fun, others are concerned about possible risks, including spread of HIV, unwanted pregnancies, violent crime, and depressed property values. The concerned citizens approach you, a local expert on AODAs, to advise them of the real risks of hosting an annual alcohol-drenched party for university students.

## Vignette 2—Boomtown Diana

Diana is an isolated mining town of about 3,500 people in West Virginia. Prospectors discovered diamonds in the area about 4 years ago. Within 2 years, the population boomed from about 2,300 to 9,700. Most of the growth was from people involved in the diamond exploration industry. About 80 percent of the new arrivals were men. A few months ago, the diamond bubble burst. Government officials discovered that the diamond potential in the area was far below original expectations. Rumors spread that the whole discovery was a hoax created by a small mining company that walked away from the project just before the truth became known. About 12 Diana residents became multimillionaires, selling their shares of the company before they took a dive. The vast majority of Diana residents have suffered in the process—either buying stocks, houses, or other businesses in the area when prices were high, and being left with little or nothing when the bubble burst.

Prior to the boom, Diana was a sleepy little town with few social problems. With rapid growth came problems such as overcrowding, slum apartments, gambling, alcohol abuse, and drug trafficking. When people were working, they had lots of money and little to do with it other than becoming involved with the aforementioned vices. Now, the money has dried up, but the problems remain. People who could afford to leave have left the town. Unemployment is high, but many others have no place else to go.

Diana has few social services. There are only three professional social workers, one doctor, one psychologist, and two nurses working in the area. A needs assessment indicates that alcoholism is at an epidemic level, with perhaps as many as 20 percent of youth and 35 percent of adults using cocaine or barbiturates on a daily basis. Within the past month, four youth and eight adults have committed suicide. Three of those were intoxicated with barbiturates in what looked to be an intentional car crash. Two used rat poison. One overdosed on cocaine. The other suicides might not be directly drug-related. Your social service agency asks you to work with the community to develop a strategy to deal with these social problems. One of your first steps is to help them understand the dynamics of the AODA issues.

# Ethics Discussion Questions

Now that we have explored how to identify community needs, how to engage communities, how to work with diverse communities, and how to apply AODA knowledge to social issues within communities, it is time to consider ethical issues that can arise when helping communities change. The following discussion questions are based on the previous two vignettes.

1.  A group from Ignatieff Residence for Seniors (IRS) in Tampona asks you, a community worker, to help them develop a coalition that would advocate prohibition of university students in their town. Your spouse owns a local hotel and tavern, which benefits from the spring break revelry. Personally, you believe that spring break needs to be toned down but not outlawed altogether. Although you believe in client self-determination, you would like the residents of IRS to see the benefits of spring break. Does the fact that your spouse runs a hotel and tavern mean that you have a conflict of interest? How do you deal with their request for assistance?

2.  As a community worker for the town of Diana, you begin to work with a coalition to "Save Diana." The members of Save Diana start to take moralistic and pathological views of the people who are using cocaine and barbiturates. They say that these people are either lazy or sick and that if they'd only take responsibility for themselves, they could turn their lives around. They begin to advocate tough laws and legal enforcement for possession and trafficking. You view the problems from an ecosystems approach, noting the relationship between AODA problems and stresses in the social environment of Diana (including unemployment, unsuitable housing, and being duped by the diamond companies). When you try to explain this, Save Diana members reject your views as naive and ask, "Are you with us or against us?" Does client self-determination include the right to discriminate or the right to advocate moralistic views against people with AODA problems? Does Save Diana have a right to your help in a campaign for "zero tolerance," even if you view their chances of succeeding as futile?

# Journaling Exercise

1. When learning about other cultures or communities and their views of AODAs, what did you learn about your own culture and community, including its views of AODAs?

2. What are your strengths and learning needs in relation to community work with AODA issues? Consider the following: self-awareness, ability to avoid imposing values or beliefs on others, planning and organizational skills, public speaking skills, ethnographic interviewing skills, advocacy skills, knowledge of specific diversity groups (identify one or two groups that you would like to know more about), and knowledge of theories for community change.

# InfoTrac College Edition

## Key words

◇ Community Development (or enhancement)
◇ Diversity (culture, sexual orientation, religion, Latin American, Native American, Jewish, Black, Asian, Pacific Islander, or names of other specific groups)
◇ Social Action

CHAPTER

# 9

~~~

# Health Promotion and Public Policy Development

Health promotion and public policy development in the field of AODAs cover a broad range of possibilities for prevention and intervention. This chapter begins with a subsection designed to help you understand how different policies fit with different models and theories, as well as strategies that focus your change efforts on different targets. The second subsection provides an exercise on how to apply a strategic problem-solving process in order to assess and plan how to create policy that deals with specific AODA issues. The following three subsections offer different approaches to analyzing AODA prevention strategies and policies. To help you review your understanding of AODA policy issues, the next subsection provides a multiple-choice quiz. The final two subsections of this chapter supply you with ethical dilemmas and journaling exercises for reflective purposes.

## Matching Programs

Refer back to Figure 3.1 in Chapter 3 (page 67) for a description of AODA theories and models of helping. For each of the following Prevention Programs, identify the models or theories that fit with the program, explaining how they fit with that program. Also, given your readings, explain the advantages and disadvantages of each Prevention Program.

| Description of Prevention Program | Models or theories that fit this program, and explanation of how | Advantages of this type of program | Disadvantages of this type of program |
|---|---|---|---|
| Example: Providing bleach kits to intravenous drug users to reduce risk of transmission of HIV/AIDS | *1. Harm Reduction Model: focuses on reducing risk of transmission of HIV rather than reducing drug use* <br> *2. Behavior Theory: teaches behavioral skills for using bleach kits rather than focusing on emotions, subconscious conflict, etc.* | *1. Starts with client (fits with SW ethic of self-determination)* <br> *2. Immediately decreases risk of HIV transmission* <br> *3. Could build trust and open up opportunities for work on other AODA issues* | *1. Might be perceived as condoning IV drug use* <br> *2. Does not deal with underlying problems related to the substance abuse* <br> *3. Not using IV drugs at all is safer than using IV drugs and using bleach kits* |
| Increasing taxes on cigarettes to reduce the number of new users, particularly among youth | | | |
| Including information on the risks of drinking and driving as part of driver education classes | | | *(continued)* |

| Description of Prevention Program | Models or theories that fit this program, and explanation of how | Advantages of this type of program | Disadvantages of this type of program |
|---|---|---|---|
| Providing public funding for nicotine patches to help people stop smoking | | | |
| Banning advertising of cigarettes, cigars, or nicotine | | | |
| Changing laws so diet pills that are currently available over the counter would require medical prescriptions | | | |

*(continued)*

| Description of Prevention Program | Models or theories that fit this program, and explanation of how | Advantages of this type of program | Disadvantages of this type of program |
|---|---|---|---|
| Providing an adult-mentoring system for children who are having difficulties at school, a risk factor for illicit drug abuse | | | |
| Helping a business find ways to reduce stress for employees so that they do not self-medicate with alcohol | | | |
| Providing a course on building self-esteem for survivors of sexual assault who might otherwise use depressants to block painful memories | | | |

AODA Prevention Programs can target four components, each with a range of subcomponents (the following are derived in part from Addiction Research Foundation, 1986):

1. The Person—(a) knowledge, (b) attitudes, (c) motivations, (d) skills, (e) self-efficacy
2. The Substance—(a) pricing/taxing, (b) competition, (c) labeling, (d) packaging (size, child-proof caps), (e) composition (including strength), (f) form (pill, liquid for swallowing, injectable, patch), (g) volume or quantity
3. The Environment—(a) advertising, (b) availability, (c) physical context, (d) socio-cultural context, (e) key influencers, (f) institutions (schools, workplaces), (g) legal sanctions
4. The interaction between the Person, Substance, and/or Environment—(a) goodness of fit (support/dissupport), (b) stress, (c) adaptation

For each of the following community problems, identify four possible Prevention Programs that target different components and subcomponents. In parentheses, include which subcomponent(s) your program targets according to the list above. Be creative so that the examples for each identified problem are significantly different. For other examples of Prevention Programs, see Prevention Online at http://www.health.org.

| Identified problem | Program targeting person | Program targeting substance | Program targeting enviornment | Program targeting interaction |
|---|---|---|---|---|
| Example: The percentage of children born with Fetal Alcohol Effects has been rising | *When women go to a medical office for prenatal care, ensure that they are provided with information about the risks of alcohol for their baby (knowledge) and offer skills training to help them cope with stress other than by drinking alcohol (1a; 1d).* | *Require all liquor packaging to include a warning label, in big print, about the risks of alcohol for a fetus (2c).* | *Work with the community to develop awareness about the risks of alcohol to a fetus and the supportive manner that they can use to confront pregnant women about drinking (3c).* | *Ensure that restaurants identify food items that contain alcohol and educate staff to look for these identifications, particularly if a female customer is pregnant (4a).* |

| Identified Problem | Program targeting person | Program targeting substance | Program targeting enviornment | Program targeting interaction |
|---|---|---|---|---|
| Elder clients in a nursing home have become compulsive Web surfers, sometimes foregoing food, sleep, and social events in order to surf. | | | | |
| Children taking Ritalin for Attention Deficit Disorder have been cutting their pills in half and selling some of them to classmates. | | | | |
| An airline company has had two recent accidents involving pilots who were drinking alcohol. | | | | *(continued)* |

| Identified Problem | Program targeting person | Program targeting substance | Program targeting enviornment | Program targeting interaction |
|---|---|---|---|---|
| In recent months, several Rastafarians from Jamaica have been charged with possession of marijuana, creating a huge conflict between police and the Jamaican American community. | | | | |
| Current research shows a high correlation between alcohol use and family violence. | | | | |

## Planning and Presenting a Prevention Program

Now that you have had a chance to consider a range of Prevention Programs, it is time to focus on how to develop a particular program. The purpose of this exercise is to give you opportunities to conceptualize and present AODA Prevention Programs or community strategies. Individually or in small groups, prepare a 20-minute presentation for the class (using audiovisual aids such as transparencies, flipcharts, or PowerPoint) based upon one of the ensuing scenarios and these questions to guide your problem-solving process:

1. What is the nature of the problem? (Assess the client's needs, making sure that the assessment is not biased by stereotypes or misinformation about the nature of AODAs; see Chapter 5 for a refresher on needs assessments.)

2. What information is needed to understand the problem? (Gather and analyze data using what you have learned about AODAs throughout this manual.)
3. What are our priorities? (Select the focus of the problem; provide rationale about why this is a priority, taking urgency, feasibility, and political motivation into account.)
4. What is the range of prevention and intervention strategies? What are the advantages and disadvantages of each? (Consider at least three options.)
5. Which strategy (or combination) is the best? (Determine the preferred strategy in light of your theoretical model, social work values, and clinical effectiveness.)
6. What are the specific goals and objectives? (Identify criteria to evaluate and determine success, such as lowered rates of particular behaviors or enhanced social functioning in areas related to the assessed needs.)
7. What activities are necessary for implementing the plan? (Determine who does what; remember that initiators of successful AODA Prevention Programs tend to work with several systems—health, mental health, education, law, social services, recreation, workplace, business sector, community groups, and spiritual-religious organizations.)

When working through this exercise, consider the "conceptual framework for preventive action," including your theoretical framework (e.g., Disease Concept, Behavioral, Family Systems, Ecological Model—see Chapter 3 for a refresher), and the focus of the prevention strategy (e.g., person, drug, environment, or interaction among them). Following the presentation, members of the class will ask questions for clarification (e.g., asking the presenters to explain certain professional terms in plain language; asking how the strategies fit with the theoretical perspectives and the identified needs).

## Scenario 1: Children on Grass

Parents in the community of Potville are concerned about drug use by their children. They have no real proof that their children are using drugs, but many parents believe that marijuana use is an increasing problem at Potville Elementary School. Suspicious parents claim they have seen children playing with cigarette rolling paper and syringes. They have noticed that their children have been "disappearing" for hours at a time during the evenings. When the children return home, they are exhausted. The children deny using drugs. They say that they are merely tired because they are playing Capture the Flag in the woods.

One group of parents is concerned that a boy named Ricardo may be responsible for bringing marijuana to Potville. Ricardo and his family moved here from Puerto Rico. He has quickly become very popular with the children. He seems to be hyper and incredibly streetwise for a 13-year-old. Another group of parents has suggested an advertising campaign called "Keep Off the Grass," believing that marijuana is a Gateway Drug to stronger and more dangerous drugs. A third group believes in zero tolerance, meaning that children caught with pot at school should be permanently expelled.

## Scenario 2: Steroid U

Steroid use at Anabolic State University (ASU) is at epidemic levels. Members of various varsity sports teams, as well as students in physical education (kinesiology), are using steroids to enhance their performance. Some researchers suggest that the reasons for increased use are related to the competitive nature of sports. Others believe that students are using the steroids to enhance their appearance. Steroids do help people build body mass in shorter time periods. They also help athletes involved in sports that require sudden bursts of power. Steroid use seems particularly common on the baseball team.

Risks of steroid use include cancer, impotence, and aggressive behavior. Some people are worried about the risk to the image of sports and the money that athletes can make. Libertarians on campus suggest that people should be able to make decisions for themselves, including the use of steroids. They believe that people should be offered harm-reduction information, such as knowing which steroids are least risky and how to moderate use to reduce risks of impotency. Conservatives suggest that ASU needs tough laws and tough penalties, "One strike and you're out" of the university. You have been selected to head the "Doping Committee" for ASU. As such, you are responsible for developing a strategy to deal with the concerns cited above.

## Scenario 3: Bingo Addictions

The local church in Bigtown, population 36,803, has been running a bingo fundraiser for the past 84 years. It has become a tradition. Townsfolk flock to the bingo hall in hopes of winning one of the big prizes—a weekend vacation at the Alehouse Hotel on Smokey Lake or a super deluxe bread maker. Until recently, no one ever thought that bingo was a problem. However, bingo has gone from one night a week to six nights a week. The church wanted to raise more money and people seemed to really enjoy playing.

Since the increase in game nights, community agencies have started to notice a rise in certain social problems: more families using the food bank, more cases of child neglect being reported, fights among bingo players requiring police intervention, and loud bingo players disrupting the peace of Bigtown after 10:00 p.m. The church decides to hire a group of social workers to help them work out a strategy to deal with the bingo problems. The church hierarchy does not want to give up the bingo fundraiser. In fact, the church has become dependent on it for its economic survival. Church leaders believe bingo is a valued sociocultural norm within the church, providing entertainment, hope, and camaraderie, particularly for seniors.

## Scenario 4: Profs on Pills

In another situation at Anabolic State University, the administration has recently cut the number of days that professors are allotted to mark final papers and exams. Ostensibly, this was done to allow students to get their grades and convocate early. The increased stress and pressure has had a profound effect: profs have been using uppers to help them grade more papers in less time. The uppers allow profs to mark both faster and for longer stretches of time. They do not have to sleep as much. Anyhow, they have all summer to sleep. In the fall, ASU could do a random drug test.

Some students see this as no problem. Others think that the uppers are causing grade inflation: profs are not only marking faster and longer, but higher. This may seem like a benefit to students, but some are concerned that grades are becoming a joke. As word spreads, the image of ASU will also suffer. Already, a national cable news station is doing a documentary on the pill-popping profs at ASU. One expert suggested that ASU regulate use rather than prohibit it, asking each professor to sign up for amphetamines at the end of each term so they can be monitored by nurses and other medical staff. ASU creates a committee to look into these problems and develop a strategy.

# Myth, Fact, or Mixed Evidence?

One of the problems with many prevention strategies and policies is that they are based on faulty information, faulty beliefs, or faulty thinking. For example, Nancy Reagan's "Just Say No" campaign in the 1980s was based on the belief that drug use is a voluntary choice and children just need to be taught how to say no to this choice. While this may have been true for some people, this program was not effective with the people whose AOD use was most problematic, for instance, people already dependent on AODs and people using AODs to cope with considerable stress in their lives (e.g., a person who is physically dependent on heroin cannot simply give up heroin by "just saying no," and a person who is using alcohol to cope with being molested by a parent is not going to be motivated to stop drinking simply because there is a "Just Say No" media campaign). For each of the following statements, identify whether the information, belief, and reasoning are valid. Provide your rationale and cite your references.

| Statement to be analyzed | Myth, fact, or mixed evidence? Explain | Reference(s) |
|---|---|---|
| Harsher criminal penalties and stricter policing significantly reduce illicit drug use. | | |
| Most people in jail are there because of drug-related crimes. | | *(continued)* |

| Statement to be analyzed | Myth, fact, or mixed evidence? Explain | Reference(s) |
| --- | --- | --- |
| Legalization of heroin use would encourage more heroin-addicted people to seek treatment. | | |
| People are more likely to engage in unsafe sexual practices (putting themselves at risk of contracting HIV and other sexually transmitted diseases) if they are intoxicated on alcohol than if they are sober. | | |
| Reducing poverty will reduce the level of drug use in a community. | | |

*(continued)*

| Statement to be analyzed | Myth, fact, or mixed evidence? Explain | Reference(s) |
|---|---|---|
| Mandatory drug treatment programs are less effective than voluntary treatment programs. | | |
| Teaching children problem-solving skills reduces their risks of developing AOD problems. | | |
| For enforcement of trafficking laws to be effective, police only need to target small, street-level dealers and not organized crime or larger importers and producers. | | *(continued)* |

| Statement to be analyzed | Myth, fact, or mixed evidence? Explain | Reference(s) |
|---|---|---|
| Physicians have a high rate of prescription drug misuse because they can prescribe their own medications. | | |
| Children who perform poorly in school are at higher risk of having AOD problems than children who perform well in school. | | |
| Images of thin women portrayed in the media as the ideal body type have contributed to an increase in the number of women with anorexia, bulimia, and other compulsive eating behaviors. | | |

# Risk, Resilience, and Protective Factors

One way to conceptualize and design health promotion and AODA prevention strategies is to identify risk, resilience, and protective factors, as well as to design policies or programs aimed at reducing risk factors, increasing resilience, or enhancing protective factors. Provide definitions and examples from AODA research for each of the following:

1. *Risk* refers to: _____

    _____

    _____

    Examples of risk factors for AODAs include: _____

    _____

2. *Resilience* refers to: _____

    _____

    _____

    Examples of resilience to AODAs include: _____

    _____

3. *Protective factors* refer to: _____

    _____

    _____

    Examples of protective factors include: _____

    _____

The following exercise is designed to help you apply these concepts to situations that emerge from your Case Profile. Select one person from your Case Profile (e.g., Julia Torres, George, Randy, or Dionne).

1. Identify at least three risk factors that might have led to this person's AODA problems.

2. Identify three aspects of resilience that this person possesses.

3. Identify three protective factors that this person did *not* have that could have helped this person deal more effectively with AODA issues personally or within the family.

4. Given these risks, resiliencies, and protective factors, identify a health promotion or AODA prevention policy that could have helped people like your chosen client avert AODA problems.

# Critiquing Current Policy

Some of the previous exercises ask you to create or develop a health promotion policy or prevention plan. This exercise asks you to consider and analyze a real policy. Identify a current AODA policy that has been developed at the national, state, or municipal level (many policies are available on government Web sites, such as the National Drug Control Policy at http://whitehouse-drugpolicy.gov). Assess and critique the policy according to the following questions.

1. Introduction: What are the key points of the strategy (if the policy contains many different strategies, you can select and focus on an aspect of the policy that interests you)?

2. Rationale: What led to the development of the strategy? (Motivating factors could include reaction to a single incident, fear, public protection, health concerns, economic concerns, or political ideologies.) Who were the prime movers of this strategy?

3. Evidence: What information, theory, research, and assumptions is this policy based on?

4. Costs: What are the costs of implementing this policy, and who will bear these costs (e.g., state government, AOD users, advertisers, medical insurance providers)?

5.    Benefits: What are the proposed benefits, during what time frame, and how will they be evaluated?

6.    Strengths: Based on your research and understanding of AODAs, what are the strengths of this policy (consider effectiveness, ethical appropriateness, fit with needs, and other relevant factors)?

7.    Limitations: Based on your research and understanding of AODAs, what are the limitations of this policy (consider discriminatory impact on different populations, challenges in implementation, and other relevant factors)?

8.    What other policy alternatives, if any, should be considered, and why?

9.    What are your personal reactions to this policy (being aware of your own attitudes, beliefs, and political perspectives—refer back to the Personal Attitudes chart in Chapter 1 to see whether and how your attitudes have changed)?

# Review Questions on Health Promotion and Policy

As you can see from the prior exercises, health promotion and policy in the AODA field can cover a broad range of issues and concerns. The following questions will test your knowledge of various health promotion and policy concepts and strategies.

1.    A community is concerned about the risks to children who might experiment with new drugs. The type of Prevention Program that they could use in order to target this risk is called:
    a.  Primary prevention.
    b.  Secondary prevention.
    c.  Tertiary prevention.
    d.  Synergistic prevention.
    e.  Antecedent prevention.

2. A coalition of professional sex workers advocates for a treatment program that helps AOD-addicted sex workers through a choice of abstinence or controlled use. This program is an example of:
   a. Primary prevention.
   b. Secondary prevention.
   c. Tertiary prevention.
   d. Synergistic prevention.
   e. Antecedent prevention.

3. A church group is concerned that children who experiment with smoking cigarettes might turn to marijuana. An education program aimed at helping these children refrain from marijuana use would be an example of:
   a. Primary prevention.
   b. Secondary prevention.
   c. Tertiary prevention.
   d. Synergistic prevention.
   e. Antecedent prevention.

4. A community is concerned about the transmission of HIV by sex trade workers who use intravenous drugs and have unprotected sex with their clients. One example of a harm reduction approach is to:
   a. Impose zero tolerance on drug use among sex trade workers.
   b. Provide clean needles and condoms, as well as education, to sex trade workers.
   c. Require drug testing for sex trade workers.
   d. Target police enforcement on sex trade workers.
   e. Promote a drug-free lifestyle in newspapers and other media.

5. Public information or advertising has been found to be most effective as an AOD prevention strategy:
   a. When it is used in combination with other prevention strategies.
   b. When it is a simple message such as "Just Say No."
   c. When the audience is general rather than targeted.
   d. When taxes or other restrictions are lowered.
   e. When the information is exaggerated and dishonest, in order to "scare people straight."

6. Alcohol problem prevention through economic means could include:
   a. Providing cheaper insurance to people who use alcohol.
   b. Putting a price cap on the amount that stores can charge for alcohol.
   c. Putting a nasty odor in alcohol to discourage use.
   d. Increasing taxes on alcohol.
   e. None of the above.

7. One of the primary social work criticisms of using policing to prevent AOD problems is that:
   a. Racial profiling by police reinforces the dignity and equality of all groups.
   b. AOD abuse is not caused by people who are bad, but by stresses in their social environment.
   c. Social workers are among the highest users of illicit drugs.
   d. Behavioral strategies are more likely to work if there is a system of punishment rather than a system of rewards.
   e. AOD use is caused by deeply engrained personality disorders that cannot be changed.

8. Drug prevention strategies can include a focus on:
   a. People's knowledge, attitudes, intentions, and skills.
   b. Drug pricing, composition, labeling, and packaging.
   c. Environment, including legal sanctions, advertising, media, sociocultural context, key influencers, and availability.
   d. All of the above.
   e. Only a. and b.

9. An example of a drug prevention strategy through the use of "control" techniques could include:
   a. Providing problem-solving skills training.
   b. Influencing people's attitudes toward drugs by promoting positive role models, such as actors who lead a drug-free lifestyle.
   c. Deporting people who are trafficking illicit drugs.
   d. Offering people methadone by medical prescription as an alternative to purchasing heroin illicitly, on the street.
   e. All of the above.

10. Of the following, the first stage of planning a drug prevention strategy is to:
    a. Develop methods for evaluation of the program.
    b. Assess the needs and nature of the problem.
    c. Determine the best target audience.
    d. Consider various options for solving the problem.
    e. Pass legislation to prohibit the specific type of drug use.

11. A zero tolerance approach to illicit drug use assumes that:
    a. Reducing harm is the most important goal of drug policy.
    b. Individual freedom includes the right to self-destruction.
    c. Drug use is an involuntary act.
    d. Drug problems arise because drugs are readily available.
    e. None of the above.

12. Proponents of decriminalization of cannabis base their position primarily on the argument that:
    a. People should be free to use whatever drugs they want without any risk of penalty from the state.
    b. Penalties for possession of cannabis can be used to deter drug use, but people should not have to be jailed or get a criminal record for simple possession.
    c. Punishment needs to be tougher to deter drug use.
    d. Taxing cannabis would allow the government to raise revenues from drug users.
    e. The government could regulate the strength of cannabis and how it is packaged.

13. Lessons of the Prohibition experience in the United States include:
    a. Government does not have the capacity or will to eradicate the customary demand for alcohol (particularly with an abrupt legislative ban).
    b. When production and sale of alcoholic beverages are outlawed, a criminal supply network emerges.
    c. The rates of problems that vary with consumption can be significantly reduced by substantially increasing real prices and reducing the ease of availability.
    d. All of the above.
    e. None of the above.

14. In order to confront employees with AOD problems, social workers can train supervisors to be alert for the following symptoms of AOD abuse:
    a. Chronic absenteeism.
    b. Lying.
    c. Spasmodic work pace.
    d. All of the above.
    e. There are no identifiable symptoms of AOD abuse, other than to give urine tests to all employees.
15. Workplace AOD programs that focus on early identification can increase chances of recovery because:
    a. The threat of job loss is a significant motivator.
    b. Work is a major cause of AOD abuse.
    c. Moderate drug use in the workplace is preferable to abstinence.
    d. All of the above.
    e. None of the above.
16. Cooperative consultation between AOD researchers and Hollywood producers, writers, and directors resulted in guidelines for television and movies that suggested:
    a. Not glamorizing alcohol use as a sophisticated or adult pastime.
    b. Avoiding the gratuitous showing of alcohol use where other drinks could be easily substituted.
    c. Demonstrating that there are no miraculous recoveries from alcoholism.
    d. All of the above.
    e. None of the above.
17. In the United States, health warnings on alcohol products must include:
    a. Warnings to pregnant women about risk of birth defects.
    b. Warnings about the addictive nature of alcohol.
    c. Warnings that alcohol is associated with intimate partner abuse.
    d. All of the above.
    e. None of the above.
18. Increasing the taxes on cigarettes is most likely to reduce cigarette use among:
    a. New users.
    b. Users who have become physically addicted to nicotine.
    c. Users who have become psychologically addicted to nicotine.
    d. Users who have compulsive personalities.
    e. Users who smoke more than two packs per day.
19. Prevention Programs that provide clean needles to heroin users are designed to:
    a. Discourage illicit heroin use.
    b. Encourage illicit heroin use.
    c. Reduce the risk of spreading hepatitis and other communicable diseases.
    d. Provide users with needles that can filter out the opiates and reduce the risk of overdose.
    e. Give heroin users a method to moderate the use of their drug of choice.

20. A utilitarian approach to prevention policies and strategies suggests that we:
    a. Recognize that the rights of an individual are more important than the rights of the community.
    b. Provide utensils to AOD users to help them stop using.
    c. Must rid our society of AOD users by whatever means possible.
    d. Need to think about the greatest good for the greatest number, and the indirect consequences of AOD abuse may be far greater than generally believed.
    e. All of the above.
21. Drug prevention programs that use an educational approach (e.g., DARE) can be evaluated by measuring:
    a. Whether AOD use increases or decreases following the program.
    b. Whether problems associated with AOD use increase or decrease following the program.
    c. Whether participants have learned and retained accurate information from the program.
    d. All of the above.
    e. None of the above.
22. Proponents of regulating psychoactive substances as a method of health promotion believe that:
    a. Psychoactive drugs are inherently bad for people.
    b. In order to promote safer use of psychoactive substances, laws should focus on how drugs are sold and used rather than making them illegal to possess.
    c. People should be free to use psychoactive substances without governmental intervention.
    d. Tertiary prevention is the only effective form of prevention.
    e. The higher the penalty for illicit use of a psychoactive substance, the less likely that people will have problems associated with use.
23. Some people claim that possession and use of illicit drugs are "victimless crimes" because:
    a. Governments cannot distinguish between nonproblem use and abuse.
    b. The victims of drug use include innocent bystanders.
    c. The only adverse consequences of drug use happen to the actual user.
    d. Drugs kill people.
    e. Drug addiction is a disease that exists in society.
24. Some drug policies and laws have been driven by economic and political factors. An example of this is:
    a. Prohibiting possession of heroin in order to reduce crime associated with heroin use.
    b. Limiting alcohol content in wine or spirits in order to reduce the risk of cirrhosis of the liver
    c. Putting high taxes on a product that the country does not produce (e.g., coffee) in order to protect a product that the country does produce (e.g., beer).
    d. Mandating no smoking in public buildings to protect people from the negative effects of secondhand smoke.
    e. Increasing police presence outside bars in order to discourage public rowdiness associated with drinking.

25. Blood alcohol concentration (BAC) refers to:
    a. The quantity of alcohol in a standard drink.
    b. The percentage of alcohol in relation to a person's body weight, in ounces per 100 pounds.
    c. The fraction of alcohol found in a person's breath, in particles per 100 cubic feet.
    d. The ratio of weight of alcohol to the volume of blood, in grams per 100 milliliters.
    e. None of the above.

26. One of the primary risks of imposing higher insurance rates on drivers with Driving Under the Influence (DUI) convictions is that:
    a. There is no way to tell if a person has been driving under the influence of alcohol.
    b. Drivers who are under the influence of alcohol are not legally responsible for their actions.
    c. Drivers with DUI convictions will be unable to purchase insurance and might continue to drive without insurance.
    d. It is unconstitutional for insurance companies to discriminate against people just because they used alcohol while driving.
    e. None of the above.

27. The problems related to the high levels of incarceration of drug users as a result of the War on Drugs policy include:
    a. A disproportionate number of minority offenders are affected by drug enforcement.
    b. The nation cannot afford the cost of this war, including the costs of incarceration.
    c. This war increases the profits for drug dealers and places additional economic burden on residents of inner cities to provide more law enforcement.
    d. All of the above.
    e. None of the above.

28. Some insurance companies will not generally fund inpatient substance abuse treatment for adolescents unless:
    a. The drug of choice is alcohol.
    b. The adolescent has a second psychiatric diagnosis, such as depression or anxiety disorder.
    c. The school authorizes treatment.
    d. The adolescent agrees to use pharmacotherapy.
    e. A government official declares the adolescent at risk of harm to self or others.

29. Outpatient treatment for an adolescent might be preferable because:
    a. This is less intrusive and less expensive than inpatient treatment.
    b. Research has found no significant difference in effectiveness of inpatient versus outpatient treatment.
    c. There is less disruption in the day-to-day activities and support systems.
    d. All of the above.
    e. None of the above.

30. The two stated goals of "managed care" for AODA clients are:
    a. Control costs and ensure quality of care.
    b. Harm reduction and moderate use.
    c. Abstinence and control of the disease.
    d. Motivate involuntary clients and keep them in treatment at least 90 days.
    e. Live long and prosper.

31. Legislators and policymakers need to provide drug enforcement authorities with direction on how to prioritize their resources to enforce laws pertaining to:
    a. Large traffickers versus small traffickers of illicit substances.
    b. Traffickers versus possessors of illicit substances.
    c. Possession and trafficking of illicit substances versus illegal diversion of controlled substances, such as reselling prescription medicines on the street.
    d. All of the above.
    e. None of the above.

32. Buying prescription pills and selling them to others can seem lucrative to a person who is addicted to the pills because:
    a. Pharmaceuticals are not as addictive as illegal drugs such as heroin or cocaine.
    b. She is not aware that she is paying more for the drugs than she can sell them for.
    c. She can sell some of the pills for a large profit and use some of the profit to pay for drugs to feed her habit.
    d. Pharmacies have no right to turn down a person who has a prescription for a drug.
    e. Doctors have an ethical obligation to prescribe drugs to a person who is complaining about pain.

33. Drug seekers sometimes fake medical conditions in an effort to obtain pharmaceutical drugs. Faking tic douloureux is a favorite approach for some drug seekers because:
    a. This is a disease that does not really exist, but is a code word to ask a physician for an illicit drug.
    b. It occurs in 95 percent of the population.
    c. The proper drug treatment for tic douloureux is cannabis.
    d. It has no clinical or pathological signs or symptoms.
    e. None of the above.

34. It is illegal to obtain pharmaceuticals by:
    a. Forging a physician's prescription and signature.
    b. Pretending to have a medical ailment.
    c. Going to more than one doctor to get pills for the same ailment.
    d. All of the above.
    e. None of the above.

35. An informed and concerned social worker decides to advocate for taking some drugs off the schedule of prescribed medicines and putting them on the schedule of illicit substances, as was done with quaaludes. A sound rationale for this law reform initiative is that:
    a. All prescription drugs should be made illicit.
    b. The risks to those who buy and use the drugs illegally outweigh the benefits of the intended medical use.
    c. Prices of drugs from pharmacies are higher than those from illicit traffickers.
    d. Drugs from the street are safer than ones from pharmacies.
    e. All of the above.

36. "Drug diversion" refers to:
    a. Trafficking in any illicit narcotic.
    b. Selling or trading in licit drugs for illicit purposes.
    c. Shooting a drug intravenously when it is meant to be taken orally.
    d. Taking a medication that diverts the toxic effects of the drug into the liver so that it will be expelled more quickly.
    e. Buying over-the-counter drugs for common colds and symptom relief.

37. Some AODA treatment programs will not hire social work graduates as counselors unless they are also:
    a. Certified specifically for addictions counseling.
    b. Licensed as a bartender.
    c. Accredited by the police force as a forensic social worker.
    d. Accredited by Alcoholics Anonymous.
    e. All of the above.
38. When a new health promotion policy is implemented:
    a. The effects of the policies should not be evaluated because there are too many variables.
    b. The evaluators should assume that the effects of the policy will be either neutral or positive in relation to AODAs.
    c. All the resources should be put into the program, not into the evaluation, because evaluation is too costly.
    d. The effect of the policy should be measured over a term of no more than one month, because people forget advertising campaigns if the evaluation waits any longer.
    e. The plan should include an evaluation that measures factors related to AODAs.
39. When the government is considering mandatory drug testing for pilots or other regulated professions, it should consider the fact that:
    a. Drug testing is a foolproof way of knowing whether someone is using drugs, even if people try to use other drugs to mask the use of prohibited drugs.
    b. Different types of drug testing (e.g., breathalyzer, blood test, and urinalysis) have different levels of accuracy for different substances and time frames.
    c. All drug-testing methods are 80 percent accurate, with 10 percent of people having false positives and 10 percent of people having false negatives.
    d. Drug testing does not infringe on a person's right to privacy in any way.
    e. Employers have no real interest in knowing whether their employees are using drugs.
40. When determining whether to allow marijuana use for pain and nausea management for patients with terminal cancer, policymakers should consider:
    a. The fact that marijuana can offer relief to certain patients.
    b. The relative effectiveness of other licit substances at offering similar relief.
    c. The risk that marijuana produced for cancer patients will be abused by others who want to use it recreationally.
    d. Ways to ensure that marijuana produced for cancer patients is used as intended.
    e. Different methods of making cannabis available (e.g., dispensing marinol tablets rather than smokable marijuana).
    f. All of the above.
41. The general time frame for changing societal attitudes through AODA prevention strategies takes:
    a. Five minutes maximum.
    b. Two to three months if you use very good advertising campaigns.
    c. Six months of tough police enforcement using lots of resources over a short period of time.
    d. One to four years, regardless of the type of prevention strategy.
    e. A generation (e.g., 20 to 40 years), using a combination of prevention strategies.

42. Communities confronting substance abuse problems typically go through four stages, namely:
    a. Use, misuse, abuse, dependence.
    b. High, low, high, low.
    c. Denial, panic, fragmentation, cohesion.
    d. Cigarettes, marijuana, cocaine, heroin.
    e. Problem recognition, problem resolution, relapse, repeat.

43. Social workers developing Prevention Programs must consider how to:
    a. Obtain sufficient resources to bolster chances of success.
    b. Preempt or deal with counterprevention that might arise from groups opposing the prevention efforts.
    c. Ensure that the prevention efforts are sustained over time and provide sufficiently intensive programs to make a difference.
    d. Ensure that the benefits outweigh the risks or unintended side effects (such as laws intended to reduce substance use that create an illegal, underground market for these substances).
    e. All of the above.

44. Which of the following is *not* an example of a substance abuse prevention program?
    a. A parenting skills program that helps parents communicate with children about substance abuse issues before their children get into trouble.
    b. Raising taxes on cigarettes to discourage young people from starting to use cigarettes.
    c. Providing mentors for youth who are at risk of developing AODA problems.
    d. Conducting a media campaign that tells people with severe AODA problems that they are good, decent people.
    e. Developing workplace policies that reduce stress and encourage employees to seek help before they develop any AODA problems.

# Ethical Dilemmas

As you have probably discovered in the above exercises, policies are fraught with issues that challenge our beliefs about the ethically correct way to deal with people affected by AODAs. Some issues are related to people's political beliefs and views about the nature of addictions, including the desired goals for people affected by or at risk for AODA problems. Other issues relate to the uncertain results of different policy approaches. In other words, even if everyone agreed upon the goals, we might not agree on what types of policies are most likely to accomplish those goals. For each of the following situations, write a 3- to 5-page paper or prepare a 15-minute class presentation. When analyzing the ethical issues, consult the NASW Code of Ethics (available at http://www.socialworkers.org)[1] and any relevant laws that apply in your jurisdiction.

---

1. Or your own professional code of ethics if you belong to another profession. See Chapter 3, footnote 6.

## Situation A: Addiction as Disability?

Many businesses and social agencies have sexual harassment policies that prohibit sexual harassment and provide for discipline, including dismissal, for anyone who breaches these policies. Recently, there have been a number of incidents in which a person who was fired because of sexual harassment claimed that he or she had a "sexual addiction" and that the Americans with Disabilities Act (ADA) should protect him or her from being fired. The legislators who passed the ADA did not intend for it to cover this type of situation. As a policy matter, should social workers advocate for ADA protections for people with sexual addictions in these circumstances? What are the conflicting social work values at stake? How would you view this situation differently if you looked at it from a Moral Model, Disease Concept perspective, Ecological Model, or Feminist perspective? Identify three policy alternatives, analyze them, and provide your rationale for which alternative is the most consistent with social work values and perspectives.

## Situation B: Duty to Warn or Protect

Assume that current laws state that information about a client having HIV is to be kept strictly confidential. However, the law also allows medical, mental health, and social work practitioners to warn others, or take steps to protect them, should they determine that a client is putting others at risk of contracting HIV. Since passage of this law, clients at addictions treatment programs have refused to discuss any behaviors related to sharing needles, fearing that their workers will have to tell their intimate partners and others at risk that they might be HIV-positive. More AODA clients have also refused to have HIV testing. This concerns workers because the current laws might be placing more people at risk, with workers having no opportunity to counsel clients in a safe, confidential helping relationship. Which social work values are in conflict? Identify at least three policy alternatives. Assess the strengths and limitations of each alternative, citing research on different types of policies for HIV reporting and confidentiality. Select and defend the policy that you believe is the most ethically appropriate and effective.

## Situation C: Slashing

A needs assessment for professional sex workers has found that many of them are survivors of childhood sexual abuse and have learned to cope by slashing themselves. When they slash, they tend to drink or use painkillers. Government officials are trying to decide what type of program to fund that will help deal with this problem: treatment based on abstinence from all AODs; harm reduction (focusing on how to use drugs and slash in a safe manner); or criminal law enforcement (targeting people who are involved in prostitution and drug use). Analyze the ethical issues related to these alternatives, taking into account values such as client self-determination, respect for all people, access to resources, integrity, public safety, individual safety, accountability, and promotion of public health. Also, read at least one GSI on survivors of sexual abuse and self-harming behaviors.[2]

---

2. GSI stands for Good Source of Information—see Chapter 1 for a definition.

# Journaling Exercise

1.  Describe your strengths and learning needs in relation to the following aspects of AODA health promotion and policy work: knowledge of governmental AODA policies at municipal, state, and federal levels; ability to critically analyze AODA policies; ability to apply a problem-solving process to macro AODA issues; ability to link different models and theoretical perspectives with macro AODA issues.

2.  Identify an AODA policy issue that has particular interest to you. Describe its significance to you, what you would like to do about this issue, and how you could go about effecting a positive change in relation to this issue.

3.  Identify a person in your community or someone who is known nationally who has been an effective advocate for AODA prevention policies or programs. What skills and attributes does that person possess that helps him or her advocate so effectively? How do these skills and attributes compare to your skills and attributes?

# InfoTrac College Edition

## Key Words

◇ Drug Prevention

◇ Drug Policy

◇ War on Drugs

◇ Moral Model

◇ Public Health Model

◇ Decriminalization

◇ Harm Reduction Model

◇ Regulation (alcohol, nicotine, drugs, pharmaceuticals)

CHAPTER

# 10

## Termination, Follow-up, Maintenance, and Relapse Prevention

This chapter brings us to what some social workers call the final phases of the helping process—termination and follow-up. These phases apply to AODA work at all levels of practice—micro, mezzo, and macro. Further, the follow-up phase could include expanding the helping process from one level of practice to another. For example, a worker helping an individual with an AODA problem might incorporate referrals for family work, or alternatively, advocacy for community change, as part of the plans made during termination and follow-up. Similarly, if government decides to decriminalize possession of marijuana, part of the plan following implementation of this policy could be to work with at-risk groups to ensure that they receive appropriate education and support. This would reduce risks associated with marijuana use.

As with other phases, termination and follow-up are not simply phases that occur at one point in the helping process. They should be considered throughout the helping process (e.g., letting a family know how long they will be in a treatment program, planning for what happens after treatment, and helping a client identify relapse prevention strategies during the beginning and middle phases of the helping process). This chapter includes a focus on maintenance and relapse prevention because the termination and follow-up phases of the helping process often concentrate on these stages of change. Still, maintenance and relapse prevention should also be raised during earlier phases of the helping process.

This chapter begins with three sections that present exercises designed to help you recognize different strategies to use with different types of termination, as well as how to recognize possible reactions to termination. The following two sections focus on identifying precipitants of relapse and applying a model of relapse prevention. The next section on referrals is geared to helping you identify appropriate resources for referrals in your community at the termination and follow-up stages. The ensuing section on follow-up looks at ethical issues that might arise during this phase of the helping process. The chapter ends with role-play exercises and assignments, and a journaling exercise to help you link theory, values, skills, critical thinking, and self-awareness.

# Types of Termination

Helping relationships can be terminated by the worker, by the client, or by mutual planning. There are also unplanned terminations, such as a client who moves, who commits suicide, or who overdoses and is moved to another level of care (e.g., admitted to a hospital or an institutional program). For each of the following scenarios, select the most ethical and clinically appropriate response by the worker. Identify the rationale for your choice, citing your course readings or class notes where appropriate.

1. Glenda's client Jeremy died of a heart attack while speedballing. Glenda had worked with Jeremy and his partner, Hal, for the past 3 months. Hal did not have an addiction problem and was a very positive influence in Jeremy's life. To facilitate termination, Glenda should:
   a. Try to forget about Jeremy and Hal as soon as possible so that she can get on with her work with other clients.
   b. Tell Hal not to allow an autopsy on Jeremy because the coroner might find out that Jeremy was using illicit drugs.
   c. Invite Hal to discuss his feelings about Jeremy's death and to assess whether he can use referrals to other services or support.
   d. Find Hal a new partner to replace Jeremy as soon as possible.
   e. Educate Hal about the risks of speedballing.

   Rationale: _____

   _____

2. Suzette is a client who used food to comfort her, particularly when she felt fear of failure at work or with intimate relationships. As a result of Cognitive-Behavioral Therapy, Suzette now uses positive self-statements and journaling to give her comfort and to avoid overeating behaviors. Suzette's therapist, Clyde, is concerned that Suzette will fall into old patterns of behavior if they stop therapy. Clyde would be well advised to:
   a. Keep Suzette in therapy forever so that she does not have a chance to relapse.
   b. Trick Suzette into having a relapse during therapy so that Clyde can help her get back to her new coping strategies.
   c. Encourage Suzette to abstain from food altogether, because abstinence is easier than controlled use.
   d. Discuss termination with Suzette several sessions before actually terminating the relationship in order to plan relapse prevention strategies, explore the use of other support systems, and help her build a sense of self-efficacy prior to terminating.
   e. Refer Suzette to a physician for appetite suppression pills that will help her when she can no longer rely on her therapist.

Rationale: _____

_____

3.  The Frist family has been coming for Structural Family Therapy for the past 3 months. At the beginning of therapy, the eldest child, Emma, was parentified, taking care of her parents who were both dependent on alcohol. Emma has now given up her role as parent, and her parents have significantly reduced their alcohol use. Emma wants therapy to continue. Her parents say that everything is under control, so it is time to terminate. At this point in the helping process, the therapist should:
    a.  Continue therapy, regardless of what the parents want, until both of them have been abstinent for at least 6 months.
    b.  Terminate with Emma, since she is not the one with the problem, and continue to work with her parents.
    c.  Terminate with the parents, since they do not want to continue. During therapy with Emma, teach her how to put Antabuse in her parent's food each day so that they will stop drinking. Make sure this plan is kept confidential.
    d.  Call child protective services to report the parents, because the parents are obviously not taking appropriate care of Emma.
    e.  Explore the risks and benefits of terminating at this time with the family; explore various options for individual, family, or group work; and let the family members decide what is best for them.

Rationale: _____

_____

4.  A community organizer was hired by a neighborhood to develop a "clean needles program" in order to reduce transmission of HIV among IV drug users. The organizer has been successful in securing a grant to fund this program and hiring former IV drug users to run it. When terminating with the community, the organizer should:
    a.  Evaluate, with the community, to what extent goals have been achieved, as well as whether and when the community organizer can terminate his work.
    b.  Continue to work with the employees he has hired, since they will always be dependent on the expertise of the organizer.
    c.  Terminate only when HIV has been completely eradicated from the community.
    d.  Test the new employees for drug use to ensure that they are not using drugs again.
    e.  Make up a good excuse for terminating so that nobody will feel angry with the community organizer for leaving the new program.

Rationale: _____

_____

5. Uri is a social worker who has been advocating for extension of Medicaid coverage to include long-term care for people with chronic AODA problems. After 2 years on this project, Uri has still not been successful in achieving this change. At this point, Uri should:
   a. Let government officials hear all his rage at them, since it is a lost cause and he might as well terminate on a high note.
   b. Evaluate why the advocacy has not produced positive results, and consult with colleagues about whether to (1) continue with the advocacy, (2) wait until a time when government officials might be more amenable, or (3) move on to other work.
   c. Let Medicaid recipients know that they can only get short-term AODA care, so they will not have any false hope about getting the care they need to handle their AODA problems.
   d. Tell Medicaid recipients that short-term care is the best type of care, even if you do not believe this, in order to produce a placebo effect so they will be more likely to get better.
   e. Quit social work because it is obvious that Uri knows nothing about AODAs, treatment, or advocacy.

   Rationale: _____

   _____

6. The Barbie Intuit Corporation had two employees who committed suicide by over-dosing on a chemical that the corporation uses in its industrial processes. A social worker named Carmen was hired by Barbie to conduct "critical incident debriefing" for other employees. The critical incident debriefing seemed to cause greater anxiety among the employees. At this point, Carmen should:
   a. Screen all employees for suicidal ideation, regardless of whether they want it or not, given the high risk of suicide in this company.
   b. Call for a government inquiry into the corporation's use of a chemical that could be used to commit suicide.
   c. Work with the company to develop a follow-up process, which might or might not include Carmen providing the follow-up services.
   d. Hold a company-wide rap session as the final meeting with them to allow employees to ventilate their anger, fear, frustration, sadness, and anxiety.
   e. Conduct an evaluation with employees to find out what they liked about the critical incident debriefing, focusing only on the positives.

   Rationale: _____

   _____

7. For 12 months, Mary-Jane has been going for treatment of cannabis dependence at a program designed for youth. She is about to turn 25 years old, which makes her ineligible for further services at this program. Her social worker should:

a. Change the records so that it looks like Mary-Jane is 23 years old and will still be eligible for services, based on a belief that the means justify the ends.

b. Terminate services with Mary-Jane, knowing that she will be fine, because most youth just grow out of drug problems, even without social work help.

c. Suggest that Mary-Jane change her name, since this is obviously the root of her problems, if not the stem and leaves as well.

d. Help Mary-Jane evaluate her progress and ongoing needs, including the possibility of a referral to services for adults.

e. Recommend a self-help program for Mary-Jane, because she cannot benefit any further from professionally led services.

Rationale: _____

_____

8. Tory has been counseling Mr. and Mrs. Lockheart to help them with their codependent relationship and their cocaine abuse. Tory has found a new job in another city and will be leaving in 3 weeks. Tory should:

a. Not tell the Lockhearts that he is moving (because this is a personal matter), and just ask another worker to meet them the week after he leaves.

b. Explain how Tory's leaving is actually a good thing for them because it will teach them not to become too dependent on people.

c. Suggest that they move to the new city so that they can continue in treatment with Tory without interrupting their progress.

d. Refer them each to individual AODA specialists, because codependence cannot be treated in a joint session.

e. Explain that he will be leaving, allow the Lockhearts to express their feelings or concerns about this, summarize progress and ongoing needs, and jointly plan what to do.

Rationale: _____

_____

# Termination as Loss

Ideally, components of termination include helping a client identify major learning or areas of growth, identifying areas for future work, helping the client synthesize the ending process and content, and helping the client make transitions to new experiences. Clients who are ready to accept termination and move on have a sense of maturity, achievement, confidence, and ability to use other sources of help and support. Often, clients experience termination of social work as a loss, and they need help from the social worker to move from other stages toward acceptance. The other stages are denial, anger, bargaining, and mourning. *Denial* of termination might manifest itself in clients not willing to prepare for termination or discuss their feelings about termination. *Anger* could be expressed directly, for example, verbal rage directed at the worker, or indirectly, for example, not following the plans that the client agreed to follow.

Anger might be seen as a transference experience or a defense against loss (e.g., a client who is angry at having lost a parent to drug-related death, but directs this anger toward the worker). *Bargaining* could mean trying to negotiate extensions or other deals with the worker, though these promises might not be in the best interests of the client. Clients in *mourning* express feelings of grief, sadness, depression, regression, or desertion (Shulman, 1999). To help you identify different stages of dealing with termination, match each of the following situations with the relevant stage:

1. Akua breaks down in tears when the social worker tells her that she has successfully completed the alcohol recovery program. Akua's face is sullen. Her worker cannot understand why Akua cannot talk about moving on, given that she has done so well up until now. Stage: _____ Explanation:

2. Hillary has been working on a controlled use program. Her drug of choice is hash. When her group counselor asks her about her plans for support when the group ends, she says that she does not want to think about that. Hillary says the group gives her excellent support, so this is all she needs. Stage: _____ Explanation:

3. The Teller family has been seeing a solution-focused therapist to help them deal with prescription drug abuse by Mr. Teller. Although they have achieved their goals, Mrs. Teller does not seem happy. She tells the therapist that Solution-Focused Therapy has been "a horrible waste of time." Upon further exploration,

she acknowledges that goals have been achieved, but she fears that things will go "back to usual" as soon as therapy stops. Stage: _____ Explanation:

4.   Quincy has been "gambling-free" for 2 months. His worker suggests that Quincy move on from intensive individual counseling to a less intensive support group. Quincy tells his worker that he has had a slip and needs a few more weeks of individual work. Quincy did not actually have a slip, but the worker had agreed to provide additional individual counseling if Quincy ever had one. Stage: _____ Explanation:

# Interpreting Reactions to Termination

Clients experience a range of reactions when the worker discusses termination, with loss (as described above) being just one such reaction. The following exercise is designed to help you consider a range of possible reactions and different ways to respond to them. For each of the following reactions, identify four different interpretations for the reaction, including possible misinterpretations. Consider reactions that might be specific to clients with AODA problems. Underline one interpretation that you think is a reasonable interpretation, and explain how you would respond to this interpretation, providing rationale from your readings and classes.

Example: Charles is a client who was living on the street and using crack. In the past 3 months, you have helped Charles control his cocaine use and find supportive housing. You and Charles agree to talk about his progress and any issues regarding termination with you during the final session. To your surprise, Charles does not show up for the last appointment.

Possible interpretations and misinterpretations (underline one that is reasonable):

    a. *Charles started to use cocaine again and was too embarrassed to come for the final session and admit failure.*
    b. *As a person who lived on the street so long, Charles became accustomed to doing things in his own time and way. Making priorities is not important to him.*
    c. *Charles has memory problems related to his former crack use, which is why he probably forgot the appointment.*
    d. *Charles is angry at me for terminating with him, but underneath the anger is fear of failure.*

Suggested strategy and rationale: *I would call and ask how he is doing, inviting him to come in for another appointment. Ideally, we would have talked about relapse earlier, so when I call him, I could remind him that he is welcome to see me whether he is remaining abstinent or has started to use again. Using cocaine at this point in the helping process might be an expression of denial of the ending. If this were true, I might reframe termination to transition, to help reduce any anxiety Charles feels around termination.*

1.    You have been working with Dorian in a 30-day treatment program for people addicted to benzodiazepines. With just 3 days left in the program, you and Dorian discuss how Dorian has not dealt with his history of child sexual abuse and how this could put him at risk of relapse. You offer to refer Dorian to a therapist to help him with these issues. Dorian says he can solve his own problems without you and refuses to discuss any further issues with you.

Possible interpretations and misinterpretations (underline one that is reasonable):

    a.

    b.

    c.

    d.

Suggested strategy and rationale:

2. You have been facilitating a group for people with gambling compulsions. When you invite group members to talk about their feelings about the group's impending ending, group members say that everything is okay and that ending is no big deal for them.

Possible interpretations and misinterpretations (underline one that is reasonable):

a.

b.

c.

d.

Suggested strategy and rationale:

3. You have been helping a group of homeless people reduce harm associated with their AODA behaviors. The group has achieved its goals and seems ready for termination. Initially, the group agrees that it is time to terminate. During the last 5 minutes of the last session, some group members start raising new questions, such as the presence of stronger forms of heroin that have been showing up on the streets. There is no time left to deal with these issues.

Possible interpretations and misinterpretations (underline one that is reasonable):

a.

b.

c.

d.

Suggested strategy and rationale:

4. You have been working with an elderly couple, Randolph and Huegette, helping them understand the importance of complying with their medical prescriptions. Both have been prescribed numerous medications for ailments ranging from depression and anxiety to heart palpitations, acid reflux, and water retention. Prior to your assistance, Huegette and Randolph often misused their medications by combining them, taking double dosages, mixing them with alcohol, or sharing each other's medications. By providing education and support, you helped them understand the risks of medication misuse, and they seemed to be taking their medications appropriately. Just as you are talking about terminating with them, they indicate that they have started to go back to their old patterns of misuse.

Possible interpretations and misinterpretations (underline one that is reasonable):

a.

b.

c.

d.

Suggested strategy and rationale:

5. You have been helping a child protection agency develop policies on how to deal with clients who come to the agency under the influence of drugs or alcohol. The week after you mention that your work with them is almost complete, they tell you that they do not need you anymore. When you ask why, they say that they have found someone who knows more about legal and ethical issues for their client population.

Possible interpretations and misinterpretations (underline one that is reasonable):

a.

b.

c.

d.

Suggested strategy and rationale:

# Relapse Precipitants and Strategies for Maintenance

Now that we have considered client responses to termination generally, we turn to a task in the termination process that applies specifically to clients affected by AODAs—how to maintain their abstinence, controlled use, or other successful changes in their AODA behaviors. DuWors (1992) suggests that the role of a professional working with a client who has achieved initial success in dealing with an AODA problem is to help the client "break the chain of compulsive reaction" that leads from sobriety or controlled use to a relapse. This chain includes 13 factors: mood, physiology, values/attitudes/history, perception, precipitating event, feelings prior to or after the precipitating event, associations, interpretations, impulse to act, awareness, evaluation, choice, and action (which could be a relapse behavior such as drinking or an alternative behavior rather than relapse). The professional first helps the client identify precedents to relapse (Annis, 1986). Then, the professional helps the client strategize ways to avoid these precedents (i.e., high-risk situations) or deal with them more constructively if faced with them in the future. To gain practice at identifying precedents and strategies, complete the following chart as demonstrated in the first example.

| Scenario | Type(s) of precedent(s) from the chain of compulsive reaction | Relapse prevention strategies |
|---|---|---|
| Example: Loubert says the last time he fell off the wagon, he was feeling very stressed. His boss had embarrassed him at work, his wife bought some furniture they could not afford, and the children were fighting when he arrived home. He said to himself, "I can't stand it anymore," and went out to a bar to get away from it all. | *The key precedent in this situation was Loubert's response to accumulated stress (a "feeling" in response to events at work and home). He seems to associate drinking with relief from stress.* | • *Have designated people at work and home help Loubert identify when he is feeling stressed before the stress accumulates.*<br>• *Use a problem-solving approach to deal with problems in ways other than by drinking.*<br>• *Use relaxation techniques such as yoga to help relieve stress.*<br><br>*(continued)* |

| Scenario | Type(s) of precedent(s) from the chain of compulsive reaction | Relapse prevention strategies |
|---|---|---|
| Janine has had episodes of depression throughout her life that do not seem to be related to specific events. When feeling depressed, she often self-medicates with barbiturates, unaware that they can actually make the depression worse. During a rehabilitation program, she was able to detoxify from barbiturates, but she is not confident that her abstinence will last. | | |
| Hannah is in a 12-Step program for people with eating disorders. She describes her vice as a "carbohydrate addiction." Although her eating patterns are under control, she says that in the past the toughest time of day for her is in the evening when she is all alone, has nothing to do, and her mind becomes fixated on pizza, pasta, and other carbs. | | |
| Yannick was mandated into a treatment program for glue users following an attempted suicide by asphyxiation on gasoline. Yannick has little insight into why he uses glue or why he attempted suicide. He has two friends who died while using glue and does not think this was such a terrible thing. | | |

*(continued)*

| Scenario | Type(s) of precedent(s) from the chain of compulsive reaction | Relapse prevention strategies |
|---|---|---|
| Corey has been in and out of cocaine addiction programs for the past 3 years. His current counselor explores periods of success, as well as periods where he lapses into old patterns of behaviors. Cory is aware that his slide back into cocaine abuse usually begins when he stops attending his NA group, starts hanging out with his old crowd, and starts jonesing (craving) for just one hit. Unfortunately, having one hit is like opening the floodgates of cocaine use. | | |
| Rothman High School implemented a "Smoke-enders Program" that helped youth overcome physical and psychological dependencies on cigarettes. Thirty-four of 42 students successfully completed the program. During a follow-up meeting, students identified the following situations where they felt at greatest risk of going back to smoking: around exam time (when they felt most anxious), when hanging out with friends at the mall, and when they felt a nicotine headache coming on. Some students said that if they only smoked once or twice a week, that would not be a problem. | | *(continued)* |

| Scenario | Type(s) of precedent(s) from the chain of compulsive reaction | Relapse prevention strategies |
|---|---|---|
| Sehra overcame a 6-year dependence on opiates after participating in a 12-Steps treatment program. She recently had a slip, when she found some old pills in her purse; this slip developed into a full-blown relapse. She said to herself, "Well, I've failed at sobriety, so I might as well just keep using." | | |

**Bonus question:** In order for an AODA social worker not to get discouraged about high rates of relapse, the social worker can:
    a.  View relapse as a natural part of recovery.
    b.  Consult with peers and supervisors for support.
    c.  Measure success not just in terms of abstinence, but look at other social indicators.
    d.  All of the above.
    e.  None of the above.

# Applying a Model of Relapse Prevention

DuWors Model, described above, is just one of many different models of relapse prevention. This exercise asks you to analyze another model of relapse prevention, including specific skills and strategies for applying that model. First, identify a model of relapse prevention (e.g., Cognitive-Social Learning, Cenap's Model, or Beechem's Model) from your primary textbook or from an additional reading. Summarize the basic tenets of this model according to the following headings:

**Originator(s) of this model (name and professional background):**

How the model defines relapse:

Theory(ies) the model is based on (Psychoanalytic, Cognitive, Behavioral, Family Systems, 12-Steps, Social Construction, etc.):

Focus of the intervention (individual, family, other systems, policy, etc.):

Key strategies suggested by the model:

♦

♦

♦

♦

Rate each of the following concepts in terms of their importance to your chosen model of relapse prevention: 1—very important, 2—somewhat important, or 3—not important:

____ Problem-solving skills
____ Complete abstinence
____ Social and economic justice
____ Separating from people and places
____ Stopping compulsive self-defeating behaviors
____ Medical compliance (e.g., taking medications as prescribed)
____ Management of irrational thoughts
____ Management of feelings such as shame, guilt, or embarrassment
____ Social skills development
____ Awareness of connections between situations, thoughts, feelings, and behaviors
____ Community empowerment
____ Management of psychiatric symptoms
____ Sense of hope
____ Avoidance of high-risk situations
____ Self-efficacy
____ Abstinence Violation Effect
____ Spiritual connection (including a sense of faith or meaning)
____ Preventing a slip from turning into a full relapse
____ Creating a new homeostasis in the family system
____ Building a support system
____ Rolling with resistance
____ Legalization of illicit drugs
____ Cured (as opposed to being in recovery)
____ Covert aversion training
____ Adaptive indulgences (lifestyle balance)
____ Self-monitoring

**Role(s) of the social worker according to this model:**

   ♦
   ♦
   ♦


**Strengths of the model:**

Limitations of the model:

Refer back to Ben's case in Chapter 6. According to your chosen model of relapse prevention, what issues do you think would be critical in Ben's ongoing recovery once he has completed an intensive work phase?

## Referrals

As we have seen through the first half of this chapter, the termination phase of the helping process includes helping clients deal with their responses to termination, as well as helping them develop a relapse prevention plan. Another task of the termination phase is to assess whether the client has any further needs so that you can make any necessary referrals. This exercise is designed to provide you with a framework for assessing ongoing needs and making appropriate referrals. Remember that referring a client does not end with giving a client the name and telephone number of an agency. Your referral role includes taking whatever steps are necessary to ensure that the referral is appropriate and that the client does not run into barriers that prevent an appropriate referral from taking place.

Review your progress with your client(s) from your primary Case Profile, including any role-plays that you have conducted with your client(s) throughout this course. Identify any ongoing needs of the client(s). Updating your ecomap from earlier in the course (Chapter 5) is a helpful way to identify a client's ongoing needs. Given these needs, identify which of the following resources might be most useful for your client(s) as you move toward termination: self-help groups, professionally facilitated groups, individual counseling, family counseling, social or communication skills training, spiritual or religious affiliation, familial or informal social support networks, medical care, pharmacotherapy (e.g., Antabuse), hygiene and self-care counseling, nutritional counseling, AOD testing, legal advocacy, housing or income support services, educational or vocational testing or guidance, or recreational groups.

In Eva's case, for example, assume that Eva has achieved her goal of controlled use of cocaine but still feels alienated from the Mormon community. Upon helping her explore what needs the Mormon community previously provided her family, she decides that it was a sense of spirituality and belonging. A referral at this stage of the helping process might include providing Eva with information about other organizations that provide spiritual support where Eva might feel accepted.

Complete the following chart with at least three potential referrals based on the client's needs and resources available in your own community (see Chapter 7 for additional information on making referrals).

| Type of service | Referral 1: | Referral 2: | Referral 3: |
|---|---|---|---|
| Name of possible agency for referral | | | |
| Contact person, address, Web site, and telephone number | | | |

*(continued)*

| Type of service | Referral 1: | Referral 2: | Referral 3: |
|---|---|---|---|
| Eligibility requirements | | | |
| Possible barriers to an effective referral | | | |
| Suggestions for overcoming these barriers | | | |

# Ethical Issues in Follow-up

No chapter would be complete without considering ethical issues that might arise in practice. Here, we focus on ethical issues in the follow-up phase of the helping process. Referring to the NASW Code of Ethics for guidance on ethical rules and social work values, identify the ethical issues raised in each of the following scenarios.[1] Also identify the most ethical response in each scenario and provide your reasoning.

1.  Henry has been on a methadone maintenance program for the past 8 months. Now that he has completed the intensive stage of the program, he does not have to see his social worker. Henry obtains his methadone from a pharmacist. During a follow-up interview, the social worker finds out that Henry has applied for a job in a construction business that involves operating a forklift and other heavy machinery. The social worker thinks that this is not a good idea, because the methadone could affect Henry's reaction time and coordination. Henry tells the social worker it is no problem because he has a high tolerance for methadone. The social worker thinks she should warn the construction company about Henry's methadone maintenance.

2.  The Abbas family has been involved in counseling for issues related to their youngest child's alcohol abuse. During the final session, the social worker tries to arrange a follow-up session with the family to explore their progress and to collect information for their program evaluation. The family says they do not want a follow-up session. The social worker tells the family that they agreed to a follow-up session when they signed the original service plan. The social worker says that follow-up is required by the agency and by the agency's funding body.

---

1. Or your own professional code of ethics if you belong to another profession, as per Chapter 3, footnote 6.

3. Janice has significant cognitive impairment as a result of chronic glue use. During the final counseling session, Janice's parents suggest that the social worker arrange for random drug testing for Janice at her special education school. The social worker suggests that this is not necessary and that it might constitute a violation of Janice's rights.

4. During a follow-up group session, one of the clients, Penelope, admits that she has purchased prescription drugs illegally. The group facilitator knows that she was on probation for charges related to similar activities. The facilitator wonders whether he must report this information to the police or probation department.

5. When a municipal government develops an after-school program for children at risk of AODA problems, it decides to put all its money into direct services. They provide no resources for follow-up or evaluation. The social worker who is implementing this program wonders if she can divert some resources from the direct services to a follow-up and evaluation component, wanting to see if the program is helpful or harmful.

# Role-Play Exercise and Assignment

In this section, we focus on the application of termination and relapse prevention theory to practice situations. Read through the case descriptions below that apply to your primary Case Profile. To prepare for this role-play, the person playing the social worker should identify a specific therapeutic framework or model of helping related to termination and relapse prevention that you want to learn and apply to this case. Using your readings on this framework or model, complete the following chart by identifying the roles of the worker, key strategies and skills that you need to use in order to implement this framework or model, and specific behaviors to avoid because they would be counterproductive to implementing your chosen framework or model. The person role-playing the worker should share this information with the observer(s), but not with the people role-playing clients. The observers should focus on the worker's ability to use this model and skills when providing feedback to the person playing the worker. This role-play should last 20 to 40 minutes.

| Theory/Author: _____ | | |
|---|---|---|
| Roles of social worker | Key strategies and skills | Worker behaviors to avoid |
| 1. | 1. | 1. |
| 2. | 2. | 2. |

*(continued)*

**Theory/Author:** _____

| Roles of social worker | Key strategies and skills | Worker behaviors to avoid |
|---|---|---|
| 3. | 3. | 3. |
| 4. | 4. | 4. |
| 5. | 5. | 5. |

## Profile A: Julia and Maria Torres—Termination Phase With a Family

This role-play builds on the family-counseling scenario from Chapter 6, in which Julia and Maria entered joint counseling. During counseling, Maria and Julia worked through issues related to growing up in a family affected by alcoholism, including chaos, abuse, lack of appropriate boundaries, and family secrets that they carried with them into their adult lives. At this point in the helping process, both Julia and Maria say that they feel ready to move on. The social worker schedules a final meeting to explore changes that they have seen through the helping process, to explore ongoing needs for support, to invite them to discuss their reactions to ending the helping process, and to help them with relapse prevention strategies (e.g., how they can help each other recognize early warnings of relapse risk and agree about what to do if these warning signs occur). Julia and Maria have both been AOD-free for just over 4 months. Refer back to your notes on the role-play from Chapter 6, as well as other assignments on this case, so that you can build on the facts and dynamics that emerged earlier (e.g., reminding clients of issues raised at earlier phases and how they overcame them).

**Social worker's confidential facts:** Using the chart on page 314, identify the roles, skills, and strategies that you want to implement in this role-play, based upon a theory you think is relevant for this scenario. Remember that Maria and Julia have come from a family with a long history of alcoholism and that many of their coping mechanisms relate to what they have learned in childhood. Also, remember that some family members are likely to be at different stages of change and may or may not be supportive of Julia's and Maria's progress.

**Maria's confidential facts:** You have been abstaining from cocaine but continue to have strong cravings for it, particularly during evenings and weekends when you are not busy at work. Sometimes you feel like you are going to go crazy trying to keep your mind off using. You do not have many hobbies or social outlets, though you enjoy helping take care of Julia's children. You are pleased that, during counseling, you were able to talk about being sexually abused by your father. Still, you do not want Julia or anyone to say anything to your father or other family members. You think you are going to be single the rest of your life, which really saddens you. The thought of ending counseling also makes you concerned about how Julia will do. You think Julia should continue counseling or she will have a relapse. You know you are not supposed to be Julia's parent anymore, but you still feel very protective of her. Convey some irrational thoughts during the session, such as, "My sobriety depends on Julia's sobriety."

**Julia's confidential facts:** You admire your social worker for all the help and support she has provided. You feel ambivalent about ending counseling, knowing it is time to move on but also feeling like you are being abandoned again. One insight you retain from the treatment program you attended was that alcohol was your best friend—something that never abandoned you. As a child, you could never trust your parents, and as an adult, there were periods where even Maria abandoned you. Without a social worker, you fear you might go back to your old friend Jack Daniels. You are also concerned about how to ensure that DJ and Dominic do not follow in your footsteps and become third-generation alcoholics.

## Profile B: George Favel—Termination Phase With an Individual

George has been staying at a supportive housing facility for people who have completed more intensive AODA treatment programs. His 6 months at the facility is almost up, and his social worker arranges for a discharge-planning meeting. Many of the instrumental issues have been handled already, including where he will live (a small apartment) and how he will support himself (a cooperative work-education program that will pay him enough to cover his basic needs). George is not currently using glue, but he has had a lot to deal with recently, including the results of a recent examination that confirmed George had significant memory impairment, likely as a result of his AODA use. In addition, George has been feeling very lonely ever since Frank moved to another city 2 months ago.

**Social worker's confidential facts:** You are concerned about how George will do on his own, but the agency has a strict policy on time limits. Refer to literature on long-term effects of glue use so that you are aware of what type of follow-up George might need to help him with his memory impairment. Consider what factors in the past led to George's glue use, and consider what types of strategies might work best in helping him continue his abstinence. Given George's current levels of cognitive, emotional, and social functioning, consider what types of referrals might be most useful at this point in the helping process, as well as how to deal with any barriers to making an effective referral.

**George's confidential facts:** If it were up to you, you'd continue to stay at the same facility. You have had so many losses in your life—loss of friends, loss of memory, loss of street life, loss of family, loss of glue, and now loss of your residence and your primary support person, your social worker. You continue to be depressive, though not suicidal. You ask the social worker if you can continue to see him or her, even if you are no longer staying at the residence. You like the social worker, though you hate when the social worker talks about discharging you—it sounds like you are being treated like some type of sewage that needs to be discharged. In terms of relapse risks, you are more likely at this point to switch to alcohol rather than go back to glue use. Alcohol seems more acceptable, and you have felt more in control when you are using alcohol than when you were huffing. In terms of progress, you believe that you have developed better problem-solving skills and that you have been successful with the first 5 steps of the NA process. Now, on to step 6.

## Profile C: Randy Lang—Termination Phase With a Group

Randy has been participating in a group program for youth with cocaine problems. The group originally had eight members, but five members have dropped out of the program, leaving only Randy, Greg, and Bob. The topics for today are maintenance and relapse prevention, even though this is just the 4th week of a 12-week program. Randy, Greg, and Bob are all in their teens and have each had many problems in school and with their parents as a result of their cocaine use. Greg was mandated into treatment as a condition of parole in relation to a drug-possession offence. Bob came into treatment following a visit to the emergency room of a hospital when he went into cardiac arrest as a result of his cocaine use. Each client has different triggers and reasons for cocaine use. Randy and Bob say they want to remain abstinent from cocaine forever. Greg says that he can use cocaine in a controlled way, but he will not "touch the stuff" while he is on probation. All three have attained initial abstinence, but they have been somewhat shaken by how their numbers have dwindled, with five of their peers already relapsed and out of the program. In addition to this group, all members have been attending Narcotics Anonymous self-help groups near their homes.

**Social worker's confidential facts:** Given that five of eight group members have already terminated with the group, it is not too early to discuss termination issues with the remaining clients (including planned and unplanned terminations). Consider whether you want to focus initially on feelings, cognitions, behaviors, or interpersonal relations, and how this fits into the model of relapse prevention that you have chosen for this role-play. If it becomes difficult trying to deal with all three client's issues at the same time, you might try focusing on one client for a few minutes (e.g., helping that client identify risky situations or exploring losses), and then help the other clients relate what has been said to their own experiences. Also, think about what types of homework might be useful for the clients.

**Randy's confidential facts:** Refer back to prior notes and descriptions of Randy's case to identify issues that you have experienced and overcome, as well as issues that still require additional work. Note that, historically, precipitants to use included peer influence and your parents' divorce. You tended to use cocaine when you were angry, though your anger toward your mother has dissipated ever since you came to realize that your parents seemed to enjoy life more since their separation. Your concerns for maintaining your sobriety include how to deal with peers when they are using drugs at parties. You do not want to become a loner or a geek, which is what you think would happen if you had to give up all your friends who use drugs. You wonder if it is okay to smoke pot, since that was never a trigger for cocaine use for you. Loss has been a major theme in your life—loss of your grandparents when they moved back to China when you were 7 years old, loss of your family of origin (with two parents living together), loss of friends who died in cocaine-related accidents, and loss of control over your life when you started to use cocaine. Cocaine gave you a false sense of control, but even that was lost when you started treatment and stopped using. The idea of the group's ending brings up memories of all these losses, giving you a mix of anger and sadness. During the session, you ask what it means to be a "dry drunk," something that you read in an AA brochure but did not understand.

**Greg's confidential facts:** You see cocaine as a recreational drug that should be legalized. You are willing to "play the game" of appearing to be cooperative, as you want to end your involvement with the criminal justice system as soon as possible. When asked about your feelings about termination, you might provide insincere answers (e.g., proud of how far you have come and sad that you will not have this support group anymore). You might also falsify some of your precipitants to drug use (e.g., seeing beautiful women and feeling sexually inhibited). If the social worker and group win your trust, you will become more genuine. Your actual triggers for use include feeling tired, believing that cocaine gives you more energy, and giving you courage to engage in risky behaviors, including motorcycle racing. With regard to your actual feelings about termination, you are not sure. You like the social worker, but your sense of bravado tells you that group therapy is too touchy-feely. You acknowledge that your cocaine use was out of control, but you also believe that you can control your use.

**Bob's confidential facts:** Still reeling from having experienced a heart attack, you are thankful for getting a second chance but fearful that you are going to "blow it." You believe that even a brief slip could result in death. Given your ongoing cravings for cocaine, you feel as if you are living on the edge of a steep cliff. You have tried to deal with cravings by meditating, running, and reading. These have worked while you have been in the program, but you fear that once you lose this support group, you will not be so strong. You are concerned that the duration of the group is too short and that the only reason the group is ending so soon is that the social worker is a student whose field practicum is ending. You are somewhat angry at the worker for not letting a "real therapist" take over this group, but you are thankful for how much attention and support the worker has provided so far. You wonder what the NA principle, "One day at a time," means in terms of relapse prevention, because it seems like if you have a relapse one day, you can just get back to abstinence the next day. You do have a strong support system, including caring parents and grandparents, and a schoolteacher who has supported you throughout all the ups and downs.

## Profile D: Dionne Thevenin—Termination Phase With an Individual

Dionne has been in methadone maintenance for 8 months. For the most part, she has stabilized, though she went into a spell of depression about 5 weeks ago when she started to have AIDS-related gastrointestinal problems. When Dionne missed two appointments, Dionne's community-based social worker reached out to her, offering support and helping her accept that she would have some ups and downs with her AIDS treatment. Now that Dionne has stabilized with her methadone maintenance, Dionne and her community-based social worker have agreed to terminate their working relationship. Dionne has another counselor at the methadone maintenance program. The purpose of this meeting is to tie up loose ends.

**Social worker's confidential facts:** You are pleased with Dionne's progress on methadone maintenance, as she has returned to work, strengthened her relationship with cousin Vedna, and seems to be responding well to her AIDS medications. You realize that AIDS is progressive and there is no cure. You want to terminate this relationship so that she can use her time with her AIDS and methadone maintenance specialists. As part of your termination, you will explore Dionne's relapse prevention strategies. In order to prepare for this meeting, think about what models of intervention you have used in prior role-plays to understand and work with Dionne. What are their implications for relapse prevention (e.g., Disease Model versus Functional Model versus Structural Model versus Psychoanalytic Model versus . . . )? Consider making use of some type of ritual to mark Dionne's progress and reinforce her self-efficacy. Also, consider offering "booster sessions," which are additional meetings intended to bolster Dionne's progress or act like a vaccination against relapse.

**Dionne's confidential facts:** You have stopped using heroin and no longer crave it. Unbeknownst to your social worker, when you went into a depression a few weeks back, you also started using barbiturates. So far, the methadone maintenance program has not picked up on this. You are embarrassed to tell anyone about your barbiturate use. You also think that it is not such a bad thing, because a lot of people take sleeping pills. You will only disclose your barbiturate use to your worker if you feel that you can trust her (i.e., that she will not judge you or make you feel guilty). Otherwise, you have agreed to work on how to ensure that you do not start using heroin again (or other drugs, if the worker raises this issue). You think that your depression might be related to a lack of meaning in your life. You are quite anxious about terminating with the social worker, because the social worker has been a great advocate and case manager for you. You have learned many skills from the worker, but you still have questions about your ability to assert yourself with various medical and psychosocial helping systems. You have learned some useful self-messages from prior work, including "Stop, look, and listen," which helps you be more aware of your environment, thoughts, and feelings. You have also learned that "Lapse is a mistake, not a failure."

## Assignment 10.1: Termination and Relapse Prevention

For this assignment, prepare an analysis of the role-play including the following information:

1. A process recording that summarizes the role-play, including an overview of the worker's use of skills and the client's responses. Also include an appraisal of the extent to which the worker followed the chosen theoretical framework or model, focusing on tasks of the termination and follow-up stages. Be sure to cover worker roles, skills, and strategies, as well as behaviors to avoid (referring back to the chart that you created to prepare for this role-play). [4 to 6 pages]

2. A critique of how well the chosen theoretical framework or model of helping fits with the client's issues as presented in the role-play, including client feelings toward termination (e.g., denial, anger, sadness, acceptance, and moving on), client belief systems, and issues in the client's social environment. Which skills were particularly helpful given the client's situation? [1 to 2 pages]

3. An analysis of how diversity issues were taken into account or should have been taken into account during this role-play, building on diversity information learned earlier in the course. [1 page]

4. Suggestions for homework by the client(s) or follow-up by the social worker that fit with the chosen model of helping. Include any referrals that you would make, identifying specific agencies or resources that are available in your community. Also, consider how you might expand helping from one level of practice (e.g., individual or family) to another level (e.g., organizational or community) as part of the plan for follow-up. [1 to 2 pages]

5. Reflection (thoughts and feelings from the worker's perspective) about the termination of work with this client (e.g., "I am anxious about how the client will do." "If the client relapses, it will be my fault." "Did I do enough?" "Does the client feel helped?" "Is it OK to be friends?" "The client surprised me when . . ."). What self-care and professional development strategies could the worker use in order to deal with any thoughts or feelings that posed significant stress, difficulty, or uncertainty? [1 to 2 pages]

**Evaluation** will be based on the following criteria: clarity of the summary of the role-play; accuracy of the appraisal of the role-play in conjunction with the roles, skills, strategies, and behaviors to avoid given the chosen framework or model of intervention and phases of the helping process; originality and level of critical analysis about the appropriateness of the chosen framework or model in reference to the presenting problems, client feelings toward termination, and client diversity factors; appropriateness and level of detail of plans for follow-up and referrals; awareness of thoughts and feelings regarding termination in the role-play; and appropriateness of self-care and professional development strategies to deal with significant issues raised in the termination phase of this role-play. The paper should be 8 to 13 pages long, including at least four relevant, scholarly references in APA format.

## Journaling Exercise

1. Write a two-page letter to the people in your work-study group (for the role-plays or for the entire class) that you would consider giving them during the last class. Letter writing is a ritual that can be used with clients as part of the termination process to deal with feelings about ending, to recognize achievements attained and work to be done, to share hopes for the future regarding AODA concerns, and to act as a reminder of how far clients have come (as a relapse prevention strategy). Your group or class has worked together for educational purposes rather than to resolve AODA issues of your own, but the parallel awareness of termination issues in the educational process can help you raise consciousness about termination experiences in an AODA helping process. How do you think that termination in your work-study group is similar to and different from termination in an AODA group process?

2. Looking back over the course (as befits the termination stage), what are your strengths and learning needs concerning the following phases and activities of the AODA helping process: engagement, screening, and in-depth assessments; identifying presenting problems; identifying client strengths; helping clients in precontemplation and contemplation stages (including agreeing upon problem for work); developing goals and objectives for work; partializing and prioritizing goals and objectives; employing theories or models of helping (identify specific ones); and implementing a plan for maintenance, relapse prevention, termination, and follow-up (refer back to the Areas of Competence chart in Chapter 1 and complete the column for the end of the course). What plans do you have in the next 5 years to follow up on this learning and continue your professional development in the field of AODA work? What are your emotional reactions in relation to the ending of this course?

## InfoTrac College Edition

### Key Words

◊ Relapse Prevention
◊ Maintenance
◊ Termination
◊ Stages of Change
◊ Loss

CHAPTER

# 11

## AODA Research and Evaluation

This chapter focuses on two types of research, research for understanding and research for evaluation. *Research for understanding* refers to any study that is designed to help us develop a more accurate or complete understanding of individuals, families, groups, organizations, and communities affected by AODAs. *Evaluation* refers to any study that seeks to assess the effectiveness of a helping process, program, policy, or other intervention for people affected by AODAs. Professional codes of ethics demand science-based practice to ensure that helping processes, programs, and policies are based on critical thinking, factual evidence, quality assurance, and the most current knowledge about what is competent, effective practice (Gibbs, 2003).

The first part of this chapter provides two research exercises: how to read research critically and how to prepare a research proposal. The second part of this chapter focuses on evaluation: how to measure success, how to use a single-system design, and how different professionals might define success, as well as a role-play assignment to provide practice in the process of conducting an evaluation interview. This chapter ends with reflective journal questions related to both research and evaluation.

## Research

### Reading Research Critically

This exercise is intended to help you read AODA research critically, taking research methods and ethical issues into account. Read through the following criteria to ensure that you can understand and apply them in a critical analysis of a research project. Consult a research text if you need additional information in preparation for this exercise.

## Criteria for Critique

1. Ethical concerns—for research on human subjects, participation was based on voluntary and informed consent by people with sufficient mental capacity (taking AOD history or use into account); reasonable steps were taken to ensure the anonymity or confidentiality of research participants; benefits of the research outweigh the risks (especially for clinical trials of psychotropic drugs or other AODA interventions); participation includes people of different sexes and ages and from diverse ethnocultural, religious, and sexual orientation backgrounds (see the National Institutes of Health Web site at http://www.nih.gov for additional information and online training for ethical issues in research).

2. Design—research methods correspond to the question that needs to be answered through the research.

3. Measurements—for quantitative research, measurements are valid (e.g., they measure what they are intended to measure; there is concurrency among different instruments; and the measurements are discriminant, capturing the complexity of the item to be measured), measurements are reliable (e.g., they could be duplicated, different people making the measurements would arrive at the same answers), measurements have high sensitivity (proportion of true positives), measurements have high specificity (proportion of true negatives); for qualitative research, researchers used methods to ensure dependability and trustworthiness of the research, such as triangulation of data and an audit of the research.

4. Sample—for quantitative research, sampling is random and unbiased, and the sample size is large enough to produce generalizable results; for qualitative research, the participants are selected purposefully, and the study provides a rich description of the research participants.

## Research Descriptions

Critique each of the following research descriptions according to whether they satisfy or violate the above criteria. What are the strengths and limitations of this research? What additional information would you like to have about this research to help you decide whether or not it is an ethically and methodologically sound study?

a. To study the effects of alcohol use by pregnant women on their fetuses, Harriet proposes to draw her sample from 20 women's alcohol treatment programs in different cities around the country. She will compare the incidence of Fetal Alcohol Syndrome and Fetal Alcohol Effects among their children (the dependent variables), using quantity of alcohol use, frequency of use, pattern of use, and gestational age of the fetus at the time the mother stopped using as the independent variables.

b. Walter proposes an ethnographic study that will look at the experiences of people in a prison-based Rational Recovery group program who were convicted of drug trafficking. Participation in this group program is voluntary, but participation will likely help anyone who applies for early parole or release from prison. Anyone who agrees to participate in the group program will be required to participate in the ethnographic study, so that the prison can test whether or not the program is doing what it intends to do. Walter will conduct focus groups with four to six clients at a time, asking questions about their experiences in the group program—for example, what was perceived as helpful and what was perceived as harmful, if anything.

c. Jane would like to find out if marijuana truly is a Gateway Drug that leads people to other types of drug use. She proposes a national survey study that will be offered to 10,000 men age 40 to 65 years old. The study will include questions about what substances they have used throughout their lives, indicating age of onset of use for each substance. They will also be asked open-ended questions about whether they felt use of one substance led to use of any other substances later in life. Based on a pilot test, Jane expects an 80 percent response rate. Her response rate in the pilot test was relatively high because the survey was offered online (Web-based), and anyone who participated in the pilot study received a free gift certificate worth $50 to a national airline. For the proposed study, participants' names will also be entered into a lottery for a prize that includes a free trip for two to any destination of the participants' choosing.

d. Celeste wants to study the effects of anabolic steroids when combined with alcohol. Before studying the impact on humans, she proposes to study the impact on sheep, including the effects on heart rate, respiration, motor activity, and mood. Mood will be studied through observation of nonverbal behavior such as facial expression, posture, and tone of braying. Celeste will compare these variables among four groups: sober sheep (without steroids or alcohol), drinking sheep (alcohol but no steroids), drug-doping sheep (steroids but not alcohol), and double-trouble sheep (alcohol and steroids). She will keep the dosages low enough to ensure that the study produces no acute problems for the sheep.

e. Dave wants to compare the effectiveness of Substance Abuse Refusal and Assertiveness Training for people with various disabilities, including blindness, deafness, mental retardation, and attention deficit disorder. In order to ensure that the research will identify statistically significant differences among these groups, Dave chooses a dichotomous measure for evaluation—drug-free versus drug-using at the 6-month follow-up interview. The research will also consider factors such as legal problems, social functioning, and vocational functioning as both dependent and independent variables.

f. Child protective services plans to study the relationship between parental cocaine abuse and physical abuse of children. The study makes use of self-report surveys, to be completed by all people whose children have been taken into foster care or group homes due to child abuse. Although the surveys will be submitted without identifying information (e.g., name or address of research participants), child protective services will also secretly contact collateral informants (family members, relatives, neighbors, and employers) to verify information provided by the primary research subjects and ensure that the responses to the surveys are reliable.

g. Identify an original research article from a scholarly journal that focuses on an AODA topic of interest to you. Critique this article using the same criteria that you used for the previous examples.

Citation for the article:

Critique:

## Assignment 11.1: Research Proposal

Review your major assignments from prior chapters and identify a "gap" in the AODA literature or knowledge base that you believe needs to be researched. Identify a possible funding source (e.g., NIDA, NIAAA, state or federal agency, private donor, social agency, or charitable foundation). Develop a research proposal that is designed to fill this gap, targeting the identified funding source and including the following information:[1]

1. Title page—including name(s) and contact information for researchers, title of research proposal, funding source where proposal could be submitted, and name of major Case Profile that this research is related to.
2. Statement of research question—identifying what AODA issue(s) this proposal is designed to explore (including goals and hypotheses for the research, if appropriate). [1 to 2 paragraphs]
3. Literature review—summarizing scholarly literature related to the proposed research, identifying what is known, and providing a rationale for the research that you are proposing. [2 to 3 pages]
4. Methods—describing the research methods, including type of research, methods of obtaining a sample or research participants, methods of data collection, copies of any instruments that will be used (attached as an appendix), and methods of analysis. [2 to 3 pages]
5. Ethical issues—describing how the research will address ethical issues, including informed and voluntary consent, confidentiality or anonymity, risks and benefits, and how you will address the special risks that may be raised by the fact that research participants may be using AODs. [1 to 2 pages, plus a consent form as an appendix, if appropriate]

---

1. Some organizations have specific formats, requests for proposals, and criteria that you could follow.

6. Diversity statement—indicating how relevant issues of diversity will be taken into account. [1 to 3 paragraphs]
7. Budget—estimating the costs of implementing the research, including costs of research staff, incentives to participate, travel, and technology to assist with research, with written justification of these expenditures. [1 to 2 pages]
8. Implications of the research—indicating how this research will contribute to the literature, as well as any other academic or practical implications of this research. [1 to 3 paragraphs]
9. Reference list—identifying references for any books, Web sites, articles, or other scholarly resources that have been cited in the proposal (at least seven scholarly, relevant references).
10. Request for proposal—including any request for proposals or criteria established by your potential funding agency as an appendix.

**Evaluation** will be based on the following criteria: clarity of research question; relevance of the research to the student's major Case Profile; strength of literature review in supporting the need for this study; feasibility of completing the study; appropriateness of research methods; appropriateness of plans for ethical issues; appropriate accommodation of diversity issues; completeness and justification of the budget; relevance and persuasiveness of references; and the fit between the proposal and the criteria of the funding source. The paper should be 6 to 12 pages. The appendices are not included in this page count.

# Evaluation

The first half of this chapter focused on research for understanding. We now turn to evaluation, which looks at how to study the relative effectiveness of an AODA helping process. This section begins with an exploration of how success should be defined, followed by a framework for implementing an evaluation with a client system. The third part of this section asks you to consider how different AODA professionals might have varying ideas about how to define and measure success. This section ends with a role-play assignment designed to help you integrate what you have learned about evaluation with the interviewing skills that you have been learning throughout this course.

## What Is Success?

How one defines and evaluates success in AODA work depends on the theoretical framework or model of helping that is being used. Complete the following chart by identifying appropriate definitions of success and ways to measure success based on each of the therapies or models of intervention identified in the left column. For each model or theory, consider whether measurement of success should focus on changes in emotions (e.g., depression, anger, mourning, recognizing and coping with feelings), thoughts (e.g., distorted cognitions such as, "My parents are to blame for my addiction."), behaviors (e.g., abstinence, controlled use, uncontrolled use), biological well-being (e.g., brain damage, liver functioning, physical dependence, general physical health), mental health indicators (e.g., schizophrenia, suicidal ideation, psychological cravings, self-efficacy), social indicators (e.g., functioning in family, at work, or with peers; resolving legal problems), spiritual indicators (e.g., sense of meaning or connection with a greater power), or quality of life indicators (e.g., standard of living, satisfaction with life). For examples of possible evaluation measures, consider some of the assessment tools identified in Chapter 5 (e.g., ASI, MAST), as well as measures from other scholarly books, articles, or Web sites (Corcoran & Fischer, 2000).

| Therapy or model of intervention | Definition of success | Two examples of methods of measuring success (where appropriate, identify a specific instrument that can be used to measure success)[2] |
|---|---|---|
| Example—Harm Reduction Model: for a needle exchange program | *Decreased biological, psychological, and social risks associated with intravenous drug abuse* | *a. Collect data on the incidence of transmission of HIV and hepatitis*<br><br>*b. Collect data on the rates of incarceration for drug-related problems and the rate of unemployment (Community Social Assessment Scale—Jasper & Eagle, 2003)* |
| Motivational Enhancement Therapy: for heroin users in the precontemplation or contemplation stages of change | | |
| | | *(continued)* |

---

2. For examples of instruments, see Web sites of NIDA, NIAAA, and SAMHSA as listed in the bibliography.

| Therapy or model of intervention | Definition of success | Two examples of methods of measuring success (where appropriate, identify a specific instrument that can be used to measure success) |
| --- | --- | --- |
| 12-Steps group: for people addicted to alcohol | | |
| Behavior Modification: for marijuana users who are working toward controlled use | | |
| Family Systems Theory: for a couple affected by codependence | | *(continued)* |

| Therapy or model of intervention | Definition of success | Two examples of methods of measuring success (where appropriate, identify a specific instrument that can be used to measure success) |
|---|---|---|
| Ecological Model: for youth with learning disabilities who misuse prescription Ritalin | | |
| Functional Model: for people using benzodiazepines to cope with stress | | |
| Psychoeducational Prevention Program: for people at risk of engaging in unsafe sexual practices while under the influence of gamma hydroxybutyrate (GHB or liquid ecstasy) | | *(continued)* |

| Therapy or model of intervention | Definition of success | Two examples of methods of measuring success (where appropriate, identify a specific instrument that can be used to measure success) |
|---|---|---|
| Cognitive Restructuring: for former cocaine users at risk of relapse because of faulty assessments of their self-efficacy and problem-solving abilities | | |
| Pharmacotherapy: use of Antabuse for people with addictions to alcohol | | |
| Detoxification: medical detoxification unit for people who are physically dependent on barbiturates | | |

*(continued)*

| Therapy or model of intervention | Definition of success | Two examples of methods of measuring success (where appropriate, identify a specific instrument that can be used to measure success) |
| --- | --- | --- |
| Crisis intervention: short-term help for clients at risk of intentionally overdosing to commit suicide | | |
| Community Empowerment: for a social worker hired by an African American community that is concerned about rave parties at which young men are using Ecstasy and Viagra | | |

## Single-System Design

As suggested in Chapter 5, single-system (or single-subject) design is a useful tool for social workers who adopt a practitioner-researcher role. Single-system design views treatment planning, intervention, and evaluation as integrated manners of practice rather than separate functions. In order to implement single-system design, the social worker and client identify goals for work, partialize these goals, and identify criteria for evaluation as the helping process progresses. The following five steps provide a basic framework for using a single-system approach:[3]

---

3. Consult a social research text for more information about this type of approach.

1.   Identify an AODA-related **goal** that you believe your client would agree to pursue in your working relationship.[4]
2.   Identify **baseline information** indicating where the client is at the beginning of the helping process in relation to the overall goal.
3.   Partialize this goal into a logical sequence of **objectives** that the client can pursue over time.
4.   Identify specific interventions or **helping processes** in which the client will take part in order to reach each of the objectives.
5.   Complete the following Single-System Goals and Interventions chart (this chart assumes that the helping process will be completed in three stages; if you want to add additional stages, prepare a chart with additional boxes).

To illustrate use of this chart, consider Imogene, a woman who is a compulsive user of the Internet. During assessment, Imogene and her worker identify that she is at the contemplation stage of change. In other words, she is thinking about changing her Internet-using behavior, but she remains ambivalent about it. At this point, it is too early to agree to a goal relating to actual change of behavior, so they agree to a goal of "Making a free and informed decision about what, if anything, to do about Imogene's Internet compulsion." (One of the key traps that clients and social workers need to avoid is choosing a goal that is too large or infeasible; goals should be challenging, but not unrealistic, so that you do not set up a client for failure. Remember, taking one day at a time can be challenging enough for many AODA clients.) Imogene and the social worker partialize this goal into three segments: first, enhancing Imogene's sense of self-efficacy; second, gathering information about the most effective ways to deal with an Internet compulsion; and third, creating a decisional-balance summary to make a decision about what, if anything, to do about the Internet compulsion (for your own examples, be sure to use different goals and interventions than the ones listed below, tailoring them to your own Client Profile; also note that the examples of instruments in the following chart are fictitious).

| **System Goals and Interventions Chart (Sample)** | |
|---|---|
| Beginning date:<br><br>*October 2* | Baseline information:<br><br>*Imogene is "very ambivalent" about whether she wants to change her behavior of Internet use (using a scale of "certain about not changing," "ambivalent about changing," "very ambivalent," and "certain about changing" by Guthrie's Ambivalence-Certainty to Change Instrument, 2004). Her ambivalence lies in her belief that she has no control over her life, and she does not think there is anything that can help her gain control over her Internet use.* |

↓

---

4. If you were actually working with the client, you would go through these steps together; for practice, you will have to use your judgment about what goal the client is willing to pursue.

| | Initial helping process(es): |
|---|---|
| | *Self-efficacy counseling with the social worker (e.g., imagery technique in which clients visualize themselves in high-risk situations and manage the situations, avoiding relapse).* |

| Initial date for evaluation:<br><br>*November 4* | Initial set of objectives:<br><br>*Gain a "strong sense of self-efficacy" to be measured by use of Hlinka & Harnish's (1986) Self-efficacy Screening Scale.* |
|---|---|

| | Second helping process(es): |
|---|---|
| | *Client and social worker to jointly explore various treatment options, including self-help, inpatient, outpatient, individual, and group processes, available within the community and abroad.* |

| Second date for evaluation:<br><br>*November 16* | Second set of objectives:<br><br>*Develop a chart that lists all the treatment options and rates them on issues such as effectiveness, risks, costs, accessibility, and fit with Imogene's issues.* |
|---|---|

| | Final helping process: |
|---|---|
| | *Social worker to provide motivational enhancement counseling, including the use of decisional balance techniques from the Transtheoretical Model and self-monitoring homework (keeping track of how much time she spends on the Internet, including patterns of use, triggers, and consequences).* |

| Final date for evaluation: | Final set of objectives: |
|---|---|
| *December 7* | *To be aware of the amount of time, patterns, triggers, and consequences of Internet use.* |
| | *To develop a clear list of pros and cons of Internet use behavior.* |
| | *To reach a high level of certainty about what to do, if anything, about her Internet addiction (as measured by Guthrie's Ambivalence-Certainty to Change Instrument, 2004).* |

Now that you have seen an example, try completing your own System Goals and Interventions Chart below. Refer back to your notes on your Case Profile, particularly in reference to the chapters on engagement, assessment, and helping individuals. Follow the five-step framework described above and complete the following chart based on this information.

**System Goals and Interventions Chart**

| Beginning date: | Baseline information: |
|---|---|
| | |

↓

| | Initial helping process(es): |
|---|---|
| | |

↓

| Initial date for evaluation: | Initial set of objectives: |
|---|---|
| | |

↓

| | Second helping process(es): |
|---|---|

↓

| Second date for evaluation: | Second set of objectives: |
|---|---|

↓

| | Final helping process(es): |
|---|---|

↓

| Final date for evaluation: | Final set of objectives: |
|---|---|

## Interprofessional Practice and Concepts of Success

In the above exercise, you were asked to identify measurements of success as if you were the only professional working with the client. In many instances, a client is working with more than one helping professional at a time. People from different professional backgrounds might have different ideas about how to evaluate the successfulness of their helping processes

(Geva, Barsky, & Westernoff, 2000). This exercise is designed to help you become more aware of how you as a social worker might define success differently than an AODA specialist from another type of professional background. Review the following case example. Using the chart below, identify your goals for work with the client, what type of help you would suggest, and how you would measure success given your chosen type of help. After you have completed your portion of the chart, meet with an AODA specialist (or student) from another professional background and ask what goals and type(s) of help that person would provide, as well as how that person would measure the successfulness of the helping process. After you have completed the other professional's section of the chart, identify the similarities and differences between how the two of you identified success. Consider which of the following factors might contribute to the differences: specific distinctions in values, professional mandate and roles, focus of training, or legal obligations.

Carol is a 23-year-old woman who abuses cocaine. Her daughter, Valerie, was born this morning and is showing signs of cocaine withdrawal. Valerie was born 13 weeks prematurely, weighing less than 3 pounds, likely because of Carol's cocaine use. While Valerie is in neonatal intensive care, she will be under the care of the following professionals: a pediatrician, pediatric nurses, a social worker, an occupational therapist, a dietician, a nonsectarian chaplain, and a cardiologist. Carol has expressed remorse for using cocaine during her pregnancy, but does not want to talk to anybody about whether or not she needs to stop abusing cocaine. Carol and her partner, Paul, want to take Valerie home as soon as possible. Paul denies that he or Carol use cocaine, even though Carol has tested positive for cocaine and Paul shows behavioral indicators of cocaine abuse.

| | Social worker | Other professional: _____ |
|---|---|---|
| *Goals for work* | | |

*(continued)*

|                                          | Social worker | Other professional: _____ |
|------------------------------------------|---------------|---------------------------------|
| Favored helping processes or interventions |               |                                 |
| How success will be measured             |               |                                 |
| Key professional values                  |               |                                 |

*(continued)*

| | Social worker | Other professional: _____ |
|---|---|---|
| Primary professional mandate and roles | | |
| Focus of training (biological, psychological, social, spiritual, etc.) | | |
| Legal obligations | | *(continued)* |

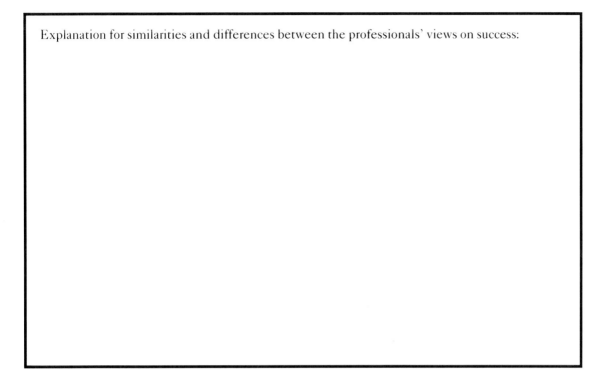

Explanation for similarities and differences between the professionals' views on success:

## Assignment 11.2: Evaluation Interview

The prior exercises have looked at various ways to evaluate success. Now, we turn to how to apply what you have learned about evaluation with a client situation, incorporating your interviewing skills to facilitate the process. Use your primary Case Profile as the basis for this assignment. Decide which client(s)—individual, family, or group—that you would like to focus on for this evaluation exercise. Assume that you have recently completed an individual, family, or group helping process, and the client(s) have agreed to a follow-up interview with you for the purpose of an evaluation. In the role-play, the social worker will conduct the follow-up interview, with a focus on conducting the evaluation. After conducting the role-play, prepare a written analysis of the role-play including the following components:

1.  How the social worker prepared for the role-play. [1 page]
2.  Rationale for choosing a particular evaluation tool or question guide (include a copy of the completed tool or guide in the appendix to this paper; consider factors such as validity, reliability, trustworthiness, diversity, and fit with theory behind the helping process). [1 to 2 pages]
3.  Summary of the interview process, including skills used by the social worker, key client responses, and how the process could have been improved. [3 to 5 pages]
4.  Implications of the evaluation for the client, the social worker, and the agency. [1 to 2 pages]
5.  Strengths and limitations of the evaluation tool or question guide. [1 to 2 pages]
6.  Description of additional evaluation methods that you would recommend for use with this client. [1 to 2 pages]
7.  References on evaluation processes in the AODA field and evaluation tools or question guides. [3 to 6 references]

**Social worker's confidential facts:** Consult your textbook and other scholarly resources for an appropriate instrument or inventory of questions to guide your follow-up interview for the purposes of evaluating your client's progress (consider factors such as validity and reliability or trustworthiness of the evaluation tool, as well as its fit with the theoretical approach that guided your helping process). Write down skills that you want to use to ensure that your client feels comfortable answering questions, whether they have been successful or unsuccessful with achieving his or her AODA-related goals. Consider whether you also want to make use of other methods of collecting evaluation data, including blood or urine tests, information from family members or other collateral contacts, or direct observation in a community setting.

**Client's confidential facts:** Refer back to your notes on prior role-plays, particularly the ones connected with the type of intervention that your social worker is evaluating (individual, family, or group). For the most part, be cooperative with the follow-up interview, but raise any reasonable questions or concerns that you as the client might have (e.g., embarrassment about not achieving all the goals that were set, concerns about confidentiality and how the information will be used, and frustration if the evaluation seems to be for the benefit of the worker more than for the benefit of the client).

**Evaluation** will be based on the following criteria: comprehensiveness of preparation; quality of rationale for choice of an appropriate evaluation tool or question guide; clarity and critical analysis of the interview process; appropriateness of implications drawn from the evaluation process; level of critical analysis of the evaluation tool or question guide; selection of complementary evaluation methods; use of relevant, scholarly, and persuasive references.

# Journaling Exercise

1. How will you know if you are successful as a social worker for people with AODAs? Identify at least two general goals and five specific objectives that you would like to achieve as a social worker in this field over the next 5 years. Devise and write a plan for evaluating your success at achieving your goals and objectives. Include a research design, how data will be gathered and analyzed, and any tasks that you will need to complete in order to ensure that the evaluation is carried out in an ethical and effective manner. Mark down key dates and timelines in your calendar should you choose to carry out this evaluation. Invite a colleague or two to conduct a follow-up interview meeting with you 1, 2, or 5 years hence (also known as a "class reunion").
2. What are your attitudes and values toward research and evaluation in the AODA field? What types of research or evaluation do you believe are most important and why? What questions or skepticisms do you have about research and evaluation in this field? How will your attitudes and values, as analyzed above, affect your approaches as a practitioner working with people affected by AODAs?

# InfoTrac College Edition

## Key Words

◇ Treatment Effectiveness (drug or alcohol)
◇ Program Evaluation
◇ Measurement and Success
◇ Validity
◇ Reliability
◇ Quantitative Research
◇ Qualitative Research
◇ Single-system Design

# APPENDIX A
# Answers

This appendix provides answers to the multiple-choice and close-ended questions throughout the manual.

# Chapter 2

## Jeopardrugs

The following answers and questions correspond to the Jeopardrugs game. Only the quizmaster should read the following. Note that the questions provided are examples of correct responses. There might be alternative questions that are also correct.

### Uppers

100  A white powdery substance that people inhale through their nose.
Answer: What is cocaine?
(For a bonus point, what is its molecular construction? Answer: $C_{17}H_{21}NO_4$)

200  The psychoactive substance that occurs in chocolate.
Answer: What is caffeine?

300  Three examples of amphetamine's short-term intoxication effects.
Answer: What are stimulation, enhanced mood, increased energy, talkativeness, restlessness, and reduced appetite?

400  Four examples of the short-term intoxication effects of nicotine.
Answer: What are relaxation (in inexperienced users: nausea, flushing, and gagging), faster pulse, rise in blood pressure, loss of appetite, and stimulation then reduction of Central Nervous System (CNS) activity?

500  The two highest risk methods of ingesting cocaine.
Answer: What are intravenous use and freebasing?

## Downers

100 A substance associated with vitamin depletion, blackouts, and FAE.
Answer: What is alcohol?

200 Four primary withdrawal effects of alcohol.
Answer: What are insomnia, headache, appetite loss, sweating, tremors, convulsions, hallucinations, and death?

300 Three specific examples of pills used as tranquilizers.
Answer: What are Valium, Miltown, and Librium?

400 The two most usual routes of ingesting/administering sedatives.
Answer: What are injecting and swallowing?

500 Three desired effects of sedatives.
Answer: What are anxiety reduction, euphoria, and sleep?

## Opiates

100 A synthetic form of heroin.
Answer: What is methadone?

200 Four primary short-term intoxication effects of morphine.
Answer: What are euphoria, drowsiness, respiratory depression, constricted pupils, and nausea?

300 Results of a codeine overdose. (At least three)
Answer: What are death, clammy skin, slow and shallow breathing, coma, and convulsions?

400 Four long-term effects of chronic heroin use.
Answer: What are physical dependence, constipation, loss of appetite, severe withdrawal, weight loss, and reduction in sex hormones?

500 Primary methods of ingesting heroin.
Answer: What are injecting and swallowing?

## Hallucinogens

100 Names of three psychedelic or hallucinogenic drugs.
Answer: What are LSD, STP, psylobin (psilocybin), PCP, and mescaline?

200 Two common types of foods or plants that contain hallucinogens.
Answer: What are nutmeg, cactus, morning glory, jimson, and mushrooms?

300 Three desired effects of hallucinogens.
Answer: What are distortion of senses, mind expansion, exhilaration, and insight?

400 Four primary risks of hallucinogen use.
Answer: What are accidental death, flashbacks, trigger-existing psychosis, episodes, and panic reactions?

500 Two examples of different ways of ingesting different hallucinogens.
Answer: What are smoking PCP and swallowing LSD (acid)?

## Pot Pourri

100 Three desired effects of hash use.
Answer: What are relaxation, increased perception, and euphoria?

200 Legal substances that are commonly used as inhalants. (At least three)
Answer: What are glue, paint, gasoline, and freon?

300 The fastest way to get the highest high by ingesting a substance.
Answer: What is inhaling or smoking?

400  Four types of substances that are associated with greatest addictive liability.
Answer: What are alcohol, barbiturates, benzodiazepines, and opiates?

500  Street names for heroin, amphetamines, and cocaine. (1 example for each)
Answer: What are horse, speed, and rock?

### From Information to Knowledge

The following are the answers to the multiple-choice questions:
1D, 2C, 3B, 4E, 5C, 6E, 7D, 8C, 9E, 10C, 11E, 12A, 13D, 14C, 15E, 16E, 17C, 18C, 19E, 20E, 21A, 22D, 23C, 24C, 25E, 26D, 27A, 28A, 29B, 30E, 31D, 32B, 33C, 34E, 35D, 36D, 37E, 38E, 39A, 40C, 41C, 42E, 43C, 44B, 45D, 46C, 47B, 48E, 49C, 50C, 51D, 52B, 53E, 54A, 55E

# Chapter 3

### Distinguishing Different Theories and Approaches

Answers to multiple-choice questions:
1A, 2A, 3B, 4A, 5B, 6C, 7B, 8C, 9D, 10A, 11B, 12C, 13A, 14B, 15D, 16A, 17B, 18E, 19E, 20B, 21C, 22B, 23B, 24B, 25C, 26D, 27C

# Chapter 5

### Assessment Quiz

Answers to multiple-choice questions:
1D, 2C, 3B, 4E, 5B, 6B, 7E, 8E, 9C, 10E, 11E, 12B, 13E, 14B

# Chapter 6

### Roles

Chemically dependent person—C, Chief enabler—F, Hero—D, Scapegoat—E, Mascot/clown—B, Lost child—A

### Review Questions

Answers to multiple-choice questions:
1B, 2A, 3B, 4C, 5A, 6D, 7E, 8C, 9E, 10B

# Chapter 7

### Review Questions

Answers to multiple-choice questions:
1A, 2D, 3A, 4C, 5E, 6C, 7D, 8B, 9E, 10D, 11D, 12B, 13E, 14C, 15C, 16B, 17E, 18D, 19A, 20B

# Chapter 8

### Review Questions on Diverse Communities

Answers to multiple-choice questions:
1E, 2B, 3E, 4D, 5B, 6A, 7E, 8A, 9C, 10B, 11B, 12B, 13B, 14D, 15C, 16E, 17E, 18D, 19B, 20D, 21D, 22C, 23E, 24E, 25B, 26C, 27B, 28A, 29C, 30A, 31E, 32B, 33B, 34B, 35D, 36A, 37A, 38B, 39E

# Chapter 9
## Review Questions on Health Promotion and Public Policy

Answers to multiple-choice questions:
1A, 2C, 3B, 4B, 5A, 6D, 7B, 8D, 9C, 10B, 11D, 12B, 13D, 14D, 15A, 16D, 17A, 18A, 19C, 20D, 21D, 22B, 23C, 24C, 25D, 26C, 27D, 28B, 29D, 30A, 31D, 32C, 33D, 34D, 35B, 36B, 37A, 38E, 39B, 40F, 41E, 42C, 43E, 44D


# Chapter 10
## Types of Termination

Answers to multiple-choice questions:
1C, 2D, 3E, 4A, 5B, 6C, 7D, 8E

## Relapse Precipitants and Strategies for Maintenance

Answer to bonus question:
D

# Cross-Reference Grid

The following chart cross-references various topics in the manual. If you are interested in following through a particular topic or case study, you can refer directly to the pages where those exercises are located.

## Case Profiles

## Diversity, 123, 131–133, 203, 221, 224, 232, 250–260, 323, 327

# Ethics, 17, 64–65, 80, 157, 224, 262, 323

Competence, 104, 117, 198, 223, 230
Confidentiality, 86, 96, 104, 110–114, 130, 143, 152, 223, 227, 291, 312–313, 326
Honesty/Integrity, 95–96, 144, 157, 313, 327
Informed consent/Self–determination, 44–45, 81, 86, 91, 112, 168, 197–198, 222, 230, 237, 262, 291, 312, 323, 326–327
Respect, 2–3, 12–13, 70, 80, 94–95, 114, 157, 184, 222, 230, 262, 291
Safety issues, 28, 53, 86, 104, 110, 121, 145, 149, 154, 157, 162–163, 197–198, 234–235, 237, 290–291, 304, 312–313

# Levels of Practice

Facilitating change through group work and treatment programs (mezzo), 18, 44–45, 56–57, 91, 95, 106–108, 138, 145, 159–162, 202–242, 301, 310–311, 317–320, 324, 326, 341–342
Helping communities and organization change (macro), 18, 55, 92, 100, 103–104, 127–128, 140–143, 243–263, 295–296, 302, 305, 333
Helping families change (micro), 15, 93, 96, 99, 119–120, 123, 128, 137, 139, 143, 147–150, 159–201, 208, 211, 295, 302, 309–312, 316, 330, 337–342
Helping individuals change (micro), 15, 19, 29, 49–59, 62–63, 66–89, 91, 95–108, 118–130, 136, 143–146, 150–156, 204–211, 284, 294–306, 310–321, 333–336, 341–342
Public policy (macro), 17, 19, 31–32, 43, 53–54, 59, 63–64, 91, 203, 264–292, 295

# Theories and Models of Intervention, 66–67, 70–74, 217, 223–227, 306–309

Behavioral, 6, 16, 52, 55, 68–69, 70, 73, 78, 113, 128–129, 145, 155, 188–191, 198–199, 230–234, 240–241, 265–267, 273–276, 290, 294, 303–306, 318, 330–331
Cognitive, 6, 16, 44–45, 66, 81, 98, 113–114, 128–129, 155, 180–181, 230, 265, 294, 303–306, 316, 320, 331–332
Disease, 2, 12–13, 26, 80, 192, 319
Family Systems, 7, 16–17, 52, 72–73, 129, 137, 147–150, 154, 161, 164–188, 295, 316
Feminist, 7, 11, 73, 87–88, 149
Harm Reduction, 16, 44–45, 52, 76, 138, 168, 237, 241, 265, 283, 285, 291, 295, 298, 301, 329
Moral, 2, 6, 74–75, 80, 240, 261–262, 291
Motivational Enhancement, 14, 16, 52, 90–115, 156, 165, 195–197, 268, 329, 333–336
Narrative, 16, 66, 70, 171
Pharmacotherapy, 16, 44–45, 49, 50, 55–58, 73, 76, 81, 153–155, 191, 209, 234–235, 237–239, 266, 312, 319–320, 332
Psychoanalytic, 72–73, 149
Transtheoretical Model, 16, 90, 99–100, 103–115, 133–135, 153, 159–165, 168, 333–336
12-Steps, 12–13, 23, 74–75, 82–83, 153, 160–162, 168, 192, 223–224, 227–229, 235, 237–238, 304–305, 318–319, 330

# Table of Concordance

This table identifies which parts of this manual correspond best with which sections of five AODA textbooks that can be used in conjunction with this manual. Note that this manual deals with ethical and diversity issues throughout the manual. Diversity and ethical issues have been highlighted in separate rows, since some texts have specific chapters on ethics and diversity.

| Barsky, 2005 | van Wormer & Davis, 2003 | McNeece & DiNitto, 2005 | Johnson, 2004 | Lewis, Dana, & Blevins, 2002 | Fisher & Harrison, 2005 |
|---|---|---|---|---|---|
| **Chapter 1: Introduction** (including definitional frameworks and attitudes toward addictions) | Chapter 1: The Nature of Addiction; Chapter 2: Historical Perspectives | Chapter 1: Definitions and Epidemiology of Substance Use, Abuse, and Disorders | Chapter 1: Social Work and Substance Abuse Practice | Chapter 1: An Introduction to Substance Abuse Counseling | Chapter 1: The Role of the Mental Health Professional in Prevention and Treatment |
| **Chapter 2: Pharmacology** (drug actions and effects) | Chapter 4: Substance Misuses, Dependence, and the Body; Chapter 5: Interventions Related to Biology | Chapter 3: The Brain Biology of Drug Abuse and Addiction; Chapter 4: The Physiological and Behavioral Consequences of Alcohol and Drug Abuse | Chapter 2: Pharmacology | Chapter 9: Drugs and Their Effects | Chapter 2: Classification of Drugs *(continued)* |

| Barsky, 2005 | van Wormer & Davis, 2003 | McNeece & DiNitto, 2005 | Johnson, 2004 | Lewis, Dana, & Blevins, 2002 | Fisher & Harrison, 2005 |
|---|---|---|---|---|---|
| **Chapter 3: Models of Helping Individuals With AODA Problems** | Chapter 3: Strengths-based Helping Strategies; Chapter 5: Interventions Related to Biology (pp. 146–162 only); Chapter 7: Eating Disorders, Compulsive Gambling, Shopping and Other Behavioral Addictions; Chapter 8: Substance Misuse with a Coexisting Disorder or Disability | Chapter 2: The Etiology of Addictions; Chapter 13: Substance Abuse and Co-occurring Disabilities | Chapter 3: Models of Chemical Dependency; Chapter 10: Substance Abuse Treatment Methods | Chapter 3: Helping Clients Change | Chapter 3: Models of Addiction; Chapter 7: Treatment of AOD Problems |
| **Chapter 4: Techniques of Engagement: Micro–Mezzo–Macro** | Chapter 3: Strengths-based Helping Strategies (pp. 78–81 only) | N/A | Chapter 4: The Art of Client Engagement | Chapter 3: Helping Clients Change (pp. 55–61 only) | Chapter 6: Client Engagement and Brief Interventions |
| **Chapter 5: Assessment: Micro–Mezzo–Macro** | Chapter 5: Interventions Related to Biology (pp. 162–163 only) | Chapter 5: Screening, Diagnosis, Assessment, and Referral | Chapter 6: Macro Context for Substance Abuse Assessment; Chapter 7: Introduction to Screening and Assessment; Chapter 8: Substance Abuse Assessment; Appendices A and B (Assessment Forms) | Appendices A to F for Assessment Tools | Chapter 5: Assessment and Diagnosis |

*(continued)*

| Barsky, 2005 | van Wormer & Davis, 2003 | McNeece & DiNitto, 2005 | Johnson, 2004 | Lewis, Dana, & Blevins, 2002 | Fisher & Harrison, 2005 |
|---|---|---|---|---|---|
| Chapter 6: Helping Families Change | Chapter 9: Family Risks and Resiliencies | Chapter 10: Family Systems and Chemical Dependency | Chapter 5: Understanding Family; Chapter 10: Substance Abuse Treatment Methods (pp. 302–304 only) | Chapter 6: Working With Families | Chapter 10: Families; Chapter 11: Children, Adult Children, and Codependency; Chapter 13: Gambling and Other Addictions |
| Chapter 7: Facilitating Change Through Group Work and Treatment Programs | Chapter 12: Mutual Help Groups: A Strengths Perspective | Chapter 6: Treatment: The System of Care | Chapter 9: The Substance Abuse Treatment System; Chapter 10: Substance Abuse Treatment Methods (pp. 300–301 only) | Chapter 4: Empowering Clients Through Group Work | Chapter 9: Twelve-Step and Other Types of Support Groups |
| Chapter 8: Helping Communities Change | N/A | N/A | Chapter 6: Macro Context for Substance Abuse Assessment (pp.153–165 only); Chapter 10: Substance Abuse Treatment Methods (pp. 304–305 only) | N/A | N/A |
| Chapter 9: Health Promotion and Public Policy Development | Chapter 13: Public Policy | Chapter 8: Regulating Drugs and Their Consequences | Chapter 6: Macro Context for Substance Abuse Assessment | Chapter 8: Preventing Substance Abuse | Chapter 14: Prevention |
| Chapter 10: Termination Follow-Up, Maintenance, and Relapse Prevention | N/A | N/A | Chapter 10: Substance Abuse Treatment Methods (pp. 306–309 only) | Chapter 5: Maintaining Change in Substance Use Behaviors | Chapter 8: Relapse Prevention and Recovery  *(continued)* |

| Barsky, 2005 | van Wormer & Davis, 2003 | McNeece & DiNitto, 2005 | Johnson, 2004 | Lewis, Dana, & Blevins, 2002 | Fisher & Harrison, 2005 |
|---|---|---|---|---|---|
| **Chapter 11: Research and Evaluation** | N/A | N/A | N/A | Chapter 7: Program Planning and Evaluation; Chapter 8: Preventing Substance Abuse (pp. 190–193 only) | Chapter 7: Treatment of AOD Problems (pp. 144-148 only) |
| **Diversity** (throughout the manual) | Chapter 6: Addiction Across the Lifespan; Chapter 10: Racial, Ethnic, and Cultural Issues; Chapter 11: Gender and Sexual Orientation Differences | Chapter 9: Treating Substance-Abusing Youth; Chapter 11: Ethnicity, Culture, and Substance Abuse Disorders; Chapter 12: Substance Abuse Treatment with Sexual Minorities; Chapter 14: Alcohol and Drug Abuse Among Elders; Chapter 15: Gender and Drugs | Chapter 1: Social Work and Substance Abuse Practice (pp. 18–25 only); Chapter 11: Populations At Risk; Appendix C: African American Women | Chapter 1: An Introduction to Substance Abuse Counseling (pp. 15–17 only); Chapter 3: Helping Clients Change (pp. 57–58 only) | Chapter 4: Culturally and Ethnically Diverse Groups; Chapter 12: HIV/AIDS |
| **Ethics** (throughout the manual) | Chapter 13: Public Policy (pp. 404–405 only) | Chapter 16: Chemical Dependency: Current Issues and Future Prospects | Chapter 9: The Substance Abuse Treatment System (pp. 278–279 only) | N/A | Chapter 15: Confidentiality and Ethical Issues |

# Bibliography

## Books and Articles

Abbott, A. A. (1994). A feminist approach to substance abuse treatment & service delivery. *Social Work in Health Care, 19*, 67–83.

Abbott, A. A. (Ed.). (2000). *Alcohol, tobacco, and other drugs: A social work perspective.* Washington, DC: NASW Press.

Addiction Research Foundation. (1986). *Prevention in the drug field: Training program.* Toronto, Ontario, Canada: Centre for Addiction and Mental Health.

Addiction Research Foundation. (1996). *The hidden majority: A guidebook on alcohol and other drug issues for counsellors who work with women.* Toronto, Ontario, Canada: Centre for Addiction and Mental Health.

Addiction Research Foundation. (1997). *Alcohol and drug problems: A practical guide for counsellors* (2nd ed.). Toronto, Ontario, Canada: Centre for Addiction and Mental Health.

Alexander, B. K., Dawes, G. A., van de Wijngaart, G. F., Ossebaard, H. C., & Maraun, M. D. (1998). The "temperance mentality": A comparison of university students in seven countries. *Journal of Drug Issues, 28*, 265–282.

Annis, H. M. (1986). *Situational confidence questionnaire.* Toronto, Ontario, Canada: Centre for Addiction and Mental Health.

Aronstein, D. M., & Thompson, B. J. (Eds.). (1998). *HIV and social work: A practitioner's guide.* Binghamton, NY: Haworth.

Baer, J., Marlatt, G. A., & McMahon, R. J. (Eds.). (1993). *Addictive behaviors across the lifespan: Prevention, treatment and policy issues.* Thousand Oaks, CA: Sage.

Barrett, M. J., & Trepper, T. S. (1991). Treating women drug abusers who were victims of childhood sexual abuse. In C. Bepko (Ed.), *Feminism & addiction* (pp. 127–145). New York: Haworth.

Barsky, A. E. (2005). Generalist practice with people affected by addictions. In J. Poulin (Ed.), *Strengths-based generalist practice: A collaborative approach* (2nd ed., pp. 298–327). Belmont, CA: Brooks/Cole.

Barsky, A. E., & Coleman, H. (2001a). Evaluacion de la adquisicon de habilidades en el modelo transteorico: Etapas de precontemplation y contemplation [Evaluating skill acquisition using the Transtheoretical Model of Change: Precontemplation and contemplation phases]. *Revista de Trabail Social, 161*, 6–26.

Barsky, A. E., & Coleman, H. (2001b). Evaluating skills acquisition in motivational interviewing. *Journal of Drug Education, 31*(1), 69–82.

Bean, P. (2003). *Drug treatment: What works?* New York: Brunner-Routledge.

Bentley, K. J., & Walsh, J. (2001). *The social worker and psychotropic medication: Toward effective collaboration with mental health clients, families and providers* (2nd ed). Belmont, CA: Brooks/Cole.

Black, C. (1981). *It will never happen to me!* New York: Ballantine.

Bloom, B. S. (Ed.) (1956). *Taxonomy of educational objectives: The classification of educational goals*. New York: Longmans, Green.

Bloom, M., Fischer, J., & Orme, J. G. (2003). *Evaluating practice: Guidelines for the accountable professional* (4th ed.). Boston: Allyn & Bacon.

Bok, M. (1998). Harm reduction: Dealing differently with drugs. *Journal of Progressive Human Services, 9*, 3–21.

Bray, R. M., & Marsden, M. E. (Eds.). (1998). *Drug use in metropolitan America*. Thousand Oaks, CA: Sage.

Brown, B. S. (1997). *Drug abuse treatment needs assessment methodologies: A review of the literature*. Washington: National Institute for Drug Abuse Resource Center for Health Services Research. Available from http://www.nida.nih.gov/about/organization/DESPR/HSR/da-pre/Brownprevention.htm

Burstow, B. (1992). *Radical feminist therapy*. Thousand Oaks, CA: Sage.

Capethorn, J. (1994). A comparison of abstinence-oriented and indefinite methadone maintenance treatment. *The International Journal of the Addictions, 29*, 1361–1375.

Carroll, C. R. (2000). *Drugs in modern society* (5th ed.). Boston: McGraw-Hill.

Centre for Addiction and Mental Health. (1999). *Canadian profile: Alcohol, tobacco, and other drugs*. Toronto, Ontario, Canada: Author.

Cloud, W., & Granfield, R. (1994). Natural recovery from addiction: Treatment implications. *Addictions Nursing, 6*(4), 112–116.

Cohen, M. (1999). *Counseling addicted women: A practical guide*. Thousand Oaks, CA: Sage.

Corcoran, K.; & Fischer, J. (2000). *Measures for clinical practice: A sourcebook* (3rd ed.). Riverside, NJ: Simon & Schuster.

Craig, R. J. (2004). *Counseling the alcohol and drug dependent client: A practical approach*. Boston: Allyn & Bacon.

Curtis, O. (1999). *Chemical dependency: A family affair*. Belmont, CA: Brooks/Cole.

Davidson, R., Rollnick, S., & MacEwen, I. (Eds.). (1991). *Counseling problem drinkers*. New York: Routledge.

Davis, D. R., & Jansen, G. G. (1998). Making meaning of Alcoholics Anonymous for social workers: Myths, metaphors, and realities. *Social Work, 43*, 169–182.

Denning, P. (2000). *Practicing harm reduction psychotherapy: An alternative approach to addictions*. New York: Guilford.

Denning, P., Little, J., & Glickman, A. (2003). *Over the influence: The harm reduction guide for managing drugs and alcohol*. New York: Guilford.

Des Jarlais, D., & Friedman, S. (1992). AIDS, injecting drug use and harm reduction. In N. Heather, A. Wodak, E. Nadelmann, & P. O'Hare (Eds.). *Psychoactive drugs and harm reduction: From faith to science*. London: Whurr Books.

Diamond, J. (2000). *Narrative means to sober ends: Treating addiction and its aftermath*. New York: Guilford.

DiClemente, C. C. (2003). *Addictions and change: How addictions develop and addicted people recover*. New York: Guilford.

Doweiko, H. E. (2002). *Concepts of chemical dependency* (5th ed.). Belmont, CA: Brooks/Cole.

DuWors, G. M. (1992). *White knuckles and wishful thinking: Breaking the chain of compulsive reaction and relapse in alcoholism and other addictions*. Seattle, WA: Hogrefe & Huber.

Erickson, P. G., Riley, D. M., Chueng, Y. W., & O'Hare, P. A. (Eds.). (1997). *Harm reduction: A new direction for drug policies and programs*. Toronto, Ontario, Canada: University of Toronto Press.

Fishbein, D. H., & Pease, S. W. (1996). *The dynamics of drug abuse*. Boston: Allyn & Bacon.

Fisher, G. L., & Harrison, T. C. (2005). *Substance abuse: Information for school counselors, social workers, therapists, and counselors* (3rd ed.). Boston: Allyn & Bacon.

Freeman, E. M. (1992). *The addiction process: Effective social work approaches*. New York: Longman.

Freeman, E. M. (1993). *Substance abuse treatment: A family systems perspective*. Thousand Oaks, CA: Sage.

Friedman, A. S., & Granick, S. (1990). *Family therapy for adolescent drug abuse*. Lexington, MA: Lexington.

Friedman, S. R. (1991). *Cocaine, AIDS and intravenous drug use*. New York: Haworth.

Geva, E., Barsky, A. E., & Westernoff, F. (2000). *Interprofessional practice with diverse populations: Cases in point*. Westport, CT: Greenwood.

Gibbs, L. E. (2003). *Evidence-based practice for the helping professions*. Belmont, CA: Brooks/Cole.

Glass, J. B. (Ed.). (1991). *The international handbook of addiction behavior*. New York: Routledge.

Goldberg, R. (1993). *Taking sides: Clashing views on controversial issues in drugs and society*. Columbus, OH: McGraw-Hill.

Goodman, A. (1992). Sexual addiction: Designation and treatment. *Journal of Sex & Marital Therapy, 18*(4), 303–314.

Gopaul-McNicol, S., & Armour-Thomas, E. (2002). *Assessment and culture: Psychological tests with minority populations*. San Diego, CA: Academic Press.

Green, J. (1999). *Cultural awareness in the human services: A multi-ethnic approach*. Boston, MA: Allyn & Bacon.

Green, R. R. (2002). *Resiliency: An integrated approach to practice, policy, and research*. Washington, DC: NASW Press.

Gruenwald, P. J. (1997). *Measuring community indicators: A systems approach to drug and alcohol problems*. Thousand Oaks, CA: Sage.

Harrison, S., & Carver, V. (Eds.). (1997). *Alcohol and drug problems: A practical guide for counsellors* (2nd ed.). Toronto, Ontario, Canada: Center for Addictions and Mental Health.

Herdman, J. W. (2000). *Global criteria: The 12 core functions of the substance abuse counselor* (3rd ed.). Bradenton Beach, FL: Learning Publications.

Herring, R. D. (1999). *Counseling Native American Indian/Alaskan Native populations*. Thousand Oaks, CA: Sage.

Inaba, D. (1990). *Uppers, downers, all arounders: Physical and mental effects of psychoactive drugs*. Ashland, OR: CNS Productions.

Inciardi, J. A., & Harrison, L. D. (1998). *Heroin in the age of crack-cocaine*. Thousand Oaks, CA: Sage.

Inciardi, J. A., & McElrath, K. (2001). *The American drug scene*. Los Angeles: Roxbury.

James, D., Mayberry, C., & Moran, J. (1994). AADAC's opiate dependency program: Evaluation of the enhanced program component. Edmonton, Alberta, Canada: AADAC.

Jensen, E. L., & Gerber, J. (1998). *The new war on drugs*. Cincinnati, OH: Anderson.

Johnson, J. L. (2004). *Fundamentals of substance abuse practices*. Belmont, CA: Brooks/Cole.

Johnson, K., Bryant, D. D., Collins, D. A., Noe, T. D., Strader, T. N., & Bernbaum, M. (1998). Preventing and reducing alcohol and other drug use among high-risk youths by increasing family resilience. *Social Work, 43*, 297–308.

Juhnke, G. A. (2002). Significant other interviews: Understanding and promoting change through others. In *Substance abuse assessment and diagnosis: A comprehensive guide for counselors and helping professionals* (pp. 101–146). New York: Brunner-Routledge.

Jung, J. (2000). *Psychology of alcohol and other drugs*. Thousand Oaks, CA: Sage.

Kar, S. N. (Ed.). (2001). *Substance abuse prevention: A multicultural perspective*. Amityville, NY: Baywood.

Katz, S., & Liu, A. (1991). *The co-dependency conspiracy*. New York: Warner Books.

Kauffman, S., & Poulin, J. (1996). Coherency among substance abuse models. *Journal of Sociology and Social Welfare, 23*(3), 163–174.

Kerr, D. (1997). *Treating gambling/substance abusing clients: A literature review*. Calgary, Alberta, Canada: Alberta Alcohol and Drug Abuse Commission.

Keyson, M., & Janda, L. (2004). *Untitled locus of drinking control scale*. Phoenix, AZ: St. Luke's Hospital. Retrieved from http://www.niaaa.nih.gov/publications/drie-text.htm.

Kinney, J. (1995). *Loosening the grip* (5th ed.). Boston: Mosby.

Kirst-Ashman, K. K., & Hull, G. H. (2002). *Understanding generalist practice* (3rd ed.). Belmont, CA: Brooks/Cole.

Klingemann, H. K., & Sobell, L. C. (2001). Introduction: Natural recovery research across substance use. *Substance Use and Misuse, 36*(11), 1409–1416.

Kritsberg, W. (1986). *The Adult Children of Alcoholics Syndrome: From discovery to recovery*. Pompano Beach, FL: Health Communications.

Levinthal, C. F. (1999). *Drugs, behavior, and modern society* (2nd ed.). Boston: Allyn & Bacon.

Lewis, J. A., Dana, R. Q., & Blevins, G. A. (2002). *Substance abuse counseling* (3rd ed.), Belmont, CA: Brooks/Cole.

Lowinson, J. H., Ruiz, P., & Millman, R. B. (1992). *Substance abuse*. Baltimore: Williams and Wilkins.

Lyman, M. D. (1998). *Drugs in society: Causes, concepts and control*. Cincinnati, OH: Anderson.

McCollum, E. E., & Trepper, T. S. (2001). *Family solutions for substance abuse: Clinical and counseling approaches*. Binghamton, NY: Haworth.

McCubbin, H. I. (1998). *Resiliency in Native American and immigrant families*. Thousand Oaks, CA: Sage.

McGoldrick, M., Gerson, R., & Shellenberger, S. (1999). *Genograms: Assessment and intervention* (2nd ed.). New York: Norton.

McNeece, C. A., & DiNitto, D. M. (2005). *Chemical dependency: A systems approach* (3rd ed.). Boston, MA: Allyn & Bacon.

McRady, B. S., & Miller, W. R. (Eds.). (1993). *Research on Alcoholics Anonymous*. New Brunswick, NJ: Rutgers Center for Alcoholic Studies.

Meeks, D. E. (1989). Alcohol addiction. In F. Turner (Ed.), *Adult psychopathology: A social work perspective*. New York: The Free Press.

Miller, G. A. (1999). *Learning the language of addiction counseling*. Boston: Allyn & Bacon.

Miller, W. (1999). *Integrating spirituality into treatment*. Washington, DC: American Psychological Association.

Miller, W., & Rollnick, S. (2002). *Motivational interviewing: Preparing people for change* (2nd cd.). New York: Guilford.

Muisner, P. (1994). *Understanding and treating adolescent substance abuse*. Thousand Oaks, CA: Sage.

Mumm, A. M., & Kersting, R. C. (1997). Teaching critical thinking in social work practice courses. *Journal of Social Work Education, 33*(1), 75–84.

National Institute on Alcohol Abuse and Alcoholism. (NIAAA). (1999). *Project match monograph series* (Volume 1 – Twelve Step Facilitation; Volume 2 – Motivational Enhancement Therapy; Volume 3 – Cognitive-Behavioral Coping Skills Therapy; Volume 4 – The Drinker Inventory of Consequences; Volume 5 – A Structured Assessment Interview for Drinking and Related Behaviors; Volume 6 – Improving Compliance with Alcoholism Treatment; Volume 7 – Strategies for Facilitating Protocol Compliance in Alcoholism Treatment Research; Volume 9 – Project MATCH Hypotheses: Results and Causal Chain Analysis). Washington, DC: National Institutes of Health.

Norcross, J. C., Santrock, J. W., Campbell, L. F., Smith, T. P., Sommer, R., & Zuckerman, E. L. (2000). *Authoritative guide to self-help resources in mental health*. New York: Guilford.

Noonan, W. C., & Moyers, T. B. (2004). Motivational interviewing. In E. McCance-Katz & H. W. Clark (Eds.). *Psychosocial treatments: Key readings on addiction psychiatry* (pp. 19–33). New York: Brunner-Routledge.

Nowinski, J. K. (1998). Family recovery and substance abuse: A twelve-step program for treatment. Thousand Oaks, CA: Sage.

O'Hare, P. A., Newcombe, R., Matthews, A., Brunning, E. C., & Drucker, E. (Eds.). (1992). *The reduction of drug-related harm*. New York: Routledge.

Philleo, J., Brisbane, F. L., & Epstein, L. G. (Eds.). (1997). *Cultural competence in substance abuse and prevention*. Washington, DC: NASW Press.

Prochaska, J. O. (1994). *Systems of psychotherapy: A transtheoretical analysis* (3rd ed.). Belmont, CA: Brooks/Cole.

Prochaska, J. O., & DiClemente, C. C. (1982). Transtheoretical therapy: Toward a more integrative model of change. *Psychotherapy: Theory, Research & Practice, 19*, 276–287.

Prochaska, J. O., & DiClemente, C. C. (1992). Stages of change in the modification of problem behaviors. *Progress in Behavior Modification, 28*, 184–218.

Ray, O., & Ksir, C. (1994). *Drugs, society and human behavior*. St. Louis, MO: Moseby.

Rogers, C. (1957). The necessary and sufficient conditions of therapeutic personality change. *Journal of Counseling Psychology, 21*, 95–103.

Rollnick, S., & Morgan, M. (1997). Motivational interviewing: Increasing readiness for change. In A. M. Washton, *Psychotherapy and substance abuse: A practitioner's handbook*. New York: Guilford.

Room, R., Janca, A., Bennett, L. A., Schmidt, L. A., & Sartorius, N. (1997). WHO cross-cultural applicability research on diagnosis and assessment of substance use disorders. *Addiction, 91*(2), 199–220.

Rotgers, F., Keller, D. S., & Morgenstern, J. (Eds.). (1996). *Treating substance abuse: Theory and technique*. New York: Guilford.

Russel, M., Martier, S. S., Sokol, R. J., Mudar, P., Bottoms, S., Jacobsen, S. & Jacobsen, J. (1994). Screening for Pregnancy Risk-Drinking. *Alcoholism: Clinical and Experimental Research, 18*, 1156–1161.

Schiliebner, C. T. (1994). Gender-sensitive therapy: An alternative for women in substance abuse treatment. *Journal of Substance Abuse Treatment, 11*, 511–515.

Shulman, L. (1999). The skills of helping individuals, families, groups, and communities (4th ed.). Belmont, CA: Brooks/Cole.

Stevens, S. J., Tortu, S., & Coyle, S. L. (1998). *Women, drug use and HIV infection*. New York: Haworth.

Stevens, S. J., & Wexler, H. K. (1998). *Women and substance abuse*. New York: Haworth.

Substance Abuse and Mental Health Services Association. (1995). *Curriculum models on alcohol and other drug problems for schools of social work*. Washington, DC: National Association of Social Workers.

Thyer, B. A. (Ed.). (1998). Psychopharmacology and social work practice (special issue). *Research on Social Work Practice, 4*(8).

Tracy, E. M. (1994). Maternal substance abuse: Protecting the child, preserving the family. *Social Work, 39*(5), 534–540.

Turpin, J., & Schmidt, G. (1999). Fetal alcohol syndrome/effect: Developing a community response. Halifax, NS: Fernwood.

Van Den Bergh, N. (Ed.). (1995). *Feminist practice in the 21st Century*. Washington, DC: NASW Press.

Van Wormer, K., & Davis, D. R. (2003). *Addictions treatment: A strengths perspective*. Belmont, CA: Brooks/Cole.

Velicer, W. F, Prochaska, J. O., Fava, J. L., Norman, G. J., & Redding, C. A. (1998). Smoking cessation and stress management: Applications of the Transtheoretical Model of behavior change. *Homeostasis, 38*, 216–233. (Summary available online at http://www.uri.edu/research/cprc/TTM/detailedoverview.htm)

Vellman, R. (1992). *Counseling alcohol problems*. Thousand Oaks, CA: Sage.

Walker, S. (2001). *Sense and nonsense about crime and drugs: A policy guide* (5th ed.). Belmont, CA: Wadsworth.

Ward, J., et al. (1992). Methadone maintenance and the human immunodeficiency virus: Current issues in treatment and research. *British Journal of Addiction, 87*, 447–453.

Watkins, T. R., & Barrett, M. (2000). *Dual diagnosis: An integrated approach to treatment*. Thousand Oaks, CA: Sage.

Wegscheider, S. (1981). *Another chance: Hope and health for the alcoholic family*. Palo Alto, CA: Science and Behavior Books.

Whitehead, P. C. (1998). *Insanity of alcohol: Social problems in Canadian First Nations communities*. Toronto, Ontario, Canada: Canadian Scholar's Press.

Windle, M. (1999). *Alcohol use among adolescents*. Thousand Oaks, CA: Sage.

Wish, E. (1992). *Drug abuse: Linking policy and research*. Thousand Oaks, CA: Sage.

## Databases for Literature Searches

*MedLine*
*PsychINFO*
*Social Work Abstracts*

Key words: addict, dependen* (using an asterisk will allow search to cover dependent and dependence), substance abuse, alcohol

## Journals

*American Journal of Addictions*
*International Journal of the Addictions*
*Journal of Addiction and Mental Health*
*Journal of Drug Education*
*Journal of Social Work in the Addictions*

## Videotapes

Dworkin, J. (2002). *Love & Diane* [VHS]. New York: Women Make Movies/Chilmark Productions.

Koppengaver, R. (2001). *Web of addiction* [VHS]. Pasadena, CA: Intelecom.

Lewis, J. & Carlson, J. (Eds.). (2000). *Cognitive therapy for addictions with Bruce S. Liese* [VHS]. Boston: Allyn & Bacon.

Lewis, J. & Carlson, J. (Eds.). (2000). *Reality therapy for addictions with Robert Wubbolding* [VHS]. Boston: Allyn & Bacon.

Lewis, J. & Carlson, J. (Eds.). (2000). *Stages of change for addictions with John C. Norcross* [VHS]. Boston: Allyn & Bacon.

Moyers, W. (1998). *Close to home.* Moyers on addiction [VHS or DVD series]: (1) The Hijacked Brain; (2) Policy, Politics, and Addiction; (3) Portraits of Addiction; (4) Changing Lives; (5) The Next Generation. Princeton, NJ: Films for the Humanities and Sciences.

## Web Sites

Alcoholics Anonymous: http://www.alcoholics-anonymous.org

Center for Education and Drug Abuse Research: http://info.pitt.edu/~cedar

Drug Enforcement Administration: http://www.usdoj.gov/dea

International Certification and Reciprocity Consortium: Alcohol and Other Drug Abuse: http://www.icrcaoda.org

Moderation Management: http://www.moderation.org

National Alliance of Methadone Advocates: http://www.methadone.org

National Association of Alcoholism and Drug Abuse Counselors: http://www.naadac.org

National Clearinghouse for Alcohol and Drug Information: http://www.health.org

National Institute on Alcohol Abuse and Alcoholism: http://www.niaaa.nih.gov

National Institute on Drug Abuse: http://www.nida.nih.gov

National Organization on Fetal Alcohol Syndrome: http://nofas.org

Prevention Online: http://www.health.org

SMART Recovery: http://www.smartrecovery.org

Substance Abuse and Mental Health Services Association: http://www.samhsa.gov

Women For Sobriety: http://www.womenforsobriety.org

TO THE OWNER OF THIS BOOK:

I hope that you have found *Alcohol, Other Drugs, and Addictions* useful. So that this book can be improved in a future edition, would you take the time to complete this sheet and return it? Thank you.

School and address: _____

_____

Department: _____

Instructor's name: _____

1. What I like most about this book is: _____

_____

_____

2. What I like least about this book is: _____

_____

_____

3. My general reaction to this book is: _____

_____

_____

4. The name of the course in which I used this book is: _____

_____

5. Were all of the chapters of the book assigned for you to read? _____

   If not, which ones weren't? _____

6. In the space below, or on a separate sheet of paper, please write specific suggestions for improving this book and anything else you'd care to share about your experience in using this book.

_____

_____

_____

_____

_____

**BROOKS/COLE**
CENGAGE Learning™

U

┌─────────────────────────────────────┐
│ ## BUSINESS REPLY MAIL               │
│ FIRST-CLASS MAIL   PERMIT NO. 102   MONTEREY CA │
└─────────────────────────────────────┘

POSTAGE WILL BE PAID BY ADDRESSEE

Attn:  Social Work Editor

BrooksCole, Cengage Learning

20 Davis Drive

Belmont, CA 94002

OPTIONAL:

Your name: _____   Date: _____

May we quote you, either in promotion for *Alcohol, Other Drugs, and Addictions* or in future publishing ventures?

Yes: _____   No: _____

Sincerely yours,

*Allan E. Barsky*

CPSIA information can be obtained
at www.ICGtesting.com
Printed in the USA
FFOW04n1231201217
44177792-43587FF